"In *Biblical Motivation: How Preaching Should Motivate according to the Word of God*, Pastor Ray Heiple works to give his fellow pastors a kindly, firm rebuke. After examining scholarly views concerning the nature of motivation, Heiple provides representative quotes showing how preachers today place their faith in various motivational schemes, rather than God's truth. The core of Heiple's book is a careful analysis of five sermons in Acts, each demonstrating that apostolic preaching motivated listeners by declaring the truth.

"When I first started this book, I wondered whether it would develop into a typical Reformed harangue against the emotions. Not at all. Heiple never denigrates the emotions. Rather, he relegates them to their proper biblical place. 'The biblical preachers . . . do not shy away from expressing passion and emotion, but all of their effort is concentrated on the truth and certainty of their message.' We are not to work to elicit feelings about the truth, but to appeal to the truth, directly. The apostles never called for any emotions other than the fear of God.

"This book was helpful, and I commend it to other preachers. It got me to think carefully about whether my preaching is more dependent on my own ability to communicate than the truth of God and the power of the Holy Spirit."

—**Tim Bayly**, senior pastor, Clearnote Church, Bloomington, Indiana; author of *Daddy Tried* and *The Grace of Shame*

"The modern church has been awash with various motivational theories, each claiming to hold the golden key to effective preaching. Dr. Heiple subjects them to insightful critique, and then offers a helpful explanation of human motivation informed by the Bible and Reformed theology. May the Lord use this book to encourage and equip preachers through whom he fulfills his promise to the church, 'And you shall know the truth, and the truth shall make you free' (John 8:32)."

—**Joel R. Beeke**, President, Puritan Reformed Theological Seminary, Grand Rapids, Michigan

"Finally—a book that builds its understanding of motivation in preaching squarely on the sermons found in the Bible itself! Dr. Heiple shows in detail how the apostles Peter and Paul sought to motivate their audiences, and how preachers today can follow in their inspired footsteps. Heiple's work evidences careful scholarship, is very enlightening, and is deeply convicting. A much-needed antidote to emotion-heavy but truth-light preaching."
—**Bailey Cadman**, PCA, retired senior pastor, Providence Presbyterian Church (PCA), Robinson Township, Pennsylvania

"I am excited about this study! Here are a few of the reasons. First, a student listened to something I said and picked a significant study. Second, it is a sound exegetical work that is clear, is well written, and does not tire the reader with unnecessary verbiage. Third, it is an excellent example of useful academic work that must not stay on the shelves of libraries, collecting dust. Fourth, it is saying something new, fresh, and needed. Fifth, it is significant for the church and not just the ivory tower of graduate school. Sixth, it helps preachers and preaching. Seventh, and most significant, it is God-centered and God-honoring. It sounds trite, but it is true: every preacher must interact with this book's position. May God use it to help revive preaching so that the needed revival and reformation of the family, church, and state may become a reality before I die and go to glory."
—**George C. Scipione**, Director, Biblical Counseling Institute, Reformed Presbyterian Theological Seminary

Preaching with Biblical Motivation

Reformed Academic Dissertations

A Series

Series Editor
John J. Hughes

Preaching with Biblical Motivation

How to Incorporate the Motivation Found in the Inspired Preaching of the Apostles into Your Sermons

Ray E. Heiple Jr.

P&R
PUBLISHING
P.O. BOX 817 • PHILLIPSBURG • NEW JERSEY 08865-0817

Preaching with Biblical Motivation: How to Incorporate the Motivation Found in the Inspired Preaching of the Apostles into Your Sermons. Ray E. Heiple Jr., D.Min., M.Div., B.A. Submitted to Reformed Presbyterian Theological Seminary, 2013, for the D.Min. degree. Supervisors: Dr. Jack Kinneer, Dr. C. J. Williams.

Italics in Scripture quotations indicate author's emphasis.

Printed in the United States of America

ISBN: 978-1-62995-282-6 (pbk)
ISBN: 978-1-62995-283-3 (ePub)
ISBN: 978-1-62995-284-0 (Mobi)

To Don Blank, who pushed me to become a preacher; and
To Bailey Cadman, who showed me how to do it.

Contents

Series Introduction

P&R Publishing has a long and distinguished history of publishing carefully selected, high-value theological books in the Reformed tradition. Many theological books begin as dissertations, but many dissertations are worthy of publication in their own right. Realizing this, P&R has launched the Reformed Academic Dissertation (RAD) program to publish top-tier dissertations (Ph.D., Th.D., D.Min., and Th.M.) that advance biblical and theological scholarship by making distinctive contributions in the areas of theology, ethics, biblical studies, apologetics, and counseling.

Dissertations in the RAD series are curated, which means that they are carefully selected, on the basis of strong recommendations by the authors' supervisors and examiners and by our internal readers, to be part of our collection. Each selected dissertation will provide clear, fresh, and engaging insights about significant theological issues.

A number of theological institutions have partnered with us to recommend dissertations that they believe worthy of publication in the RAD series. Not only does this provide increased visibility for participating institutions, it also makes outstanding dissertations available to a broad range of readers while helping to introduce promising authors to the publishing world.

We look forward to seeing the RAD program grow into a large collection of curated dissertations that will help to advance Reformed scholarship and learning.

John J. Hughes
Series Editor

Foreword

When I was first asked to serve on the committee to oversee this dissertation, I was intrigued by the topic but somewhat skeptical that it could be parlayed into a work of great depth or substance. Biblical motivation in preaching? I had never come across any works on this specific subject, and my first thoughts about it were simplistic. I knew that the motivational model of human-centered emotionalism popularized by television preachers was to be avoided, but could one articulate a comprehensive, biblical doctrine of how a sermon should properly motivate the hearer? I agreed to the task partly out of curiosity, but mostly because of my confidence in Mr. Heiple's ability to tackle such a topic, however difficult it may have first seemed to me.

I was not surprised that the end result was an outstanding piece of scholarship. I expected as much from my friend and student, Ray Heiple. I *was* surprised that a topic I first viewed with a little skepticism had taken the form of a dissertation that I found myself recommending to every pastor I know.

Mr. Heiple brings out the point that motivation lies at the very heart of preaching, and that every sermon is preached on some notion of how people are motivated to respond. These notions are sometimes consciously articulated, but for many preachers they remain undeveloped assumptions. Most preachers of the Reformed persuasion could tell you what motivations should *not* be used, but a great number of the same preachers have likely not thought through and employed a coherent, biblical model of motivation. The following work will lead pastors a good way down the path of discovering and applying a biblical model of motivation in preaching that honors the Lord, upholds his Word, and produces conviction in the hearts of conscionable hearers.

Motivations color every human act with the light hues of virtue, the darker shades of corruption, or the gray tone of suspicion. Motivation often reveals the heart even more than the act it produces. When it comes to the motions of faith, motivation means everything, as Jesus so powerfully reminded us in Matthew 6. Therefore, biblical motivation in preaching is a subject that we cannot afford to overlook. If we would preach the Word with the right motives, we must lay the right motives before our hearers, and pray that our gracious God would sovereignly use them to produce true faith and sincere obedience.

In nineteen years of pulpit ministry, few works have impacted my view of preaching like this one. I am delighted to recommend it to pastors, seminary students, homiletics professors, and anyone who takes pleasure in God's Word and the preaching of it. I pray that God would use this work to strengthen the preaching of his word with biblical motivation that brings many to their knees before Christ.

C. J. Williams
Professor of Old Testament Studies
Reformed Presbyterian Theological Seminary
Pittsburgh, Pennsylvania

Preface

The experience of getting a book published stirred up a variety of emotions in me. The emotions began when P&R Publishing first expressed interest in the work, and they continued to ebb and flow throughout the approval process, during the copyediting, proofreading, and even now as I write this preface. Some are beneficial emotions of excitement, satisfaction, and desire. They help me to stay focused and to work in a timely and attentive manner. I am trying to keep them going. Others are impeding emotions of anxiety, stress, and worry. I have to resist and suppress them so that I can stay diligent, continue working, and meet all my deadlines. However, all of the emotions came as a result of my knowing and assenting to each of the successive tasks I had to accomplish in order to get this book published. They came as I learned and was convinced of the truth of the information I received. It was the instructions, as I understood and believed them, and as they interacted with the rest of my character, which produced the emotions. That is the way emotions are always produced. We do not consciously choose to feel a certain way or to have this or that emotion. We can cherish certain emotions or try to control and hold them back, but emotions and feelings for the most part simply come. They come differently to different people. They flow out of who we are and what we believe as we interact with our environment.

Man is an emotional being. Man is a rational being. Man has physical strength. Man has an intellect. These things are all good in that they are necessary elements of human nature as God has created it. When a person loses some ability in any of these areas, whether from a genetic defect or from some accident after birth, it is a tragedy which we ought to mourn and do all that we can to remedy with our science, technology, and medicine. Man, in the way that God created him in the beginning, both male and female, was, to use the old philosophical language, a *perfect* being. That is, man did not lack anything in his being to be what God created him to be: the sinless and righteous image of God, glorifying and enjoying Him forever as he exercised his God-given dominion over the creation, filling and subduing the earth and being fruitful and multiplying. Had man not sinned surely all of his powers in body and soul would have been used perfectly forever. We would never have to worry about someone abusing his abilities in a way that is against the nature of those abilities, whether intentionally or out of ignorance. But since man did fall into sin, such is not the case.

This book examines a subject—motivation—that is in need of a lot more examination. Not from secular psychologists, but from theologians and ministers of the gospel. In fact, one of the main reasons why motivation so desperately needs to be studied by the true doctors of the soul—the teachers of the Word—is because of all of the clutter and confusion heaped up around it by the secularists. And because we in the church have for too long neglected the soul and its powers. We do not even know what a soul is anymore. If we cannot put it under a microscope and map its DNA, it doesn't exist for us. But the soul is not physical! It has no matter, atoms, or cells. You cannot measure a soul. You cannot weigh a thought. The soul and its powers belong to the realm of being. And to directly study being one must go beyond physics, after physics, which is to say *meta*physics. Yet our almost idolatrous confidence in science and physics has for all practical purposes slain metaphysics. (Apart from a few antiquated Roman Catholic theologians, does anyone even study metaphysics anymore? Where are the Protestant evangelical metaphysicians? Please call me when you find them. I would like to join up. I hope they accept novices.)

Soul and body make up the individual human being. What

affects the soul affects the body and vice versa. We can measure, observe, and describe how the body is affected by thoughts and desires. Emotions, though occurring in the *soul* (which is to say the *heart*, which in turn is to say the *mind*) affect the body. Emotional states can be measured by the heart rate, blood pressure, perspiration, body temperature, and other physical indications. Different kinds of thoughts can be quantified according to recorded brain waves. Yet these bodily accompaniments are the effects and not the causes of activities which occur in that nonphysical, noncorporeal entity which we call the soul. The soul is not measurable. The soul is not observable. Yet the soul is real. Identical twins with exactly the same DNA, raised at the exact same time, in precisely the same way, by the same people, in the same environment, consuming the same kinds of food and water, and participating in the same exercise and experiences, have entirely different thoughts, affections, desires, senses of humor, likes, dislikes, and personalities. Though exactly the same physically and bodily, they are two distinct, different people because each one has his own individual soul.

Psychologists by definition study the soul, and motivation takes place in the soul, so psychologists are right to talk about motivation. When someone is motivated they are moved to action. Motivation begins when a person becomes aware of a present motive or motives. He considers them and understands them; whether he is correct in his understanding does not matter. What matters is that he has an apprehension of the motives that are before him. Then at some point the apprehended motive or motives has become effectual to the point that what was a potential incentive has been received and accepted by the person. The motive has persuaded him to do something; whether merely in his mind or also in his body, he has assented to and not rejected the motivation that was before simply *there*. Now it is his motivation. This is true for what has been classified as both "external" and "internal" motivation. When a person becomes motivated, the potential or possible motivation of which he was previously aware, of which he was previously merely considering, though possibly quite unconsciously, he has now adopted and is acting upon it and by means of it.

Many factors are involved in the motivation process but the one that has dominated modern psychology for more than fifty years is emotion. People can be moved by emotion. In fact they are quite easily moved by emotion. Emotions are powerful. They are easy to excite and stir up, and they can just as easily be turned or controlled. Very little thought is required to bring about an emotional state. In fact we often react with strong emotion before thinking things through, sometimes getting ourselves into trouble. As noted above, emotions are part of our human nature; therefore, emotions in and of themselves are good. It is good that we are emotional beings. God made us that way. It would be bad for us to be nonemotional or unemotional beings. If one were to lose one's ability to have emotions, it would be a tragedy and a malady for which one should seek treatment. Emotions are part of our created natures and as such they are good.

Like the rest of our powers, however, emotions can be used for evil. They can also be misused in a way that is not in accord with their natures. So, for example, seeing that God has not given us emotions in order to determine good from evil, to judge something to be good or evil based upon one's emotions would be to judge wrongly, even if you happened to make the correct judgment. It would be like an algebra teacher requiring her students to complete a regimen in the weight room to "study" for their exam. Increasing their physical strength will not help them to correctly apply the quadratic formula—for that they need to engage in mental exercise. Similarly, we must not look to emotions to do what they were not given by God to do. Even when we do so unintentionally, we misuse God's good gifts resulting in harm to ourselves.

In this book I present a thesis on how preachers ought to seek to motivate when they preach a sermon and how Christians ought to seek to be motivated when they listen to a sermon. My evidence to support this argument is based upon five sermonic events recorded for us in Scripture in the book of Acts. From my study I am convinced that there is a biblical way, a correct way, for a sermon to motivate. The preacher should seek to motivate and the listener should seek to be motivated according to this biblical way. Whether or not a person actually is effectually motivated in a sermon is God's business, but both preacher and listener are still responsible to do things the right way. Such is the case with all Christian duties; whether praying, evangelizing, worshipping, or anything else, we are always to seek to do things rightly. We leave it to God to sovereignly move as He sees fit. We pray for Him to help us and bless us but even then we pray, "Thy will be done." A cursory look at the contemporary scene reveals that to be motivated or to seek to motivate in an unbiblical way is not only a possibility for churches but is the majority report in today's church. As goes without saying, doing anything in an unbiblical way is not pleasing to God. Specifically, to motivate in an unbiblical way is manipulative and sinful. In Christianity, the ends cannot justify the means.

My thesis is that a sermon ought to motivate by its content as it is presented and proven to be true. The preacher ought to show that what he is saying is from God and therefore is true and should be believed by everyone who approves of the truth. The listener, if he is a Christian, ought to be seeking to see and be persuaded by the truth of the Word of God. In Scriptural preaching events, unbelievers are shown to be converted when the Holy Spirit (savingly) convinces them of the truth of the message. So the preacher's goal and aim is the same for both believer and unbeliever: to present and prove the truth of his message. A message or report persuades or motivates as it is believed. It is more likely to be believed when it is demonstrated to be true. However, even if the message is true and shown to be true, people can still refuse to believe it. Such is especially the case with regard to the truth of the Word of God, the truth which fallen man naturally hates. When a sinful man rejects God's true Word, he is guilty and will be judged. God's Word, though perfectly true, only benefits those who believe it. Those Jews who failed to enter the

Promised Land were not able to enter it because the gospel which they heard did not profit them. It did not profit them because they did not believe it. Those who believe are moved by faith to respond and they enter God's rest (see Heb. 3:18–4:3).

Therefore, the instrument of biblical motivation is faith, as God is pleased to give it or strengthen it. As a preacher I cannot make an unbeliever come to faith. I cannot make a Christian grow in his faith. But I can give the means by which both can occur: the truth of the Word of God. Furthermore, I ought to do all I can to show that the particular part of the Word of God that I am preaching is true, for my goal is to persuade by the truth. Listeners have a similar duty when a sermon is preached. As Christians you and I cannot make ourselves believe more today than we did yesterday, but we can focus our attention on the Word of God and ask God to help us grow in believing it. I would argue that it is only as we see and are convinced of its truth that our faith in God's Word grows. As they hear sermons Christians should do all that they can to see the truth of the message, to allow it to remove their doubts, and to let it answer their questions. Only as we are convinced of and persuaded of the truth of the message preached can we be rightly motivated to grow in our believing in and doing what God says.

Although I specifically reject emotion as a means of biblical motivation for the preacher and for the listener, I do not reject emotions! I hope and pray that no one will say that my work advocates for a sterile or emotionless preaching event. That is not at all what I am trying to say. If you listen to any of my sermons or come to my church you will know that is not the case. You will see and hear me express emotions. You will see and hear me plead with listeners to believe in God's Word and to do what it says, and to do so sincerely from the heart, from the whole man. I hope and pray that God's Word moves my listeners, including their emotions. Emotions are a vital part of our humanity and we should seek to express them in a God-honoring way. It would be rebellion against God and our very natures to seek to be without emotion. I hope and pray that beneficial emotions are stirred up in you in a preaching event. But I hope and pray that those emotions flow from your being convinced of and of having believed in the truth of the message, that it is the truth heard and believed that causes you to feel in God-honoring way. Right emotion can only be produced by believing in right doctrine. However, for the preacher or the listener to deliberately seek motivation through emotion without regard to right doctrine is to abuse emotion and use it in a way for which it was not designed. Converted people must seek to be transformed through the renewing of their minds—that is how they will prove that good, acceptable, and perfect will of God (Rom. 12:1–2). They must be motivated through their faith, for whatever does not come from faith is sin (Rom. 14:23).

Motivation that comes from intentionally appealing to the emotions or stirring up feelings does so without any regard for the truth of the message. I cried at the end of *Old Yeller*, and then went out and hugged my dog. Adherents of false religions are often strongly motivated. The one is fiction, the other idolatry. Feelings cannot on their own authenticate or embody truth. Only that motivation which flows from faith in God's Word of truth can generate emotions that are pleasing to God.

Moreover, emotions and feelings are not the same. Experts in the field will tell you this. The best Christian counselors know this. I do not go into the distinction in this book, but there are differences between them. One of the more obvious differences is that emotions always have some physical manifestation: sweating, increase in heart rate, and so on, whereas feelings can be wholly concealed. The reason is that while emotions touch both body and soul, feelings are generated entirely within the soul, the nonphysical aspect of our personhood. We are living in a day in which feelings have been given permission to trump objective reality. A person who is genetically, biologically, and unchangeably male can now call himself female, or vice versa, and our world says it's true. His feelings are more determinative for what is real than truth or fact. I do not believe this is simply relativism taken to its logical extreme. I think something more profound is going on here. In and of itself this particular example is sinful and wrong, even absurd. Male and female are two distinct cellular realities, observably and demonstrably absolute and undeniable. Yet man is more than what can be observed, measured, and weighed in a laboratory or petri dish. And that nonphysical, incorporeal aspect of our being has been neglected, disallowed, and even mocked for far too long. The human soul is real. It is crying out to be heard. Could it be that in the mysterious providence of God, today's sinful denial of "male and female He created them" is not simply a naked rejection of the truth of God (as if there ever was such a thing), but comes camouflaged (as rebellion is so wont to do) under something truthful: that man is more than physical? Like a voice from the metaphysical realm, though irrational and ludicrous, yet by its sheer force it compels the physical realm to acknowledge its reality, even to the point of making it promote the preposterous. Call it the revenge of the metaphysical or the humiliation of the physical. Maybe if theologians and preachers had been teaching rightly the reality of the soul and its powers, we would not be at this strange place of denying what is undeniably true and affirming what is patently false. The soul is real. It has affections and desires. It is no more an authoritative voice than any piece of our sin-laden creation, but it has power, and we ignore or deny it to our own peril.

All of these things were not at all in my mind when I chose this topic on which to write my dissertation. One of my professors, Dr. George Scipione, a biblical counselor for over thirty years at the time (over forty now), was explaining to the first doctoral cohort at Reformed Presbyterian Theological Seminary (RPTS) how a doctoral project needed to examine something not before studied. We had been talking about counseling and discipleship and about why people do the things that they do. Dr. Scipione mentioned how confused and distorted the study of motivation had become, not just outside the church but also within it and that a good topic for a doctoral dissertation would be to go through the Bible and examine how God motivates people. As one of the students in that cohort, his suggestion did not particularly interest me at the time, but I remember thinking something to the effect of "Well, if I can't think of anything better, that could work." Once I seriously began to look at the topic, however, I saw how motivation touched nearly everything in which I had an interest. Soon, in order to in any way adequately deal with the topic, I had to seriously narrow the focus from how God motivates people in the Bible to how five sermons in Acts sought to motivate their listeners.

Although I credit Dr. Scipione with giving me this topic, I take all the blame for every way in which this work falls short of its goal. It is my prayer that despite its shortcomings it would be used by God to help Christians to seek to be rightly motivated by the Word of God through their faith in its truth, and recognize and reject all emotional manipulation that would bypass the mind, and to even be the beginning of a Protestant and evangelical focus on the objective reality of the soul and its powers, that some light could shine on a place that has been in the dark for far too long.

Acknowledgments

This book would not have been published without the strong support of my examiners at Reformed Presbyterian Theological Seminary (RPTS): Dr. Jack Kinneer and Dr. C. J. Williams. I thank them for all of their help and encouragement. I want to thank Judith Dinsmore and Elizabeth Bortka for their excellent work in getting this manuscript ready for printing. Without them it would barely be readable, let alone publishable! I pray for our sovereign Lord's richest blessings upon them and their families. I also want to thank John J. Hughes and everyone else at P&R Publishing for their interest in this work. May our good God be pleased to bless them through it. Finally, I want and need to thank my faithful wife Robin and my children Calvin, Daniel, Jacob, and Sarah for their love, respect, and support in life and in ministry. I would not be able to do anything without the grace that God gives me through each and every one of them. May God forgive and cause to quickly be forgotten all the errors in this book. But may He be pleased to mightily bless and multiply any truth that is in it.

Introduction

One of the most solemn charges given in all of Scripture is contained in Paul's second letter to Timothy, where he declares to the younger preacher:

> I solemnly charge you in the presence of God and of Christ Jesus, who is to judge the living and the dead, and by His appearing and His kingdom: Preach the word! Be ready in season and out of season; reprove, rebuke, exhort, with great patience and instruction. For the time will come when they will not endure sound doctrine; but wanting to have their ears tickled, they will accumulate for themselves teachers in accordance to their own desires; and will turn away their ears from the truth, and will turn aside to myths. (2 Tim. 4:1–4 NASB)

Preach the word! Under the inspiration of the Holy Spirit, Paul wanted to so impress upon Timothy the great importance of preaching the Word of God that he would never forget it. In fact, Scripture views preaching so highly that in comparison to baptism, which was commanded by the Lord Jesus in the Great Commission of Matthew 28:19–20, Paul can even say, "For Christ did not send me to baptize, but to preach the gospel, not with wisdom of words, lest the cross of Christ should be made of no effect" (1 Cor. 1:17).

The Westminster Assembly echoed this high view of preaching. Question 155 of the Larger Catechism declares:

> How is the Word made effectual to salvation? The Spirit of God maketh the reading, *but especially the preaching of the Word*, an effectual means of enlightening, convincing, and humbling sinners; of driving them out of themselves, and drawing them unto Christ; of conforming them to his image, and subduing them to his will; of strengthening them against temptations and corruptions; of building them up in grace, and establishing their hearts in holiness and comfort through faith unto salvation.[1]

According to the Westminster Divines, it is "especially the preaching of the Word" that the Holy Spirit uses to save and sanctify His people according to the sovereign good pleasure of God. Consequently, there should be little disagreement in Reformed circles with the proposition that preaching is the most fundamental and important duty in the calling of a *preacher*.

If we take our definition of preaching from Question 155 of the Larger Catechism, how then shall we preach? Particularly, what elements of motivation should the preacher seek to incorporate into the sermon, so that the end product would be better suited to be used by the Spirit in His work of enlightening, convincing, humbling, driving, drawing, conforming, subduing, strengthening, building up, and establishing the hearts of sinners "in holiness and comfort through faith unto salvation?" This book seeks to discover how God, in His own sermonic speech to His people, sought to motivate them, and to then set forth the ways in which the preacher can emulate Him. There are many books, methods, styles, and approaches to preaching. Much of it today is concerned with applying or moving the text in order to influence attitudes and behaviors, but my question is: Can we identify the elements of motivation inspired by the Holy Spirit in those sermonic addresses to the people of God found in Scripture? Can

[1] WLC 155 (emphasis mine).

we take our method of motivating in a sermon directly from the sermons of Scripture?

Before we can turn to the Bible, we need to define what motivation is, how it is given, and determine our criteria for identifying motivational elements in the text. For that, we need to at least briefly consider a representational sampling of the current field of motivational theory, particularly with regard to how it has been identified and applied in religion, the church, and preaching. In this first part of my book, my method will be to examine what various authors say about motivation and how it is to be most effectively used, especially in a Christian context. Apart from showing consistency or inconsistency, I will try not to extol or criticize the individual arguments or methods, except where they specifically look to Scripture for justification. Since my purpose is to identify from Scripture the biblical way to motivate, I will address appeals to Scripture as they come up in order to affirm or reject them. Finally, as patterns and similarities become evident, I will seek to aid the reader by calling attention to them and drawing conclusions that will be revisited later in the book.

1

Promoting Motivational Theory to the Church

Forty years ago, when psychological motivational theory was still somewhat new, Gary Collins sought to promote some of its alleged benefits to church leaders. In his influential work, Collins opines that difficult theological concepts could be more effectively taught by making the teaching activity as meaningful as possible.[1] He argues that since boredom, meaninglessness, and hopelessness are the common plagues of modern life, the main challenge of the church is "to get people interested, enthusiastic, and involved in spiritual issues."[2] Yet Collins recognizes that people perceive things differently based on their knowledge, past experiences, current interests, emotions, hopes, and expectations. He gives, as an example, the way in which people of different backgrounds might view the same piece of land. The architect considers the home he could build, the farmer thinks about the crops he could plant, the geologist imagines the rocks he could find, and the artist envisions the painting he could create.[3]

Collins goes so far as to classify emotion *as* motivation.[4] He

[1] Gary Collins, *Man in Motion: The Psychology of Human Motivation* (Carol Stream, IL: Creation House, 1973), 24.

[2] Ibid., 9.

[3] Ibid., 44–45.

[4] Ibid., 49.

claims, "Emotions are so influential in motivating our behavior that some psychologists have even suggested dropping the term 'emotion' from psychology textbooks altogether and using the term 'motivation' instead."[5] Yet, he notes that emotional overload can have the opposite effect, resulting in de-motivation. For example, whereas the mildly anxious student is motivated to study harder,[6] "high stress and anxiety can hinder our motivation."[7] Collins says the desire for need reduction (I'm hungry so I eat), stimulation (going on a roller coaster or eating an expensive steak), unconscious habits, goals, and incentives all play a part in the complex way in which people are motivated.[8] Moreover, he notes that beliefs, attitudes, opinions, and values, which all interact with emotion to influence the way people think or act, could themselves be affected or changed by persuasion. In fact, even God uses motivation to persuade: "The Holy Spirit can and does motivate."[9] Thus, the right use of persuasion looms large in Collins' theory for the future benefit of the church.[10] Collins exhorts, "In the church we must be aware of how people are motivated and attempt to use this knowledge in motivating Christians to be more diligent in their service for Christ."[11] Collins' triad of persuasion, emotion, and personal factors will be taken up again and again by others.

[5] Ibid., 52. Here he cites M. D. Vernon, *Human Motivation* (Cambridge: Cambridge University Press, 1969), and R. S. Lazarus, J. R. Averill, and E. M. Opton, Jr., "Towards a Cognitive Theory of Emotions," in *Feelings and Emotions: The Loyola Symposium*, ed. M. B. Arnold (New York: Academic Press, 1970).

[6] Collins, *Man in Motion*, 51.

[7] Ibid., 64.

[8] Ibid., 56–64.

[9] Ibid., 64.

[10] Ibid., 108–9. He cites Acts 26:28, where Paul "almost persuaded" Agrippa to become a Christian.

[11] Ibid., 65.

2

Motivational Theory in Academia

Edward J. Murray on Motivation and Emotion

One of the early pioneers in the field of motivation, Edward J. Murray, set forth some of the difficulties experts were wrestling with right from the beginning: "The field of motivation and emotion is so disorganized,"[1] he writes in his seminal 1964 work, *Motivation and Emotion*. Psychologists were disagreed over such basic issues as whether motivation and emotion should be one area or two, he notes, and some wanted to eliminate them both entirely from the field of psychology.[2] In his work, Murray seeks consensus by defining motivation as the answer to the question of why a man does what he does. He claims that part of the confusion was because "science" was for the first time entering an area previously dominated by philosophy and religion, in order to discover how motives were affected by one's biology and experience.

Like others, Murray matter-of-factly distinguishes between internal and external motivation. He refers to the internal component as "drive" and the external as "goal" or "reward." He did not agree with some who were advocating a third categorization of "conscious

[1] Edward J. Murray, *Motivation and Emotion* (Englewood Cliffs, NJ: Prentice-Hall, 1964), vi.

[2] Ibid.

desire," or "want."[3] Instead, he emphasizes that there was a "general agreement that a motive is an internal factor that arouses, directs, and integrates a person's behavior."[4] Thus, while *motivation* was both external and internal, *motives* were understood to be internal. Like Collins a little later, Murray sees the importance of motivation as a means of influencing behavior. He notes that success in all kinds of business depends upon giving the customers the product they want. (Today we would probably say success is better achieved by giving customers the "want" for your product.) His point is that by understanding a person's motivation (what he wants), we are able to influence him toward good action or hold him responsible for bad. Here Murray cites as an example the American justice system where the punishment for murder depends upon the killer's motivation—was it premeditated or was it provoked?[5]

Murray's work is important to my research for several reasons. He marks the point in time when motivational theory made a final break with the system of "instincts" of the Freudian model, which by the 1920s had officially categorized over six thousand different instincts, including the "instinct to avoid eating apples in one's own orchard!"[6] In the transition period between instinct and motivation, some flirted with various "drive theories" where the energy that impels to action was categorized under such headings as hunger drive, thirst drive, sex drive, and so on, but Murray's approach of understanding these drives as psychological needs seemed to already be the majority position in 1964.[7] Additionally, Murray gives a good overview of the various strands of motivational theory competing for ascendency right at the time when the field was coming into its

[3] Ibid., 7–8.

[4] Ibid., 7.

[5] Ibid., 2.

[6] Ibid., 5–6.

[7] Ibid., 6–7. Consider also that Abraham Maslow's famous "hierarchy of needs" was first fully expressed in *Motivation and Personality*, which was published ten years earlier, in 1954.

own. In particular his view of the relationship of emotion to motivation anticipates certain views of preaching that we will consider in the church context. Finally, Murray represents a strong break with the peculiar strand of motivational theory that was stilted in the mechanical determinism of influential American psychologist John B. Watson. According to Murray, that classical behavioral-based motivation theory, which held that an organism has a drive that continues until the stimulation that produced the drive is reduced (what we know today as "drive-reduction" theory), had as its ultimate goal of action a state of nirvana, or no stimulation. Yet Murray keenly points out that the universally-acknowledged *undesirable* state of boredom flies in the face of this theory. He concludes rather that people seek neither too much, nor too little, stimulation.

For at least the last thirty years, high schools and colleges have regularly taught Maslow's hierarchy of needs, but Murray goes further than Maslow in allowing, even at a basic level, acquired needs born out of love. He cites as support the functional autonomous motivation of Gordon W. Allport demonstrated in Allport's famous example of the wealthy ex-sailor who began his career simply needing work to buy food, but then fell in love with the sea and longed to return from an entirely different motive, the first one being no longer operative at all. Neither is there any animalistic instinct or hormonal drive needed to explain his behavior.[8] Murray cites examples where new stimulations are sought out and desired (seeing new sights), whereas old ones can grow tiresome (an overplayed song). Likewise, he notes that children are motivated to activity merely for the pleasure of doing it: running, jumping, climbing, and so on.[9] Murray tries to incorporate the emotions, desires, growth, and change that all people go through into his presentation of motivational theory, resulting in a view of man that differs from other pioneers in the field and is closer to man's actual nature as set forth in Scripture.

[8] Ibid., 72.
[9] Ibid., 76–79.

Murray's Error: Emotions Are *Motivation*

Ironically, the theme of Murray's book—how motivation interacts with emotion—is the weak point in his presentation. In chapter 5, "Emotional Motives," he notes that science identifies emotions as feelings and reactions aroused by external stimuli, which can be positive or negative and endlessly distinguished.[10] Murray, however, frames his own definition of emotion in relation to motivation: "[A]n emotion is an externally aroused motive with important bodily accompaniments."[11] Here, Murray makes a very significant error that many will follow and that accounts for much of the emotionally manipulative preaching in contemporary evangelicalism: emotions are motives. Again, if we combine his definitions of *emotion* and *motive*, we get: "[A]n emotion is an externally aroused internal factor that arouses, directs, and integrates a person's behavior with important bodily accompaniments."[12]

Murray offers a detailed example to prove his assertion that emotions *are* externally aroused motives:

> Imagine a man who is driving along a road when another car suddenly darts out of a driveway. The man is frightened, he feels a sinking sensation in the pit of his stomach, and his muscles tense up. The effect on his behavior is dramatic—he jams his foot down hard on the brake pedal and rapidly turns the steering wheel. There is a screeching of the brakes followed by the sickening sound of breaking glass and crumpling of fenders. The man sits for a moment and then the fear turns to anger—this idiot has frightened him, upset his schedule, and caused damage to his car. The anger also has dramatic effects on his behavior—he sets his jaw and strides toward the other car. Then, he sees that the other drive is injured, with blood streaming down his face. The man has

[10] Ibid., 56.
[11] Ibid., 51.
[12] See ibid., 51, 57.

> a wave of nausea, a twinge of guilt, and a strong feeling of compassion. Once more behavior is mobilized—the man administers first aid and calls for an ambulance.[13]

Murray concludes that emotions have a powerful motivating effect on behavior.

The primary problem with this analysis is Murray's failure to take into account the heart and mind of the main actor in the illustration. The man's emotions or feelings do not "mobilize" his behavior at all. It is the man's heart and mind, his character and faith, which determine, not only his actions, but his emotions. Put another kind of man in this example and when he sees the person hurt, he feels glad and robs him! Still another man worries about being blamed for the accident, abandons the victim, and drives off. We can easily imagine many different reactions, all equally plausible. The accident creates a crisis where action and emotion are elicited, but it is the virtue or lack of it in a man's heart, which in turn is the product of what he believes about himself, God, and others, that causes him to act *and to feel* the way he does. The emotion does not bring about the behavior, *what the man believes* does. And what the man believes also determines the emotions he feels, and to what degree he will allow himself to act out of them.

Theodore A. McConnell's Quest for Meaning

An interesting example of how the fields of psychology and religion were interacting at this early stage in the development of motivational theory is the book *The Shattered Self: The Psychological and Religious Search for Selfhood* by Theodore A. McConnell, published in 1971. Noting how psychology and theology irreconcilably differed on the concept of the self, McConnell examines six different models of the self as set forth by twentieth-century psychology and

[13] Ibid., 48–49.

claims his study "indicates some major areas of relationship and dissonance between these and a variety of theological perspectives."[14] His goal was to "begin exploring the relationship" between the psychological models and the theological perspectives.[15] The models he highlights most positively are the functional autonomy of Gordon W. Allport, where motives develop autonomously corresponding to one's personality; the logotherapy of Viktor Frankl, where the search for meaning is man's most motivating force (not power, as Nietzsche claimed, nor pleasure, as Freud contended); and the hierarchy of needs model of Abraham Maslow, where man is motivated from basic physical needs to more complex cerebral and social needs.

McConnell asserts that the quest for meaning is the most motivating force in man.[16] He claims that a person's identity is only found in the cause that he chooses to get behind. The "tension between what is and what ought to be" (according to the judgment of the individual) characterizes the self. Selfhood is the striving for meaning as a result of this tension. He calls this quest for meaning, a person's self-transcendence toward a chosen "ought."[17] McConnell finds comparable emphases on meaning and transcendence in the writings of neo-orthodox theologians Karl Barth, Rudolf Bultmann, Emil Brunner, and Reinhold Niebuhr, and in Dietrich Bonhoeffer's relation of suffering to meaning.[18] Thus, McConnell concludes, both the humanistic psychologists and the neo-orthodox theologians see the strongest motivating force as the meaning inherently experienced in striving to accomplish some desired good as determined by the self. McConnell's existentialism is palpable throughout his analysis, and probably accounts for this proclivity toward neo-orthodoxy and the existentialist search for meaning being the identifying factor

[14] Theodore A. McConnell, *The Shattered Self* (Philadelphia: Pilgrim Press, 1971), xi.

[15] Ibid., xii.

[16] Ibid., 54–55.

[17] Ibid., 56.

[18] Ibid., 57–58.

of the self. I see the same existentialist philosophy fueling those preaching methods that teach that the most effective way of motivation is by utilizing or validating the individual's search for meaning or purpose in this life.

Beyond This Creath Davis Goes

Going further and deeper than McConnell, Creath Davis declares in his book *Beyond This God Cannot Go* that the most powerful motivation results when the Christian pursues meaning through a life of love. According to Davis, knowledge is a necessary part, but not a sufficient source, of motivation. A man's values—what he esteems—is what will impel him to action: "Rational knowledge is necessary if man is to act, but it is not adequate to furnish the dynamics which thrust men into action. . . . Man is by nature a value-pursuing creature. He uses his reason to pursue what he esteems."[19] Furthermore, Davis sees values as a prism through which a man subjectively creates the world in which he lives.[20]

Davis avers that all Christians are given the same mandate from God, which is to "try to remake this world on the pattern of heaven." He cautions that accepting and pursuing this task requires a great deal of motivation.[21] And when Christians see that they cannot change the world, problems occur. Their motivation regresses to fear of punishment and hope of reward, both in this life and in the life to come. Now they are motivated by the expectation of society to get involved in certain activities that are considered to be religious and good. Fear of disapproval spurs them to act. Their goal is to maintain peace and keep everyone happy. But in avoiding criticism they sacrifice joy.[22]

[19] Creath Davis, *Beyond This God Cannot Go* (Grand Rapids, MI: Zondervan, 1971), 135–36.

[20] Ibid., 136.

[21] Ibid.

[22] Ibid., 137.

> Fear of punishment and hope of reward. . . . Anyone caught up in these motivations will be paralyzed, unable to take any action about which he feels he is not absolutely certain. . . . He must be able to quote a specific verse of Scripture for each decision to avoid the possibility of making a mistake. In theological circles this is usually called "legalism."[23]

In addition to confusing Christian obedience with legalism, it is clear from the broader context of his work that Davis, in the quote above, redefines *faith* as "believing that I can change the world." Thus, it is when a man no longer believes that he can change the world, when he loses *this kind* of faith, that he regresses to a motivation of fear of punishment and hope of rewards and begins to be paralyzed in his activity. Davis calls this type of motivation "more negative than positive." It still "prods us into action, but it will be without spontaneity or creativity."[24] When one no longer believes that what one does can change the world, spontaneity and creativity exit and despair and pessimism enter.[25] Faith is central to Davis' concept of motivation, but his faith is not a trust in Christ for one's justification. Faith is one's personal conviction of the plausibility that through oneself, this world will become more like heaven.

Since Davis' faith cannot sustain itself, his dilemma is to find a motivation strong enough to overcome declining into a legalistic life ruled by the Scriptures fueled with a hope of reward and fear of punishment. He found the solution to his dilemma in *love*. "The most creative, dynamic motivation that exists is love . . . a love which runs as deep as life itself for Jesus Christ and for what He purposes."[26] Davis counts Peter as an example of being motivated by this kind of love. Davis avers that after Peter denied Christ,

[23] Ibid.
[24] Ibid.
[25] Ibid., 136.
[26] Ibid., 138.

> He saw the same accepting love in the face of Christ that he had seen from the very beginning—and it broke him up. He went out and wept bitter tears of repentance. Now he knew what unconditional love, acceptance and forgiveness was all about, and it melted the coldness in his heart.[27]

Consideration of Davis's Scriptural Support

One of the problems with this kind of analysis and the conclusions Davis draws from it is that he makes a definitive statement that an emotional experience of Peter produced a change in his understanding and heart, without a single word of Scripture confirming this interpretation. We do not know, because Scripture does not say, what Peter saw, knew, or what it did to his heart when he saw Jesus' face. We know Peter looked at Jesus and then he went out and "wept bitterly" (Luke 22:62). But even here, the three passages that record this event all specifically say that it was not the look Jesus gave to Peter that caused him to go out and weep bitterly, but rather Peter's remembrance of the words of Jesus that he would betray his Lord:

> Then he began to curse and swear, saying, "I do not know the Man!" Immediately a rooster crowed. *And Peter remembered the word of Jesus* who had said to him, "Before the rooster crows, you will deny Me three times." *So he went out and wept bitterly*. (Matt. 26:74–75)

> A second time the rooster crowed. *Then Peter called to mind the word that Jesus had said to him*, "Before the rooster crows twice, you will deny Me three times." *And when he thought about it, he wept*. (Mark 14:72)

> And the Lord turned and looked at Peter. *And Peter remembered the word of the Lord, how He had said to him*, "Before the

[27] Ibid., 139.

> rooster crows, you will deny Me three times." *So Peter went out and wept bitterly*. (Luke 22:61–62)

Even Luke, who alone speaks of Christ looking at Peter, explicitly states that it was when Peter remembered Christ's words that he went out and wept. Christ's look played a part in Peter's remembrance, but it was his remembrance of Christ's words and not his interpretation of Christ's look that is credited as causing Peter's emotional reaction in all three gospels. Therefore, Davis incorrectly asserts, "To see what Peter saw in the face of Christ will either awaken a deep, passionate love for Him within us, or it will destroy our ability to love at all."[28] Clearly, Davis' position is that one's experientially provoked emotions more powerfully motivate than rational, propositional truth, even when it is from the lips of Jesus.

In Davis' theory of motivation, love, like faith, is redefined. Love is not identified according to its biblical description of keeping God's commandments in an obedience that is not a burden but a delight (see Ps. 119; 1 Cor. 13; 1 John 5:3), but rather love is deep feeling and affection. Love is emotion, and as we have seen, emotion is either inseparable from or equivalent to motivation according to many theorists. Thus, Davis interpreted Jesus' restoration of Peter in John 21, where Jesus repeatedly asks Peter if he loves Him, as being successful to the degree that Peter loves, or is emotionally attached to, Jesus. According to Davis, Peter will carry out his calling to the degree that he is motivated by his love for Jesus.[29] Love, then, is understood in terms of emotion, not of rational, volitional commitment.

Now Davis does not, in this work, promote a method or style of preaching to engender this kind of motivating love. Instead, he declares that we get this kind of love by diligently asking God for it. As with his earlier definition of faith, Davis' concept of love appears

[28] Ibid.
[29] Ibid., 140.

to be most concerned with its impact on one's experience in this world. He emphasizes that the more we have of this kind of love, the more we will be poured out for others. Yet he claims man, in his selfishness, is often afraid to want or ask for this kind of love.

Davis is important to this work because he is an early proponent of motivation through a redefined faith and love, which are fueled by emotion, emptied of their vertical component, and valued exclusively for their potential improvement of this life. Davis' negative view of reward and punishment and obedience to God's law are also common themes in works on motivation.

Motivation in Self-Help Works

Motivational works of the more general self-help variety take this same "improvement of this life" emphasis and individualize it for personal gain. A typical example is Don McMinn's *Strategic Living: How to Set and Accomplish Life-Changing Goals*, published in 1988. McMinn's book is straightforward in its concern: "The presence or absence of motivation is often the sole difference between energized action and accomplishment, and apathetic inactivity and failure."[30] Seeking to correct what he says is a common error, McMinn instructs that true motivation is neither intimidation, nor manipulation, nor stimulation. These three impostures can produce results, but intimidation destroys joy, manipulation kills trust, and stimulation, which targets the emotions, is temporary at best.[31]

So what is motivation? Unfortunately McMinn cannot tell us! He does declare, however, that it is very important: "Motivation is an essential ingredient for productivity."[32] He quotes Paul J. Meyer, president of Success Motivation Institute, to instruct us that the motivation that will drive you to permanent and sustaining

[30] Don J. McMinn, *Strategic Living: How to Set and Accomplish Life-Changing Goals* (Grand Rapids, MI: Baker, 1988), 58.

[31] Ibid., 58–59.

[32] Ibid., 61.

success "must be personal, deep-rooted, and a part of your innermost thoughts. All other motivation, the excitement of a crowd, the stimulation of a pep talk, the exhilaration of a passing circumstance, is external and temporary. It will not last."[33] Motivation itself is "that mysterious, often unexplainable element."[34] It is crucial in that it is "the on/off switch that operates a huge, almost limitless machine—you!"[35] Moreover, McMinn insists that motivation can only be gotten internally: "[Motivation] *starts* from within. It is logical; it makes sense (although in time it can become emotional). And motivation is lasting; it won't wear off."[36] He knows that it is somehow "tied to our desires and affections,"[37] but admits he cannot tell us how:

> But what motivates us? Only you can answer that. . . . Past experiences, future hopes, present pressures, a magazine article, a deep conviction, the example of a hero, the suggestion of a friend, a personal preference, a selfish desire, a vision from God, a natural talent—all these and more can combine to produce—motivation.[38]

McMinn tries to point us in the right direction to help us get our own motivation. He instructs that because motivation is highly contagious, we should seek to be around *motivated people*: "I'm referring to people who really produce." Being around motivated people "will act as a catalyst for our latent potential."[39] Likewise, good planning will help us to see how we can get what we want, then if we want it badly enough, and the plan makes the effort required to get it seem reasonable and within our power, we will be motivated to execute

[33] Ibid., 59.
[34] Ibid., 61.
[35] Ibid., 60.
[36] Ibid., 59.
[37] Ibid., 61.
[38] Ibid., 60–61.
[39] Ibid., 62–63.

the plan, thereby getting what we want.[40] Additionally meaningful action and needs motivate, whereas fear of failure, complacency, laziness, procrastination, and stagnation do not.[41] McMinn concludes his purely pragmatic but honest approach with a strong plea:

> So the words of exhortation are—*get motivated.* Eliminate the hindrances to motivation, embrace those activities which promote motivation—and get motivated. Look for, pray for, that fire that burns within. You won't accomplish many meaningful things in life without the motivation factor.[42]

With respect to this book's study of the motivational elements in the sermonic passages of Scripture, the interesting thing about McMinn's approach, which as mentioned above is entirely utilitarian in aim, is his rejection of all emotional appeals from his category of "true motivation." In particular he noted as an example that any effect from the thrilling or stimulating or rousing speech soon wears off.[43] Ironically, as my book will later seek to demonstrate, those advocating emotional appeals in sermons do so with the claim that these kinds of sermons *most effectively* motivate.

Motivation in Scientific Research and Experimentation

At this point I want to turn to a combined studies analysis and see how research and experimentation can contribute to this project. This studies analysis, edited by Theall, examined the models and research of nine authors, the field work of four others, and took into consideration the writings of other fields of inquiry.[44]

[40] Ibid., 63.
[41] Ibid., 63–74.
[42] Ibid., 76 (emphasis in original).
[43] Ibid., 59.
[44] Michael Theall, ed., "Motivation from Within: Approaches for Encouraging Faculty and Students to Excel," Marilla D. Svinicki, series ed., *New*

I will look at several of their studies, which are pertinent to my project of motivation in preaching. Theall's group sets up a few axioms through which the various methods that they examine are considered. First, it defines *motivation* as "a construct that describes how individuals respond to sets of conditions in light of their own perspectives, attitudes, and beliefs."[45] Second, their analysis affirms both intrinsic and extrinsic motivation with the following distinction. Rewards are viewed as external but the decision to pursue the reward must come from within. Therefore, efforts to motivate should "target their values, needs, and orientations, [so] that an understanding of the individual allows teachers or others to provide sets of conditions that will prompt positive intrinsic motivation."[46] Finally, the authors acknowledge that motivation cannot be measured directly, but must be inferred or deduced from observed actions. Motivation provides "a possible concrete causal explanation of behavior."[47]

Wlodkowski's Framework

The first system they analyze is propounded in "Motivation and Diversity: A Framework for Teaching," by Raymond L. Wlodkowski. Wlodkowski saw a problem with earlier studies of motivation, which he says continued up through the 1980s, where psychology focused too much on the individual and factors within the individual to the neglect of exterior factors such as the culture. Wlodkowski claimed to represent a more socio-constructivistic approach which placed a greater emphasis on the social context. The goal of this approach was to get educators away from externally motivated grades, categorized by Wlodkowski as artificial and mechanical, in order to find intrinsic systems that were perceived to be more fair and more student-oriented. Proponents of

---

Directions for Teaching and Learning, 78 (Summer 1999), 105.

[45] Ibid., 1.

[46] Ibid.

[47] Ibid., 7.

this method view traditional grading systems as a negative, extrinsic application of a rewards and punishments model. On the contrary, intrinsic systems are those in which "teachers and students create opportunities, experiences, or environments that are likely to evoke motivation." The latter models alone can support respect and social equity toward all students, according to Wlodkowski, because only an intrinsic system can respect different cultures and thereby create a learning environment both accessible and acceptable to students of all backgrounds.

Notice how in Wlodkowski's study, the emotional, subjective, and internal are inherently good. They provide more opportunities and are more likely to be motivational. They are styled personal, constructive, fair, respectful, student-oriented, whereas the external, objective measures of rewards and punishments are referred to as mechanistic, individualistic, negative, stifling, and not supportive of social equity for all students. In fact, in Wlodkowski's method, "extrinsic" inherently means bad, "intrinsic" inherently means good.

Wlodkowski's findings are based on his "Motivational Framework for Culturally Responsive Teaching" (Wlodkowski and Ginsberg, 1995). This framework recommends that teachers include and combine all of those motivating factors and conditions which they have evaluated as being intrinsically motivating to all kinds of students. According to their research those conditions are: "establishing inclusion," that is, making students "feel respected and connected to one another"; "developing attitude," that is, "creating a favorable disposition toward the learning experience through personal relevance and choice"; "enhancing meaning," which is achieved by including the "students' perspectives and values"; and "engendering competence," by making the students believe that they "are effective in learning something they value."[48] They conclude that their model, because it considers the cognitive process in a way that integrates and includes social activity and interaction, is superior to the older

[48] Ibid., 10–11.

linear psychological models, which focused on perception, then thinking, and action.[49]

For our purposes of recognizing motivational elements in sermons, Wlodkowski presents a method of motivation that is entirely feelings-based and subjective. Motivation and emotion have merged to the point where objective truth, reality, and fact have no place whatsoever, unless as a hindrance to the motivation and emotion, which has, in Wlodkowski's framework, become no longer just the method but the goal and aim of the education process. Consequently, emphasizing external rewards and punishments impedes the education process. I have found that this approach of many modern educational models—wherein internal motivation is both the method and the goal of education—has been adopted by some of the motivational preaching methods, as I hope to demonstrate. I will examine the Scriptures to see to what degree internal feelings and emotions are viewed positively and rewards and punishments negatively in the motivating method of the Holy Spirit in Scripture.

The ARCS Model

The second study Theall's group analyzes is "Using the ARCS Motivational Process in Computer-Based Instruction and Distance Education," by John M. Keller.[50] The ARCS model purports to adapt to and meet the motivational needs of a given group of students. It sets forth a seven-step systematic model by which motivational factors are worked into teaching.[51] The ARCS model analyzes motivational needs based on what it identifies as the four dimensions of motivation. They claim that the four dimensions were developed based upon the combination of a variety of studies done on human motivation. The four dimensions make up the ARCS acronym: attention (A), relevance (R), confidence (C),

[49] Ibid., 12.
[50] Ibid., 39–47.
[51] Ibid., 39.

and satisfaction (S).[52] Rather than incorporating a flat number of motivational exercises for everyone, the ARCS model purports to be adaptable to the motivational level of the student. Through various exercises the model seeks to capture and keep the student's attention, then give him tasks relevant to the subject to perform, which as he succeeds in them builds his confidence, which in turn increases his satisfaction.

The ARCS model views motivation in an entirely utilitarian approach. The underlying assumption is that students who are highly motivated in an activity will work harder and perform better because they want to. Here, motivation is *not* the end goal, but simply a tool that can enable students to work more efficiently. The simple objective of the ARCS model is for the student to better learn the material—the doctrine, if you will—of the subject to which it is applied. The computer is programmed to internally motivate each student subjectively, with constant feedback according to results. The ARCS model anticipated some modern video-game-based learning systems.[53] It is important for my study because it statistically shows that motivation techniques can be effectively used to influence behavior and increase learning.

The CORE Elements

The third method of motivation in education examined is called the "CORE Elements of Student Motivation in Problem-Based Learning," by Marjorie M. MacKinnon. This method purports to motivate students to want to learn, not simply by memory, which it views negatively, but by combining what it calls the four elements of student motivation known as CORE.[54] The study comments on the research that has shown Chinese students consistently

[52] Ibid.

[53] Richard D. Blunt, "A Causal-Comparative Exploration of the Relationship Between Game-Based Learning and Academic Achievement: Teaching Management with Video Games," (Ph.D. diss., Walden University, 2006), 24.

[54] Theall, "Motivation from Within," 49.

outperforming Western students on examinations. These students are typically more demanding of teachers, constantly requesting detailed notes, models, sample essays, and a variety of other study materials especially before exams. The CORE method criticizes the Chinese system for requiring students to depend upon memorization in order to succeed in the classroom and for demanding more of teachers.[55]

MacKinnon adds another criticism of the Chinese system, which is due to its performance-based orientation: students will often proceed all the way through elementary and high school without experiencing anything other than examinations testing their knowledge of instructional content that was delivered through information-communicating lectures. Thus, the students perform better than American students, but as that is an extrinsic, mechanistic measurement, it is not deemed as important as acquiring the CORE elements of student motivation, which, as will be shown, have become not only the method but the goal of the education process.

MacKinnon lists these elements as Community, which is defined as the relationship of students with one another and with their teachers; Ownership, where the students are intrinsically motivated to become responsible for their own progress by being made to perceive themselves to be autonomous and self-sufficient; Relevance, which according to MacKinnon is typically considered the most important motivational factor in problem-based learning (PBL); and Empowerment, which is produced as students see that they have the skill and ability for personally accomplishing something they believe is valuable.[56] According to MacKinnon, excelling in the CORE elements, not memorizing new information, is the goal of the education process. In a surprisingly direct appeal to the hierarchy of needs pyramid developed half a century ago by Maslow,

[55] Ibid., 50–51.
[56] Ibid., 52–55.

she argues for the superiority of this model because the CORE elements more successfully meet human needs for affinity, self-esteem, and self-actualization.[57]

Accordingly, instead of trying to raise test scores, she counsels that teachers ought to focus on things like discovering how they can build a better sense of community in their classrooms.[58] The Chinese system is perceived to be problematic because it merely produces students who are high achievers academically, and she assesses it to have the second weakness of producing students who will have to always rely on memorizing facts and information in order to continue to excel in the learning process.[59] On the contrary, MacKinnon explains, acquiring the CORE elements, that is, being motivated by having good interpersonal relationships, seeing the relevancy of assignments, while perceiving oneself to be self-sufficient and one's skills valuable, is the measure of a good education in this model.

Cooperative Learning

The fourth method of educating through motivation studied by Theall et al. is "The Motivational Benefits of Cooperative Learning," by Theodore Panitz. Cooperative Learning (CL) seeks to make individuals dependent upon the group in meeting objectives. Citing other research, Panitz claims that because CL focuses on enhancing the self-esteem of students, it is better at motivating them to more fully participate in their academic process.[60] Additionally, Panitz declares that his research shows that Cooperative Learning is superior to other models for the following reasons: it increases students' satisfaction as they learn, for it engenders student mastery over against the old accumulation of facts method that renders them more reliant on outside sources of information; it reduces anxiety in students who in the old system could be called upon to answer

[57] Ibid., 56.
[58] Ibid.
[59] Ibid., 50–51.
[60] Ibid., 59.

a question they did not know because in CL the group is responsible for the answer, not the individual (Panitz claims that few, if any, mistakes occur in a CL setting); and it focuses on developing a nonthreatening environment where different feelings are respected, minorities and majorities work together, and positive attitudes are developed by emphasizing inclusion, connection, helping, and interaction at all levels, creating an atmosphere of cooperation and acceptance. Finally CL is superior to other education models because it is "particularly effective at increasing the leadership skills of female students and at getting male students used to turning to women for help in pressure situations."[61]

While at the top of this list of benefits Panitz states that CL "promotes mastery," yet he does not seem to mean that test scores improve in this system. In fact, he later boasts that CL significantly reduces examination anxiety because there are few if any tests! Although he adds that "CL provides many opportunities for alternate forms of student assessment,"[62] his study is simply not interested in comparing itself to traditional methods of education based upon traditional measurements of learning (tests). Once again motivation that is measured by displays of positive emotions is the means as well as the end. The *successfulness* of Cooperative Learning is determined by how it makes the student feel about himself and others, not by the amount of factual information that he learns in a particular subject.

Theall and associates offer some concluding comments on their evaluation. The goal for educators in the classroom (and for our purposes we could say for preachers in the pulpit) is to create an environment that facilitates and encourages motivation. They argue from scientific research that human beings cannot directly and effectively motivate other human beings. However, what they can do is create the environment that is most conducive to people motivating themselves.[63] This conclusion flows from the rejection

[61] Ibid., 60–62.

[62] Ibid., 60.

[63] Ibid., 80. Motivation is assumed to be exclusively internal.

of all external or extrinsic motivation as being legitimate motivation, which has become the orthodox dogma of the experts. Only when the desire is somehow born within one is one's motivation truly internal and therefore authentic and desirable. Any motivation that is given to one directly from outside of one is by definition forced, artificial ,and wrong. They cite multiple studies to argue that the environment that best promotes internal motivation is the one

> giving positive reinforcement, conveying enthusiasm, creating awareness of value, maintaining global awareness, cultivating personal responsibility, fostering supportive interpersonal relationships, linking individuals' intrinsic self-interest with the program, structuring experiences that show real-world relevance.[64]

Theall states that their findings yields a consistent pattern where six particular factors are emphasized: inclusion, attitude, meaning, competence, leadership, and satisfaction.[65] In other words, if we can create an environment or context that fosters these six factors, we will be providing the greatest opportunities for truly internal motivation to occur and develop, which includes positive emotions, student comfortability, inclusion, acceptance, and acculturation. This is the goal at which the models are aiming.[66]

Once again we will read "congregant" for "student" in order to apply these findings to our question. Theall's own conclusion lends implicit support to this application as he declares that the implication of his group's analysis goes well beyond the classroom:

> The consistency of the models clearly suggests that inclusion in a coherent community can raise awareness and enhance positive attitudes, that these benefits can bring meaning

[64] Ibid., 81.
[65] Ibid., 105.
[66] Ibid., 103.

> and value to academic and workplace situations, that the effort expended by those who perceive meaning will result in greater success and heightened levels of competence and confidence, and that a great deal of intrinsic satisfaction will result.[67]

It will be interesting to see if we can find any Scriptures that support this emphasis on positive emotion, individual self-esteem, and group cohesiveness as the main goal of instruction.

A Cross-Cultural Perspective on Motivation

Another study particularly looked at how a positive self-image affected academic performance. Wondimu Ahmed and Marjon Bruinsma explored how the collective culture of Asians versus the independence emphasis of the West might affect what had heretofore been thought to be universally applicable axioms in theories of the self and motivation. Like previous studies, their experiment affirmed, in the main, the widely held theory that the more positive one felt about oneself academically, the higher would be one's academic achievement.[68] In fact, on this main issue the difference between the Asian and European groups was statistically insignificant.[69] For both Asians and Europeans, those who thought more positively about themselves academically did indeed perform higher academically. What the study does not demonstrate is *how* feeling positive about oneself *is related to* higher academic performance. Was one the cause of the other? Were both the result of being self-disciplined and having studied? Or were both the product of contriving a fool-proof way of cheating?

[67] Ibid., 107.

[68] Wondimu Ahmed and Marjon Bruinsma, "A Structural Model of Self-concept, Autonomous Motivation, and Academic Performance in Cross-cultural Perspective," *Electronic Journal of Research in Educational Psychology* 4, 3 (2006), 566–67.

[69] Ibid., 566.

The one notable difference was "that in the Asian sample autonomous motivation does not seem to be of equivalent value in determining outcome [as it was in the European sample]."[70] Here autonomous motivation refers to "doing a task . . . for the pleasure and satisfaction derived from [it]," or when an activity is performed for external reasons, which have been accepted as personally valuable.[71] What this means is that the study found that Asian students more consistently performed well academically even when they did not enjoy the task or agreed that an assigned task was personally valuable, or to say it another way, Asian students performed well even when they were *not internally motivated.* Asian students still did a good job when they did not want or value the job that they were given. The authors theorize that this is a product of the collectivistic emphasis of the East over against the stressing of the individual in the West, but this theory is not proven. The difference could just as easily be due to an emphasis on achievement in the East vs. self-esteem in the West! For this book the significant outcome of this study is the finding that *Westerners do better at those things about which they feel good.*

Thus far, our analysis of motivational theory, as it has been formulated and tested by academicians and theorists for several decades, has revealed at the very least a consistently close affinity for including or even equating motivation with positive human emotions and self-esteem but what about the religious literature? Let us now briefly consider what studies that have specifically looked at the motivation in the church context have found.

[70] Ibid., 569.
[71] Ibid., 555–56.

3

Motivational Theory in the Church

Zagzebski's Divine Motivation Theory: Motive as Affective Emotion

First, we look at a study called *Divine Motivation Theory*, by Linda Trinkaus Zagzebski. As a major philosophical treatise seeking to ground all good and evil in motivation, the motivation of God Himself, and published in this century, it's appropriate for this book to consider Zagzebski's theory in some detail. According to John Lippitt, University of Hertfordshire, UK, reviewer for *Faith and Philosophy*, Zagzebski argues that man is motivated, not compelled, to virtue. The book "puts forward 'a theological virtue ethics in which morality is driven by the attractiveness of the good.'"[1] Zagzebski describes her divine motivation theory as "a strong form of virtue theory with a theological foundation."[2] She states that one of her goals is to uncover whether morality attracts or compels, which she describes as "the difference between virtue theories and duty theories."[3] Her thesis is unambiguously declared: "My purpose in this

[1] John Lippitt, review of *Divine Motivation Theory*, by Linda Trinkaus Zagzebski, *Faith and Philosophy* 25, 4 (October 2008), 451.

[2] Linda Trinkaus Zagzebski, *Divine Motivation Theory* (Cambridge: Cambridge University Press, 2004), xi.

[3] Ibid.

book is to present an ethical theory driven by the concept of the good."[4] Her method is to avoid "an ethic of obligation" in order "to see how far we can get with an ethic of the good." Thus, she says her study intentionally eschews Aquinas, Kant, and most *modern* ethicists, as she places them within the camp of obligation. Her goal is to develop "the attractiveness of the good."[5]

For the purposes of my book we will not be following Zagzebski's thesis so much as her presentation of how God motivates us. Interestingly, on this subject Zagzebski immediately ties in the concept of emotion. In fact, she summarizes divine motivation theory as a theory based on emotion: "An affective perception of the world is what I believe constitutes an emotion. What follows is an ethical theory based on the emotions of a perfect being."[6] Once more we see a study making an intimate connection between motivation and emotion. In fact, Zagzebski defines *motive* as an emotion that brings about action: "A motive is an emotion causing an act."[7] And again, "I call an emotion a motive when it initiates action . . . motives are emotions that cause acts."[8] Thus, her "theory makes the moral properties of persons, acts, and the outcomes of acts derivative from a good motive, the most basic component of a virtue, where what I mean by a motive is an emotion that initiates and directs action."[9] Consequently, with this emphasis on emotion and action, the goal of divine motivation is to morally persuade. Moral persuasion takes place when we get a person to make the moral judgment we want them to make. "When he is morally strong, a motive sufficient for action accompanies his judgment; when he is morally weak, a motive insufficient for action accompanies his judgment."[10] And

[4] Ibid., xiii.
[5] Ibid., xii.
[6] Ibid., xiv.
[7] Ibid., 97.
[8] Ibid., 72.
[9] Ibid., 1.
[10] Ibid., 9.

so persuasion comes about when we give a person a strong enough *motive* to cause him to act, which is equivalent to giving him a strong enough *emotion* to cause him to act. Notice how the weakness or strength of moral action is based upon whether the motive impels action.

Ends and motives are closely related in Zagzebski's theory. Although motives can exist without ends, every end necessarily has a motive.[11] She states that to ask why a person has a certain end in an act is to ask questions of motive.[12] Yet, breaking with some of the previous theorists we have examined, Zagzebski avers that a motive is not the same thing as an end. She offers an illustration to prove her point: A searching person may be looking for his keys, but it is not correct to say that his motive is to find his keys. That is his goal, aim, end, or even purpose, but his motive is to get to work on time, to not get in trouble with his boss, to not have the embarrassment of being late, and so on. She concludes, "Means-end explanation tells us why an agent acts . . . but a further explanation is needed for the fact that he has the end that he has."[13]

Here, notice that although Zagzebski clearly and repeatedly defines a motive as an emotion, none of the possible motives she offers in this illustration are emotions. We could argue that behind his motive to not get in trouble with his boss or to not suffer embarrassment for being late was the emotion of fear, but Zagzebski does not make this connection. Rather, she refers to not wanting to get in trouble or being embarrassed as the motives themselves. Even more difficult to explain is the first motive she offers: to get to work on time. What emotion could be behind this motive? Here, at least, Zagzebski seems to, perhaps inadvertently, allow for a sense of duty to be a motive impelling one to act without the accompaniment of a prior emotion behind the motive of duty. However, to be fair, in another place Zagzebski seems to qualify her equalization of motive

[11] Ibid., 72.
[12] Ibid., 98.
[13] Ibid., 22–23.

to affective emotion; perhaps allowing for something else to come in with the emotion and be an additional cause of action: "A motive is an emotional state. . . . Emotions are typically identified by the way they feel. . . . A motive is a (partly) affective state in the agent's psyche that moves him to act."[14] Calling a motive an emotional state is not the same thing as identifying a motive as an emotion having risen to the level of causing an action. I call attention to this possible inconsistency in a method that explicitly identifies motives as emotions to point out the difficulty in accounting for even simple actions entirely from an emotional cause.

Zagzebski rejects what she calls *classical utilitarianism*, the idea that the motives of an act do not determine the morality of the act, but are found to be good or bad only according to the outcomes they produce.[15] On the contrary, in divine motivation theory, the ends do not justify the means. Zagzebski argues that outcomes can be good or bad directly or indirectly depending upon the end (goal) of the action. She offers a few examples: I tried to hurt him but benefited him instead; I showed compassion only so that I could look good to others. Here the "end" is the goal of the action, which is explicitly stated: I tried to hurt him; I attempted to look good to others. Likewise the outcome both times is revealed: I benefited him; I showed compassion. The ends in both cases were bad, yet the outcomes both times were good.

She states that in divine motivation theory, the "motive" is the emotion driving the action, while the "end" is the goal of the action. The "outcome" appears to be the result of the action, although never explicitly defined.[16] Thus, people can commit the same act with entirely different motives, which may change the act from being good to bad, or vice versa. Zagzebski concludes that ultimately the motive makes an act good or bad, not the outcome of the act. And the end is likewise determined by the motive. A good motive makes

[14] Ibid., 73.
[15] Ibid., 174.
[16] Ibid., 101–3.

for a good end and a bad motive makes for a bad end, but the outcome may be good or bad irrespective of the motive and end.[17] Here she argues that motives have intrinsic value and ends have extrinsic value. Motives are always either good or bad, which in turn directly determines the value of the ends.[18] She claims that objective good will result from objectively good motives.[19]

The Source of Morality

A difficulty here arises when we recall that Zagzebski defines *motives* as affective emotions. Therefore, since the motive determines whether an act is good or bad, and since motives are affective emotions, emotions themselves must be either good or bad. Furthermore, since in Zagzebski's theory it is emotions which have risen to the level of motives that cause actions, to what degree can a moral agent be responsible for bad behavior, unless he is able to volitionally cause his own emotions? How can we ground morality, and therefore, moral responsibility, in feeling and not in volition, and still be left with the *oughtness* that is necessary in an ethical system? Or to go back even further, how can emotions be right or wrong in themselves, and if they are, how can it be *right* that I be faulted (or commended) for how I feel?

These questions are important to my research because much of today's understanding of motivation is related closely to emotion. Zagzebski seriously grapples with some of these questions. She proposes that morality is neither the arbitrary creation of God imposed on man, which she identifies as *voluntarism*, or morality from God's will; nor is it based upon eternal truths binding both God and man, which she calls *intellectualism*, or morality from God's intellect; but rather "all moral value derives from God's motives."[20] She states that all moral agents have motives which "function both as explanations

[17] Ibid., 23.
[18] Ibid., 105.
[19] Ibid., 106.
[20] Ibid., 185.

of and justifications for an agent's acts. . . . Since God is the perfect agent, God's motives are the perfect motives."[21]

Now once again we need to remember that Zagzebski defines *motives* as emotions that move the one who is motivated. Emotions become motives when they are strong enough to move their owner. Therefore, when she attributes all moral value ultimately to God's motives, it can only mean that all moral value derives from the emotions of God that affect Him to action. In divine motivation theory, morality does not flow from God's will or mind, but from His motives, which according to her definition must be His affective emotions. Here Zagzebski qualifies this necessary conclusion of her method, depending upon whether or not emotionality is an aspect of our nature or personhood. She argues that if it flows from our personhood, and if God is a person,[22] then and only then are God's motives God's emotions. She defines a divine virtue as when God's perfect motives perfectly bring about their intended end, if there is one.[23]

At this point Zagzebski defends the view that God has emotions. She admits the historic view that God, a perfect being, cannot be acted upon by another so that His state fluxes according to circumstances, but argues that God's perfection may require certain emotions at certain times.[24] She appeals to Aquinas' theory of God's analogous knowledge, and asserts that God can have analogous emotions and still be unchanging.[25] Without using the word, she seems only to be seeking to affirm the necessity of anthropomorphisms in Scripture, where God, in Calvin's expression of it, condescends to speak truth to us in a way that is adjusted to our nature, so that we are able to meaningfully and accurately grasp, though not fully comprehend, God's nature and being. Moreover she states that

[21] Ibid., 204.

[22] Ibid., 192. Here she asserts that there is strong evidence "that the Christian God is personal."

[23] Ibid., 204–5.

[24] Ibid., 206–7.

[25] Ibid., 208.

her theory does not require God to have emotions exactly the way humans do but only that "the divine states that are the counterparts of human emotions are motivations."[26]

Zagzebski understands God as a moral being who acts, and since she has made morality dependent upon motive, she states that she is only concerned that God is affirmed to have motives. Moral agents necessarily act from motives. God is a moral agent. Whether or not these motives actually are, or are considered to be, analogous to human emotions is irrelevant to her position. Human motives are then identified as good to the degree that they imitate God's motives. Thus, human goodness is achieved by imitation of God's motives and not be conformity to His commands. Whether or not the Christian God is a person or personal, virtue is motivation-based and by way of creaturely imitation of the divine being.[27]

Since morality flows from motives, and ultimately God's motives, Zagzebski argues that ethics ought to be grounded, not in the revelation of God's will, but in the imitation of His motives. She identifies the motive most in accord with the Christian tradition as love. Other traditionally Christian motives such as forgiveness, mercy, loyalty, and generosity all flow out of love. Imitating these motives as they occur in God is how we imitate God.[28] Thus she identifies love as both an emotion and a motive; but we must remember that since Zagzebski calls it a motive, and since motives are only those emotions that rise to the level of causing action, love as motive cannot be separated from action. Accordingly, she names several sub-motives that derive from love, and in these we can more readily see the action that she would have love to perform: "mercy, forgiveness, generosity, and loyalty." She does not explain the relation love has to God's commandments as Jesus repeatedly does (John 13:34; 14:15, 21–24; 15:9–12), or to evil as Paul and Peter do (Rom. 12:9; 1 Cor. 13:6; 2 Thess. 2:10; 1 Pet. 3:10). Also, whether or not it

[26] Ibid., 211.
[27] Ibid., 213.
[28] Ibid., 219–20.

is possible to have love as an emotion that can merely remain on the feeling level and still be *love*, even though it never rises to the level of a motive by impelling to action, is not addressed by Zagzebski, nor can we know, therefore, whether such *love* would be considered by her to be good or bad. However, her intention to remove morality's source from the realm of God's will, the traditional view which she calls divine command theory, to that of His motives remains clear:

> Divine Motivation (DM) theory has significant advantages over Divine Command (DC) theory. The theories are structurally parallel in that DM theory makes moral properties derive from God's motives, whereas DC theory makes moral properties derive from God's will.[29]

What about Sin?

Here we could ask, but how does resting God's moral nature on His motives, rather than on His will expressed in commandments, affect our understanding of the nature of sin, which has always been defined as breaking God's law? Though she does not go into this subject in great detail, Zagzebski does not shy away from the possibility of a completely new definition of sin:

> For several decades, there has been a shift of focus from the idea of sins as discrete acts to the idea of sin as a pervasive individual and social condition. Sin is now seen as less like a crime and more like an orientation of person and community away from God.[30]

This conclusion is consistent. If the good of morality is viewed as imitating God's motives, then the bad of morality must be found in being oriented away from, both individually and communally,

[29] Ibid., 258.
[30] Ibid., 229.

imitating these motives. It would seem that if I am not motivated as God is motivated, that is, if I do not have the same emotions impelling me to action that God has impelling Him to action, then I am found to be a sinner. Even as the mathematician and astronomer Johannes Kepler (1571–1630) sought to "think God's thoughts after Him," so it seems in divine motivation theory the moral person *ought* to seek to feel God's feelings after Him. What name, other than sin, Zagzebski would give to breaking God's commandments is not developed, nor is, for that matter, what name, other than virtue, she would give for keeping them.

Zagzebski's divine motivation theory claims that man will be moral to the degree to which he has God's motives, not to the degree to which he keeps God's commandments. Morality flows from God's motives, which are, or are equivalent to, the emotions out of which He acts. Zagzebski argues that since God cannot will contrary to His nature, His will must rest on His nature. This deduction leads her to then assert that God's will rests on His motivations.[31] In other words, God's motivations are more foundational to His nature than His will. She seems to make this final contrast in order to once again press the superiority of her divine motivation theory to the traditional view of morality, or divine command theory.

Although Zagzebski's work earnestly wrestles with historical questions about God's nature and strives to affirm an objective moral order that is greater than man, her attempt to replace commandment with motivation cannot escape the question that would seem to dismantle her whole theory: Is a man *obligated* to keep this moral order based on motivation, not command? The *oughtness* of her theory undermines what it seeks to establish. If man is not obligated to seek God's motives, then all of human ethics and morality, even imaging God, are reduced to being various options. There is no possible basis for holding it right to seek God's motives or wrong to not seek them. However, if man is obligated to seek God's motivation

[31] Ibid., 285.

then we are back to divine command, the very theory from which she is trying to escape.

In spite of this inconsistent conclusion, Zagzebski's research not only philosophically reinforces some of the connections we have already seen regarding the relationship of emotion to motive, and leading to persuasion and to viewing positive emotions as good and commandment and duty as bad, but it also inadvertently gives a sound warning to any method or system that would attempt to redefine such basic concepts as sin and morality. Such attempts will have to avoid the immense danger of being self-refuting.

Rational Psychological Hedonism: Motivation by Pursuit of Happiness

Taking a similar theme of deriving man's motivation from his Maker, Richard Hazelett and Dean Turner sought to trace the roots of human motivation to God. Their book appears to have two interrelated purposes. First, it is an apologetic work defending the premise that human society functions best with the idea of a loving God, from whom alone morality can truly exist.[32] Second, from the necessity of a loving God for the best possible human society, the book develops and promotes a philosophy of living called "rational psychological hedonism.[33]

They begin by declaring that "in one way or another all people need and seek happiness."[34] Human history is proof that belief in God is the best way that man has found to pursue this happiness:

> Historically, the basic theistic worldview has endured for four to five millennia and has motivated its adherents to

[32] Richard Hazelett and Dean Turner, *Benevolent Living: Tracing the Roots of Motivation to God* (Pasadena, CA: Hope Publishing House, 1990), inside cover.

[33] Ibid., 244.

[34] Ibid., inside cover.

> build several civilizations spanning the globe. In cultural history, religion without philosophy has proven more constructive in the eliciting of moral behavior than has philosophy without religion.[35]

Economic prosperity is a necessary part of human happiness, yet the authors note how state socialism has "abysmally failed" in bringing economic prosperity to those nations practicing it. Every form of socialism "renders genuinely satisfying daily work next to impossible" and in fact "state socialism tends to tyranny."[36] Without the possibility of economic prosperity, socialism cannot succeed in the long term as a viable motivation for man's happiness. "State socialism may motivate a society for a time, until the mass of people thoroughly experience its hollowness."[37] Yet the authors claim that the free market system does little better without the force of "ethical principles to restrain and guide it."[38] They assert that the Judeo-Christian ethic has historically brought this beneficial restraint to capitalism. "The sacrifice of some private interest for the public good is a theme of Christianity and Judaism and indeed of the responsible elements of other faiths."[39]

They add that the Christian worldview was necessary for the development of modern science as we know it. The Christian embrace of natural laws, laws observable and logical, is the true foundation for science—the skeleton necessary for the body to walk. The authors argue that this fact explains why modern science did not develop in China, or Islamic countries.[40] It also explains why man is not able to find the happiness he seeks. The authors cite Charles Finney to declare one of the principal arguments of their

[35] Ibid., 9.
[36] Ibid., 18–19.
[37] Ibid., 31–32.
[38] Ibid., 22.
[39] Ibid., 32–33.
[40] Ibid., 34–48.

book: "The reason why all mankind do not find happiness, when they are so anxious for it, is that they are seeking *it*. If they would seek the glory of God and the good of the universe as their supreme end, *it* would pursue them."[41] Mankind's problem is that he seeks that which he will only get by seeking God. If he would seek God then in whatever he did he would find happiness, or rather, it would find him:

> Having the conviction of the existence of a caring God, anyone can pursue a goal or task that is widely and deeply rewarding. . . . People who deny the theistic worldview thereby undercut in principle their own motivational foundations and thereby commit a kind of non-simultaneous contradiction. . . . Such a procedure is unscientific, if not absurd.[42]

The motivation necessary to bring to mankind the happiness desired by the humanist is only found in the worldview of the theist. They offer sex as an illustrative example. Sex is used as a motivator in virtually all aspects of human society. Yet, history and experience have taught us that "sexual motivation is dangerous when it comes only from the loins."[43] However, the authors assert that "sexually inspired motivation within a faithful monogamous union can strengthen the race both biologically and culturally."[44] Therefore, they conclude, "One must look beyond humanism for viable religion and ethics."[45] It is "theistic religion [that puts] morale in morality."[46]

[41] Charles Finney, "Selfishness Not True Religion," *Lectures to Professing Christians* (1837); quoted in Hazelett and Turner, *Benevolent Living* 97 (emphasis in original).

[42] Hazelett and Turner, *Benevolent Living*, 123–24.

[43] Ibid., 189.

[44] Ibid., 184.

[45] Ibid., 209.

[46] Ibid., 144.

Although it is not clearly developed by the authors, they imply that theism brings a freedom to pursuing morality (intrinsic motivation?), which humanism would restrict by external pressures. "Freely acting theists can achieve the alleged benefits of humanist collectivism without its stifling problems."[47] The freedom seems to flow from the "idea of a loving God," as being the necessary foundation of morality, which is the avowed premise of the book.[48] The argument would run like this: Because man necessarily pursues his own happiness, once he sees that logically speaking, the only way to achieve that happiness is to seek God, man will now be sufficiently motivated to seek God and thus achieve his own happiness. They call this theory of human motivation *psychological hedonism*:

> The theory that we do pursue our own pleasure or happiness as the *sole* essence of our motivation internally speaking is called *psychological hedonism* . . . The theory has recommended itself to many, including the present authors, as affording the only reasonable way to talk about motivation or even to talk about the making of ethical choices.[49]

As stated earlier, the authors refine their own particular version of psychological hedonism by the qualifier "rational." Therefore to summarize their view: Psychological hedonism holds that all men pursue their own happiness. They adduce Matthew 6:24 ("No one can serve two masters") to argue that there can be only one motivator to pursuing our happiness, of which God proves to be the most effective.[50] Consequently, once the facts about God and human happiness are rationally demonstrated and understood, "the only rational thing to do is to pursue such inward value" by pursuing God.

[47] Ibid., 208.
[48] Ibid., inside cover.
[49] Ibid., 239 (emphasis in original).
[50] Ibid., 240.

This book reiterates some of what we have been seeing with relation to the importance placed upon human motivation being found in terms of what is positive or pleasant. Thus, they talk about the idea of a loving God being motivating, but not about the motivating factor of a fearful God or a holy God. Similarly, the prospect of human happiness is accepted as a universal desire, but nothing about the universality of human guilt, shame, fear, or even a (regenerate) desire for holiness for its own sake. They assert that history shows that what best motivates man has been seen to be almost universally equivalent to what pleases man, or what is usually called "internal motivation." When rewards or punishments are mentioned, they are referred to as "external" or "extrinsic" motivation, and are seen to be either inferior to the internal variety, or altogether negatively as counterproductive and therefore "de-motivating." I will later examine Scriptural sermons to see if they give this same congruency to man's pleasure and his motivation.

Scottie May and the Superiority of Intrinsic Motivation over Extrinsic

The next work, from the *Christian Education Journal*, by Scottie May, takes the same premise that we have consistently seen at the theoretical or experimental model—that internal motivation is superior to external—and applies it to the concrete practice of children's memorization of Bible verses. The author states that "extrinsic motivation comes from what one can earn or avoid." He gives the example of getting a happy face sticker for memorizing verses.[51] Without offering any real proof, he asserts that this method does not produce the results of Psalm 119:9, 14, 20, 34, 47, 74, 97, 99, and 105—of loving obedience, turning from sin, and growing in knowledge.[52]

[51] Scottie May "A Look at the Effects of Extrinsic Motivation on the Internalization of Biblical Truth," *Christian Education Journal* 7, 1 (Spring 2003), 48.

[52] Ibid.

On the one hand he states that from at least the (Babylonian) exile on, a large portion of a child's "Christian" education, consisted of memorization with the purpose of the learner becoming "a person of holiness."[53] But then he opines that Bible memorization clubs and programs, as well as rote learning in public schools, coincided with the apex of the philosophy of behaviorism that viewed humans as the products of external forces.[54]

May begins to argue for his method by admitting that certain studies have shown the benefits of rote learning in mathematics, sequential skills, and in self-control.[55] He then goes on to note numerous studies that show that extrinsic motivation has many negatives. One particular study, which he says includes

> decades of research . . . showed that tangible rewards, when used to motivate people, substantially undermine learners' curiosity, interest, self-motivation, and persistence. Simply stated: Tangible rewards decrease intrinsic motivation—the learner's desire to do the task for its own sake. It's as if rewards actually backfire.[56]

Here we notice that in this specific study extrinsic motivation is considered negatively, not because of whether or not it succeeded or failed in terms of its goal of getting the children to memorize Scripture, but because it was found to "decrease intrinsic motivation." Once again the method of learning known as intrinsic motivation has become the goal of the learning process. Those specific qualities here mentioned, "curiosity, interest, self-motivation (called autonomous motivation in other studies), and persistence," comprise the very definition of intrinsic motivation, and have come to be valued for their own sake to the point that the actual

[53] Ibid., 51.
[54] Ibid., 52.
[55] Ibid., 53.
[56] Ibid., 55–56.

memorization of Scripture and becoming persons of holiness are no longer the criteria for success.

May attempts to justify his criticism of extrinsic motivation. First, he argues that it promotes expending the minimum effort to get the reward. Short term compliance can result but he claims there is no power to produce long term change. He cites Scripture to support his point:

> Ps. 119:11—"I have hidden your word in my heart . . . " which has become the cornerstone verse in many memorization programs, has been mis-applied. The word "hid" actually means in this context to treasure, to hold dear—the very thing that rote memorization leaves entirely out.[57]

May then recommends ways to get children, not to treasure verses in their hearts, but to become intrinsically motivated to memorize them.[58] Once again what is called "intrinsic motivation" is considered to be superior because of how it better succeeds at making the child enjoy and choose to participate in the learning process. Thus, even as May criticizes extrinsic approaches for not getting the child to treasure Scripture in his heart, nothing he proposes achieves this either. He maintains only that his method will get the child *to want* to participate in the learning process, and for that he considers it superior.

It would be interesting to see which method actually succeeded in getting the child to memorize more verses, or to memorize the verses more accurately. But proponents of May's type of intrinsic motivation would more than likely say such a comparison would entirely miss the main point of how the child felt, or how he was internally motivated throughout the process, which is the same thing. And since that is the *superior* goal, that is their success.

[57] Ibid., 59.
[58] Ibid., 61

Paul Jones' Ultimate Intrinsic Motivator: Joy

Extending this same premise of the superiority of feeling good about yourself in the education process to adults, the next study I will consider is by Paul Jones in the journal *Weavings*. Jones proposes joy as a powerful tool for church leaders. He defines *joy* as "yearning," in order, he says, to better account for the tension of the Christian life, where we can have joy in sorrow, joy in persecution, and so on, and offers various Scriptures to justify this definition: the shepherds were filled *with fear* at hearing the great joy (Luke 2:10); Mary Magdalene departed from the tomb *with fear and great joy* (Matt. 28:8); the disciples *disbelieved* for joy (Luke 24:41); Christians are to find joy *in suffering* (Col. 1:24; James 1:2); Jesus endured the cross for joy *while despising* the shame (Heb. 12:2); the bones of David, God had broken may rejoice (Ps. 51:8); and we sow with tears and reap with joy (Ps. 126:5).[59]

According to Jones the question of motive "may be the major dilemma of the contemporary church. . . . Why should anyone become a Christian?" His answer is that the delight of being a Christian is its "only justification" and this delight should be the true experience of every Christian.[60] Reaching back to his historic roots, Jones states that Methodism began with the "*instrumental* motivation" of seeking to escape God's wrath. Jones then argues that today's church, having lost this fear, must offer potential members a "*supplemental* motivation" to join their fellowship.[61] Under supplemental motivation he includes location, friendliness, activities, and programs, which he sees as "cultural, social, and personal services that supplement what is available in one's immediate environment."[62] However, these motivations all realize their greatest power when they are able to tap into joy.

[59] W. Paul Jones, "Joy and Religious Motivation," *Weavings*, 8 (N-D, 1993), 39–40.

[60] Ibid., 40.

[61] Ibid.

[62] Ibid., 41.

Jones explains today's widespread interest in "spirituality" as the yearning for joy.[63] According to Jones, Christianity is best suited to satisfy this yearning for joy:

> *The true gift which Christianity has to offer is an intrinsic way of being*. Christian existence is self-validating, needing no other justification than the experience itself—joy as delight. . . . This process called "salvation" begins with a lack, a sadness, an emptiness—yearning. Self-interest drives us to try to satisfy it in varied ways. Yet society's offerings cannot really touch where we ache. They only tease us with hints that intensify the yearning. The profound hunger in each of us is for a joy whose delight needs no justification other than the experience itself.[64]

Few statements could better apply to the subject of intrinsic motivation, as it has come to be defined both secularly and religiously, more than this: "needs no justification other than the experience itself." If Jones can find a way to make Christianity achieve intrinsic motivation (and then vice versa), he will be applying the latest theories in the purest possible fashion. Jones appears to see this golden ring and he reaches for it. He argues that growth in grace

> begins as a self-interested yearning for wholeness and moves from instrumental through supplemental toward intrinsic motivation. As Christian life becomes increasingly intrinsic, true evangelism occurs—spontaneously. . . . When the church is a community of joy, evangelism occurs as contagion.[65]

Here Jones postulates the explosive power that will result from merging Christianity with intrinsic motivation: Christianity will

[63] Ibid.
[64] Ibid. (emphasis in original).
[65] Ibid., 43.

spread like a disease! Since intrinsic motivation is getting people to autonomously want what you are offering, how could it not?

Pragmatic Considerations of Motivation

If correct, the success of Jones' theory depends upon rightly diagnosing and then tapping into what people want. This next study we will consider, by Kennon L. Callahan, takes that same recipe for success but goes a step further in analyzing current cultural and generational trends to predict what people will be most longing for, so that pastors can use this knowledge to more successfully motivate them: "In the coming decade, the motivations of compassion and community will stir the grassroots to action and generosity."[66] Here, the outcomes of "action and generosity" are the promised results of using the right motivation. Callahan is not as interested in defining these outcomes so much as promoting the next big motivations. He warns: "Pastors and leaders who continue to approach the congregation with the motivations of challenge, reasonability, and commitment will be disappointed. They will simply see an increasing motivational gap between themselves and the grassroots."[67]

Callahan explains that the reason why leaders need to update their motivational methods is because the increasingly mobile family unit has created new longings or needs that pastors will need to tap into if they want to be effective. "Today, with extended family scattered, their longings for community have become desperately and profoundly urgent. They want to hear about belonging and caring."[68] After justifying his diagnosis of the family, Callahan turns his analysis to the current motivational practices of the church.

[66] Kennon L. Callahan "The New Reality in Motivation," *Leadership* 20, 4 (Fall 1999), 31.

[67] Ibid.

[68] Ibid.

> We have had in recent years a focus on program-driven churches, purpose-driven churches, and vision-driven churches. They talk the language of commitment. But when you look behind the scenes, you see those churches work because somebody is delivering the compassion and community.[69]

Here, Callahan argues that the change he predicts is already occurring. Unbeknownst to church leaders, families within their congregations are already looking for compassion and community, and it is only to the degree that their current programs are tapping into these new motivational emphases that they are succeeding. Church leaders need to recognize this phenomenon and purposely adjust how they are seeking to motivate their audiences in order to capitalize on it: "The pastor's task is to connect with his leaders on the basis of compassion and community, then together to motivate the congregation with this same spirit."[70]

Thus, to summarize Callahan's theory: The cultural situation of fragmented mobile families has prevented families from naturally developing compassion and community. People are now longing for what the family is no longer able to provide. Wise church leaders will recognize this situation and find ways for the church to intentionally offer this compassion and community that people are no longer getting from their families. An active and generous congregation is the result of a church providing people with the compassion and community that is missing in their family. One additional result is numerical church growth: "Increasingly, unchurched people will be drawn to churches that care. High-compassion, high-community congregations will thrive in the coming years." "Unchurched people," that category the popular church growth and seeker-sensitive movements most want to reach, "will be drawn to churches that

[69] Ibid., 32.
[70] Ibid.

care."[71] Callahan's method calls for identifying and meeting the latest longings of the culture without any consideration whether those longings are right or wrong, or should be addressed by the church and not rather the family or some other entity.

In the same issue of *Leadership*, Leonard Sweet compares eBay use to the current state of the church. Sweet makes the point that eBay is successful because it creates that community that postmodern people are longing for. On eBay you can "find people with similar interests . . . a single purpose . . . where . . . they tell the stories most central to who they are and find people eager to hear them." Sweet claims that in these forums, people "participate so fully and have their lives changed by the experience." Then he offers the church as the place where this should also happen, asking "And isn't that what the gospel is all about?"[72] Sweet develops an acronym to help church leaders remember how to adjust to the latest trends. He declares we are "living in EPIC times." Therefore, "to connect with postmoderns, the church will [need to] become more Experiential, Participatory, Image-driven, Communal."[73] As confirmation to his own observations, Sweet notes that a few months earlier, the journal *American Demographics* (April 1999), "esteemed the quest for experiential faith one of the nation's most important cultural trends."[74] Once again, uncritically adapting to the way things are is promoted purely for its pragmatic value.

With similar pragmatism but resulting in a different conclusion, several articles in *Evangelical Missions Quarterly* argue for motivational methods based more on universal principles than on the culturally relevant approach seen in *Leadership*. Though one study deals with motivating volunteers and the other with being a motivating teacher, they both emphasize the necessity of building

[71] Ibid.

[72] Leonard Sweet, "The Quest for Community," *Leadership* 20, 4, (Fall 1999), 34.

[73] Ibid., 33.

[74] Ibid.

relationships like a family in order to successfully motivate. The universal application of these principles is explicitly stated in the earlier of the two articles: "Although the specific methods may vary, some, if not all, of these principles will work in almost any culture."[75] The benefit of incorporating elements of motivation is again stated in broad terms by both articles: "As we learn how to motivate those with whom we work, we can accomplish greater things for God's kingdom"[76]; and, proper motivation is often the difference between a student doing well or doing poorly.[77]

In later chapters I will seek to determine to what degree, if any, the sermons in Scripture motivate based upon what will most likely work in a particular setting, or by discerning and then giving people what they feel they want most.

[75] David Stevens, "Getting the Job Done Requires Motivating Your Volunteers," *Evangelical Missions Quarterly* 29, 1 (January 1993), 15.

[76] Ibid.

[77] Mark A. Olander, "How to Be a Motivating Teacher," *Evangelical Missions Quarterly* 40, 2 (April 2004), 230.

4

Motivational Theory for Pastors

As we turn to those studies dealing specifically with motivation as it relates to church leadership, the latest literature can be described as a combination of the satisfying of needs approach similar to Maslow, the supremacy of the search for meaning as in Frankl, and the autonomous self-motivation comparable to Allport, with an emphasis on the importance of *positive* emotions. Experts today assert that the most desirable, effective, successful, or—by some other adjective—*best* way to pastor a church and to preach motivating sermons is to know and speak to the needs of the audience in such a way that they will want to listen and respond. Additionally, much of the literature sees preaching motivating sermons as merely one of the most important tools in achieving the greater goal of having a successful church, which ultimately means having a church full of internally motivated people.

Pastoring as a Means, Not an End

The first article I will consider as we apply the topic of motivation particularly to the office of minister is an interview with Jim Collins, in *Leadership Journal*, 2006. The subject of the interview is a discussion of Collins' *Good to Great* books, especially as it relates to Christian ministers, hence the title of the interview, "The Good to Great Pastor." In his first *Good to Great* book, targeting the business world, Collins began by defining what he meant by greatness. The book examined those leaders and businesses defined by Collins to be "great," with the goal of trying to find out how they reached the summit of their field, so that the readers could apply those principles in order to become great in theirs. Obviously Collins' definition of greatness was of crucial importance to the success of his book, since it offered the goal of greatness as a motivation to purchase and read it. Consequently, in this interview, the interviewer, seeking to apply Collins' principles to pastors, began with the question, "How do you define 'greatness' in a church?"[1]

Collins answered that according to his original research, any organization must have three things to qualify as great:

> 1. Superior performance relative to its mission in the world.
> 2. A distinctive impact on its community. So you'd say, "If this church disappeared, it would leave a serious hole in this community."
> 3. Endurance, or making an impact over a long enough time that it's not dependent on the personality of one leader. If a church is effective during one pastorate, it may be a church with a stellar pastor, but it is not yet a great church.[2]

Collins then discusses how greatness in the business world differs from greatness in a church.

> The biggest distinction is the role of money. In the business world, money works both as a fuel to achieve greatness and as a measure of greatness. . . . But in a church, money is only a means or an enabler of true performance, which is successfully reaching people with the message, creating a sense of community, and contributing to the community.[3]

[1] "The Good to Great Pastor: An interview with Jim Collins," *Leadership* 27, 2 (Spring 2006), 48.

[2] Ibid., 49.

[3] Ibid.

Superior performance is still the goal, but performance is not measured by money. The last part of the quote gives us Collins' threefold definition of "true performance" for a church: (1) successfully reaching people with the message; (2) creating a sense of community; and (3) contributing to the community. The leadership, and particularly the pastor, of the church needs to be striving to achieve these three goals with everything that they do.

Although the interviewer asked no follow-up questions for Collins to further define these three very general marks of "true performance" for a church, Collins did elaborate on the importance of establishing clear goals. In Collins' description, goals do not need to be quantifiable, but they do need to be describable. Here he asserts that

> Lots of goals—beauty, quality, life change, love—are worthy but not quantifiable. But you do have to be able to tell if you're making progress. For a church, a goal might be: *Young people bring other young people here unprompted.* Do they talk about the church with their friends? You may not be able to measure that, but you can assess it.[4]

If greatness for a church is defined by the three overarching goals listed previously, here in this latest citation, Collins gives us an important principle in achieving this greatness: Very specific subordinate goals must be defined and then worked toward in order to achieve true performance. So, for example, we can assess that we have successfully reached the youth of our church with our message (true performance mark number one) when they bring their friends to it unprompted and when they naturally talk about church with their friends.

According to Collins the most important factor in getting a church to move toward this greatness, is "getting the right people

[4] Ibid., 49–50 (emphasis in original).

in key seats."[5] These people then begin not by laying forth a vision to which they will immediately seek to motivate people to achieve (Collins specifically denies the efficacy of the visionary leading method), but rather, by first determining the "brutal facts" as to why their church is not currently great. Only then will they be able to plan the best course toward higher, or true performance.[6] Collins asserts that the older way of thinking, where you set a vision and then build momentum toward it, really does not work. "The vision emerges from small successes. . . . What actually happens is you build momentum and see that something is actually working and then you see how far it can go."[7] As this last quote illustrates, what works in getting you closer to your goals determines your procedure in Collins' system.

Collins' method has less of an emphasis on motivation than what we might expect, considering how the studies we have looked at elevate its importance. Motivation comes in later, once the more fundamentally crucial step of getting the right people into key positions has been accomplished. Collins' position seems to be that if you have the right people leading, motivation will not be as much of an issue. The right people will make a proper use of motivation.

Although Collins offers little to my book in terms of directly speaking to how sermons should motivate individuals, he accurately represents today's majority report on the subject of preaching: Everything a pastor does, including preaching, should be consciously undertaken with a view to how it will impact the greater goals for the church as a whole. My research has found that today, preaching is overwhelmingly valued and even viewed more as a means to an end, than as an end in itself. The right method of preaching is then determined by how it can best contribute to what seems to be assumed by writers in the field as the ultimate goal of all church activity: the horizontal well-being and numerical growth of the church as

[5] Ibid., 50.

[6] Ibid.

[7] Ibid.

a community. A case in point is that two of Collins' three marks of true performance for a church have as their goal the creation and development of a *community*. Applying Collins' marks specifically to preaching, it seems safe to say that the overarching focus of the sermon should be about "creating" and "contributing to" the community. When these two marks are met, you will have the first one as well: reaching the people with the message, for the message is *community*.

The message becoming the goal is exactly the same phenomenon we saw with intrinsic motivation. As the means to achieve the goal of better outcomes in education, educators sought to intrinsically motivate individuals in order to get them to autonomously engage themselves in the learning process, which would, it was theorized, result in more effective or more accurate learning. But eventually the successful establishment of intrinsic motivation supplanted the goal of learning, with the result that educational methods are evaluated by how well they produce internally motivated students. So also it seems that creating a community as the means for a church to grow in its goal of glorifying God has itself become the chief end of the church in today's literature. Church ministries, leadership, and, as we will see in the studies that follow, preaching are viewed as successful or good to the degree they contribute to the creation, sustenance, and growth of the church as a community.

Pastoring as a Means to Motivation

Another article in *Leadership* illustrates this emphasis on the church community as it addresses the way a pastor should minister to a "declining congregation." The author of the article is a pastor who immediately contrasts his current church, which is "healthy," from a "declining church." Today, no one familiar with the literature on these subjects needs "healthy church" or "declining church" defined for them. A healthy church at the minimum means a church growing numerically, whereas a declining church above all else means a church that has shrunk or is shrinking numerically. Yet, as you read this article and others like it, the healthy church is considered healthy more for its positive, cooperative attitude than for its numerical growth. In fact, hopefully as will be seen in my analysis, numerical growth seems to be the most telling indicator of the relative health of a church rather than the goal itself. The health of the church, however, *is* the degree to which it is composed of internally motivated people.

The author, Bob Moeller, argues that five different types of people will be found in any declining church. The pastor will stop the decline when he understands the five distinct groups and implements the correct strategy that is specifically designed to motivate each one.[8] Here, the unspoken assumption is that decline can and will be reversed with the proper application of the right motivation. Even as internal motivation is the solution that will make a declining church healthy, so what must ultimately have gone wrong with that church in the first place is that the people were not properly motivated. Thus, the numerical decline of a declining church is really just the clearest indicator of a lack of proper motivation to bring the church together in a common cause. The article's conclusion justifies this assertion: "When various groups in a declining church, separated and isolated by discouragement, link up again in a common cause, the tide of events will change."[9]

Moeller goes through the five different groups and explains how to motivate each one. According to Moeller each group is motivated by having its particular needs met. These needs, though different in details, are all at bottom a desire that their own specific concern for and contribution to the church be acknowledged, appreciated, and valued. If the pastor can grant this single desire in the various ways it is manifested in each group, Moeller assures him that they will all pull together to follow him and support his efforts to get the church to grow numerically. Here are Moeller's five groups

[8] Bob Moeller, "Saving a Sinking Ship," *Leadership* 17, 2 (Spring 1996), 47.
[9] Ibid., 51.

with the identifying distinctive of each: 1. the Pioneers—founding members; 2. the Curators—children of founding members; 3. the Dysfunctionals—people who are attracted to troubled churches; 4. the Stand-By Passengers—people who are attracted to successful churches; and 5. the Remnant—people who are already internally motivated and actively serving.

It is common to misunderstand the Pioneers by thinking their biggest problem is being unwilling to change. Not so says Moeller: "Pioneers' deepest need is for someone to understand and appreciate what they have accomplished."[10] If the pastor can find tangible, public ways to show them recognition and thanks, the Pioneers will be happy to help out with his new programs.[11] Likewise, the Curators are not opposed to change itself; they merely "wish to preserve the history and legacy of a previous generation." The resistance comes in when "Any change in program or worship is seen as an affront to the church's founders . . . [for] the curators' goal is not renewal but preservation." This last point is seen by Moeller as the key to understanding how to effectively motivate the Curators.

> The place to begin motivating curators is to assure them you share their deep desire to see the church doors stay open. You must convince them the best chance of survival is to make certain adjustments.[12]

According to Moeller, Dysfunctionals "are people attracted by the confusion and chaos of long-term disintegration . . . they fear newcomers and growth."[13] Dysfunctionals are the most difficult to motivate, requiring strength, grace, boundaries, and turning the other cheek. Even while modeling cheek-turning love to Dysfunctionals, Moeller counsels it is important to keep them out of

[10] Ibid., 48.
[11] Ibid.
[12] Ibid., 48–49.
[13] Ibid., 49.

leadership positions. The hope seems to be that if you show them a good example long enough, and minimize the damage they can cause on your efforts, some of the Dysfunctionals may be motivated to change the dysfunctional way in which they live and contribute to the church.[14]

Moeller's Stand-By Passengers are those busy young families who are not going to stay around long if they do not see things improving, and therefore, Moeller says, "you have only a short window of opportunity to persuade the Stand-By Passengers to stay."[15] Stand-By Passengers are motivated by hope. That is, you need to give them tangible signs that things are getting better. Pastors need to exude confidence that things are going to get better, and show this by bringing their families to every program. If numbers begin to go up, many of the Stand-By Passengers will stay.

Finally, Moeller speaks of the Remnant. They "remain because they are convinced God will revive their church."[16] They serve, volunteer, and come to programs regardless of the numbers. Moeller does not use the word, but this category of people, as he describes them, are what others would label "intrinsically" or "internally" motivated individuals. Moeller simply sees them as walking by faith, not by sight, convinced that the church will fulfil God's purpose. Not surprisingly Moeller concludes, "It's not difficult to motivate this group. They pray, they serve, and they rarely complain."[17] In effect their already present motivation just needs to be directed to support the pastor's efforts at righting the ship.

Very clearly, Moeller represents the point of view that sees motivation as a key aspect of a healthy church. Here, motivation is realized as each person finds the church meeting his need for love and acceptance in community. In fact, what Moeller envisions as a healthy, growing church is indistinguishable from what others

[14] Ibid.
[15] Ibid.
[16] Ibid., 50.
[17] Ibid.

would call an internally motivated church. The pastor's task in bringing renewal to a declining church is to get people to buy into what he is doing in such a way that each disparate group finds its greatest desire (or need) met so that they become an active participant in the work. In other words his goal is to see the people internally motivated so that they take it upon themselves to seek to be a loving, growing community where everyone is affirmed as an important and significant part of a greater whole.

Roger Thompson's Definition of Christian Motivation

The next article I will consider takes the same fundamental view of the importance of motivation but rather than seeking to apply it to correct a particular problem like a declining church, it attempts to define a general concept of *true motivation*. In this article, Roger Thompson admits that while motivation can be abused into mass manipulation or flow from the unbiblical view of man of B. F. Skinner, motivation itself is simply something leaders must do. To ignore the dynamics and principles of motivation is to court disaster. In seeking to define what Christian motivation is (or should be), Thompson begins by telling us what it is not (or should not be). Guilt, says Thompson, is a poor motivator that cannot be effective beyond the short term. Guilt can give no joy nor is it worth the effort. Guilt requires a lot of work and yields minimal results. Yet one of the main sources of motivation used by church leaders is guilt. He claims guilt is often why people are constantly moving from one church to another.[18]

Thompson affirms that all Christians have to deal with real guilt in their lives. He says that real guilt is the result of sin and slothfulness and is exposed by the Holy Spirit. Here, Thompson seems to be distinguishing between the guilt we should have as a result of sin,

[18] Roger Thompson, "The Christian Art of Motivation," *Leadership* 15, 3 (Summer 1994), 52, 54.

and the guilt that is artificially and wrongly used to get people to do what they do not want to do. The real guilt that the Holy Spirit produces is good in that it leads people to repentance and forgiveness. But this guilt is not meant to motivate the Christian life.

In setting forth a distinctly Christian view of how to motivate, Thompson appears to affirm the common distinction between external and internal motivation. His position then is that a truly Christian motivation will be entirely internal. As we have been seeing, internal or autonomous motivation is viewed as more authentic, genuine, or even "good," since when one is internally motivated, one is doing what one wants and chooses to do; but external motivation, which is to in any sense be made, pressured, or forced into doing something that one does not, from oneself, sincerely desire to do, is regularly seen as inferior, less effective (at least in the long term), and ultimately less good or even just plain bad. As we examine Thompson's *true motivation*, it becomes clear that, to use the language of theorists in the field, what he is really talking about is *internal motivation*: a motivation that flows from a heart that has chosen and on its own desires to act in support of the leadership's direction.

Accordingly, since Christianity is to be from the heart, a Christian use of motivation, by definition, will not settle for the, at best, lesser variety of motivation. Thus, Thompson admits that many people in the church are motivated by guilt. But this kind of motivation always results in less than wholehearted commitment and effort. Congregants would be confident and happy if they had that kind of motivation which Thompson identifies as true, calling it "genuine biblical motivation." Thompson claims that this true motivation depends on three things: right rewards, right relationships, and right reasons.[19] The cure for guilt-fueled activity, which is clearly viewed as an undesirable situation, is wholehearted service, which is achieved by applying genuine biblical motivation. This kind of motivation

[19] Ibid., 54.

depends upon establishing the three factors of right rewards, right relationships, and right reasons.

Right Rewards

First, true motivation depends upon right rewards. Thompson here says that our view of motivation and rewards should be shaped by our being created in God's image to have dominion and to work. Since God created us for work, true motivation necessarily involves finding reward in your work. Thompson claims that this principle is so basic to our creation that the Bible does not even argue the point, it simply assumes it. There is a natural reward that comes to a person as he works. Provided, however, that his work is seen by him as worthwhile. Busy work has the opposite effect and demotivates rather than motivates. However, the more worthwhile the work is and the more a person sees himself accomplishing it, the greater the reward. Thompson concludes accordingly that the greatest reward is when a person sees their contributing to a work that they know to be eternally significant.[20]

In applying this principle to the church Thompson declares that "whenever we begin a new program, [we need] to ask, 'Can my people find legitimate and immediate reward in participating?'" Thompson understands that this principle can be abused but he claims examples of the proper use of rewards by Paul with Timothy and Jesus with His disciples (though he does not cite any specific instances). He argues that there is a place for incentives, extrinsic rewards and other kinds of reinforcement. We just need to make sure that they are kept in their proper role of functioning alongside other aspects that are just as necessary and important.[21]

Here we must not confuse Thompson's "extrinsic reward" with "extrinsic" or "external" motivation as we have thus far seen it defined in the literature on the subject. Clearly Thompson is arguing for an

[20] Ibid., 55.
[21] Ibid., 57.

extrinsic reward that, especially at the beginning of a spiritual enterprise, can and should be used to *truly*, that is, to *internally* motivate. Thus, Thompson is not conflating extrinsic reward with external motivation. The important thing at this point is that Thompson has uniquely found a place for reward in his theory of what he variously calls true, biblical, or Christian motivation, or what we have seen is technically referred to as "internal motivation." In Thompson's method an extrinsic reward can truly or internally motivate!

Right Relationships

Thompson again draws from the creation account of Genesis to argue for the second component of Christian motivation: right relationships. Here he notes how God created men and women as relational beings. They needed to continue in their relationship with each other and with God. It was God's design that in these relationships they would experience His unconditional love and have assurance and meaning. They would know that they mattered. Thompson argues that mankind was not created with a nature that allows him to impersonally move from one incentive to the next. He asserts, "To move from one achievement to another, without intimate personal partnership with people and God, is meaningless. The greatest achiever of all time, Solomon, concluded that."

Although Thompson is speaking directly to the concerns of my book when he seeks to establish his definition of motivation from Scripture, and although it does not prove whether or not this second component of true motivation is biblical, yet I must point out that Solomon clearly did not conclude that achievement without relationship is meaningless. Such a distinction was not part of Solomon's reflections. Solomon concluded that work, relationships (e.g., his thousand wives) or anything else, unless one is intentionally doing all to the glory of God *in obedience to His revealed will*, is meaningless. Thus, Solomon's conclusion in his own words: "Let us hear the conclusion of the whole matter: Fear God and keep His commandments, for this is man's all" (Eccl. 12:13). That everything that does not contribute to fearing God and keeping God's commandments is meaningless *is* the conclusion of Solomon.

Regardless of this misapplication of Scripture, the point Thompson is making is that relationships sustain motivation. He claims that "Motivation that lasts is fueled with love, respect, and appreciation. Much spiritual work, by its very nature, precludes external incentives. How precious at those times is the cadre of care givers."[22] People are motivated when other people are affirming them and their work as important and worthwhile. That is a point that is hard to argue with, even apart from a correct attribution of Scripture!

Right Reasons

Thompson's third ingredient of true motivation is right reasons. Under this heading Thompson talks about the motivating power of giving people purpose. He claims that a sense of oughtness or duty cannot sustain long term motivation. Even the most committed people will get tired of doing the same thing repeatedly if they do not perceive a worthwhile purpose in it.

> A sense of duty isn't enough for long haul motivation; a sense of purpose is. . . . The repetition of behavior without purpose can sour even the most faithful. Scripture repeatedly warns us of the dangers of performance without purpose, sacrifice without love. It is the essence of pharisaism. Giving is to be cheerful, work "as unto the Lord," service "in love," and correction "in gentleness."[23]

Thus, giving people a sense of purpose seems to be what Thompson means by the "right reasons." He equates this sense of purpose with doing things sincerely or even willfully. So giving, for example,

[22] Ibid., 58.
[23] Ibid.

in order to be done rightly, must be cheerful. Thompson negatively identifies purposeless performance with loveless sacrifice, even as he approvingly connects doing things with purpose to loving service and gentle correction. So doing things from the right reasons, is doing things with purpose, which means doing things sincerely or from the heart. Thompson contrasts the sincerity and love that a sense of purpose can give, with a sense of duty, which he says cannot sustain long term motivation. Thompson seems to regard trying to motivate through a sense of duty the same way he viewed motivating by guilt. It is inferior, or even dishonest, since one is not doing what one loves. His position, then, holds that to do something out of duty is akin to doing it insincerely.

Love vs. Obedience?

I just want to note here that this conclusion is only true if love and obedience are necessarily contraries, or if one *cannot* love one's duty. Along these lines, Thompson makes the very common mistake of citing the Pharisees as those who did the right things but not from the heart. They are presented as having obeyed, but not from the right reasons, not with purpose. Bryan Chapell also makes this error when he describes the Pharisees as examples of those who did all the right things but did them with all of the wrong intentions.[24] On the contrary, Christ quarrels with the Pharisees precisely because they did *not* do the right things!

> Then the scribes and Pharisees who were from Jerusalem came to Jesus, saying, "Why do Your disciples transgress the tradition of the elders? For they do not wash their hands when they eat bread." He answered and said to them, "Why do you also transgress the commandment of God because of your tradition? For God commanded, saying, 'Honor

[24] Bryan Chapell, *Christ-Centered Preaching* (Grand Rapids, MI: Baker, 1994), 208.

> your father and your mother'; and, 'He who curses father or mother, let him be put to death.' But you say, 'Whoever says to his father or mother, "Whatever profit you might have received from me is a gift to God"—then he need not honor his father or mother.' Thus you have made the commandment of God of no effect by your tradition. Hypocrites! Well did Isaiah prophesy about you, saying: 'These people draw near to Me with their mouth, and honor Me with their lips, But their heart is far from Me. And in vain they worship Me, teaching as doctrines the commandments of men.'" (Matt. 15:1–9)

The sin of the Pharisees, according to Jesus, was not that they kept the law for the wrong reasons, but that they did not keep the law and instead replaced it with their man-made traditions.

Clearly Jesus taught that the Pharisees were guilty, not so much of insincere obedience, but of actual disobedience. In Mark's account, Jesus adds, "and many other such things you do," (Mark 7:8). Thus, Jesus claims that this was only one example of an endemic problem. Consequently, let us learn the chief error of the Pharisees from the lips of Jesus: substituting man-made traditions for the commandments of God. They did not love God's law to a fault as is so often claimed; they hated it to such a degree that they substituted their own rules in place of it.

Accordingly, on another occasion Christ prophesied to the Jewish leaders that it would be their failure to keep the law of Moses that would be their ultimate undoing. Jesus does not say "Your problem is that you love Moses too much to come to Me," or even "You obey the writings of Moses but you do so for the wrong reasons." No, according to Jesus the reason they did not believe in Him was that they did not believe in Moses:

> Do not think that I shall accuse you to the Father; there is one who accuses you—Moses, in whom you trust. For if you

> believed Moses, you would believe Me; for he wrote about Me. But if you do not believe his writings, how will you believe My words? (John 5:45–47)

Those who love God's law will love Jesus. Those who hate God's law will hate Jesus. Although He often censured their hypocrisy, it was not their insincere obedience that Christ called attention to time and time again but rather their actual disobedience in their duplicitous actions on which our Lord always set his focus (see Matt. 23, Mark 12, Luke 20). Once again, although an improper citation does not prove or disprove a point, I will continue to draw attention to how Scripture is or is not being properly used, so that when we look at Scriptural sermons to discover their motives, we can readily recall and avoid these errors.

Having God's Purpose

Thompson avers that in order to sustain true or genuine motivation, the Christian must be continually realigning himself to the purpose of God. It certainly goes without saying that if having the right reasons is a necessary ingredient of true motivation, and if having the right reasons means having purpose, then having God's purpose would be the most motivating thing one could do. God's purpose is by definition the ultimate purpose. But how does one have and keep God's purpose?

Thompson's answer is twofold. First, he argues, we need teamwork. Teamwork is the way to keep the right perspective and not lose sight of our goal.[25] We cannot do it alone. We are relational; we need the help of other people. He likens teamwork to a safety net where people help each other when they fall. At this point he appropriately cites Ecclesiastes 4:10, which emphasizes this very point. Thompson states that together we can help one another to *not* lose sight of our ultimate purpose. In addition to teamwork, and very

[25] Ibid.

important to the topic of how sermons should motivate, the last half of Thompson's answer is that the pastor must give people this ultimate purpose through his teaching and preaching:

> I try to teach and preach how God's timeless plan is translated into human action. Even while propounding the Great Commission, it helps to give illustrations from living models. By using our sermons to point people to positive examples of faithfulness, we help build a motivated congregation.[26]

God's purpose, or ultimate purpose, is here referred to as God's timeless plan. Therefore, the way in which ministers keep people in touch with God's purpose, what he also calls the ultimate purpose, is by teaching and preaching on how God's timeless plan is put into human action. To this end, setting forth real life models as examples is helpful, examples of people who modeled the kind of faithfulness to God's purpose for which we should all be striving.

In a nutshell, Thompson's Christian motivation is accomplished as Christians seeking the right rewards, enter in and maintain the right relationships, and as the pastor provides them with the right reasons—God's purpose—by communicating how God's plan is translated into action in our lives with the help of teamwork, which is best seen through people who have modeled it.

Here we have a concrete and specific method of applying motivational principles to preaching: Sermons motivate through illustrations of positive examples of faithfulness. My book will test this method with the sermons of Scripture to see if the Word of God confirms it. Thompson is to be commended for seeking to establish his principles from Scripture, and also for being the first author on motivation that we have thus far examined who tried to do justice to the Bible's emphasis on the positive use of reward.

[26] Ibid., 58.

One final thing to notice about Thompson's method is the similarity to what we have observed with regard to internal motivation being its own reward. Thompson concludes his article on *true motivation* with a conscious equalization of means and end: "Self-sustaining fellowship with God is its own reward. And people will reach that goal if they are given the right rewards, the right relationships, and the right reasons." Self-sustaining fellowship with God by having the right rewards, relationships, and reasons appears to be both the means and the end of all Christian ministry, including preaching. Throughout our study, there appears to be this general agreement among theorists relating to motivation in the church: When church leaders use methods of "true" (internal) motivation, by sincerely and relationally giving a sense of purpose, the result will be a congregation that is truly (internally) motivated to live sincere, relational, and purposeful lives.

5

Motivational Theory in Preaching

The next few articles, from *Preaching Magazine*, directly address the topic of preaching and motivation.

Preaching That Prioritizes Motivation over Message

Well-known minister, author, and speaker John Maxwell gave an interview based upon his book *Everyone Communicates, Few Connect*. The subtitle is, "What the Most Effective People Do Differently." According to Maxwell, "connecting is all about asking questions."[1] Maxwell says he first began to see the difference between connecting and communicating at a Zig Ziglar rally in 1975.

> Up until then, I thought as a leader-pastor that I was to get people to buy my vision . . . but Zig that day said, "No, no; go their way. Go where they are. Get off the mountain, go down to where the people are. Walk slowly through the crowd, put their interests first. Help them with whatever they're struggling with, and they'll turn around. You'll influence them, and they'll begin to follow you."[2]

[1] "Communicating or Connecting? An Interview with John Maxwell," *Preaching* 26, 1 (July/August 2010), 5.
[2] Ibid.

Maxwell explains how dramatically his life changed once he believed in Ziglar's word. He began to hang out with people who were different than himself, people who did not come to church, in order to find common ground with them as the first step to connect with them. Maxwell exhorts that pastors, especially, need to get out of their world and into "the world that desperately needs to know the good news," in order to find common ground. When you get on the same ground as your audience they will "sense that you know and care. Once that understanding, caring link is there, then they're ready to be led and influenced, ready to hear the Good News, but not until then."[3]

Maxwell says that pastors mistakenly think that just giving people the Word of God will change their lives. They assume that because it is God's Word and it is true, it will motivate people if it's just handed to them. But the reality, Maxwell claims, is that people won't accept that Word unless they first accept the people giving the Word—"you and me . . . Once people buy into me and I have bought into them and who they are, then we can start making some movement and connecting."[4]

Surely it is sound advice for discipleship or shepherding or other such roles of a pastor that in order to gain a hearing he must build trust through real, personal relationships, but Maxwell is not talking about those roles. He's talking about preaching. For him, willingness to hear God's Word is what the pastor must impart to his audience before he can effectively preach to them. We must motivate before we can bring the message. Doctrine comes after and flows out of motivation. This order is very important for my book, and as we will see, it is the exact opposite of historic Reformed teaching. Maxwell cites Jesus as the "Master Connector." He says Jesus "was always where the people were, was always asking questions that would stir their hearts a little bit, always connecting with

[3] Ibid., 5.
[4] Ibid., 6.

them, always putting them first—then out comes the message."[5] Pastors and Christians need to get out of our Christian world and into the business world of the people around us. In the Christian world the key word is relationship. We influence one another in our relationships with them. According to Maxwell what connects with the business world is respect. Respect is not given freely, however; you have to gain respect by being excellent at what you do. Maxwell explains that if he were still a lead pastor, he would have his listeners work on gaining respect in their work places and their lives before witnessing to those around them: "You're going to be able to break people into the Kingdom, but don't share Christ with them until you've got their respect, because it's a message that will land absolutely nowhere."

If he were still preaching every week, he would meet with unchurched and uninterested people and "bounce ideas off of them" to see what caught their attention. He concludes "I would put a lot more of that teaching into my messages."[6] The superiority of such messages, according to Maxwell, is that even though they would have been less polished, they would have been more authentic, from the heart.

Maxwell's emphasis on building relationships where you connect with people, who are then more willing to be influenced by you, speaks again to the internal motivation that we have been seeing so often. Getting people to *want to* follow you is the goal, here it is called "connecting," and that goal is achieved by getting people to sense that you care about them and what is important to them. As Maxwell declared earlier, the starting point is getting people to accept you. Once people accept you they will be more open to accepting your message.

[5] Ibid.
[6] Ibid., 8.

Preaching That Communicates Through Connecting

In another article in the same issue of *Preaching*, Maxwell expands on his idea of connecting over communicating to talk about the next step, which is communicating through connecting. The greatest teachers, leaders, and speakers see themselves primarily as guides, Maxwell claims. "Because they value others, they work at connecting with the people they are teaching or trying to help."[7]

The good teachers and leaders get people to follow them. But the way to get people to follow you or to learn from you is for you to first go to them and learn about them. Maxwell instructs, "when you are trying to connect with people, it's not about you—it's about them . . . You have to change the focus from inward to outward, off of yourself and onto others."[8]

According to Maxwell there are several reasons people do not realize the simple principle he learned from Zig Ziglar—that in order for you to get people to help you get what you want, you have to first help them to get what they want. The first is immaturity. Like small children we are naturally selfish and we do not see it. Maxwell says that it is important that we fight that selfishness because only through maturity can we begin to focus on others and be able to connect with them.[9] The second is ego. Maxwell warns, "Leaders, speakers, and teachers can develop a disproportionate sense of their own importance."[10] When all we are looking for is approval and applause it is impossible to connect with others. The third is failure to value everyone. Because we must work *with* others to succeed, Maxwell explains that success "requires you to see the value that others possess."[11] Like a good businessman who learns how to speak his

[7] John Maxwell, "It's All About Them," *Preaching* 26, 1 (July/August 2010), 11.

[8] Ibid., 12.

[9] Ibid., 13.

[10] Ibid.

[11] Ibid.

customers' language, when we have valued others enough to truly get to know them, that value will become evident to them. Insecurity is the final reason people fail to focus on and therefore connect with others. When we are insecure about how others receive us, we become even more self-focused, creating a negative cycle that precludes truly connecting with anyone.[12]

Maxwell asserts that we can also fail to connect with others when we give the impression that we or what we have to say is more important than our audience. However there are certain things you can do to show your audience you care for them. You can: express appreciation as quickly as possible; do something specifically *for* them, and let them know it; expect the audience to enjoy you; and finally, let your audience know how much you enjoyed them. Maxwell concludes, "You can connect with others if you're willing to get off your own agenda, to think about others and to try to understand who they are and what they want."[13]

Maxwell focuses on what the speaker can do, before, during, and after the speech to connect with the audience because connecting will enable the audience to enthusiastically receive and apply your message to their lives, or to put it another way, connecting will (internally) motivate them. So, whereas Thompson's article looked at how to frame the message in order to better enable the audience to be internally motivated, Maxwell focuses on how the speaker should comport himself for the same purpose of internally motivating the audience. Here is another concrete method of how a speaker motivates his audience that we can use to consider the motivational elements of Scripture.

Preaching That Assumes Less

Pastor and seminary professor Rod Casey wrote a similar article calling for a certain focus in preaching that will better motivate

[12] Ibid., 14.
[13] Ibid.

your audience. Casey's method involves preachers "assuming less" in their preaching. Pastors make a mistake when they assume that people will be interested in what they are saying because it is in the Bible. Casey zeros in on the problem with a concise analogy: "Too many preachers fail to ask themselves what every successful fisherman asks. They fail to ask what bait will hook their listeners."[14] Casey explains that the reason we do not ask what kind of bait will hook our listeners is because we wrongly assume the listener is already internally motivated to listen. Casey says that is typically not true for the listener. To be more effectively engaged in the motivation process, the preacher must realize that "The learner is more motivated to engage the sermon's subject when it addresses life crises the learner is experiencing. . . . When preachers speak to the crises that hold learners hostage, the learners are motivated to engage the sermon's content."[15] In Casey's method the subject of the sermon is able to be more inherently motivating to the listener when it speaks to some current crisis in his life.

Casey instructs that in order to know what to preach that will hook the greatest portion of his audience, the preacher should identify

> common themes that constitute inner crises. . . . The internal conflict of people in the pew may include an unsatisfied longing, unresolved rationality, moral dilemmas, relational alienation and an impending fear of human mortality. "Less assumptive" preaching won't assume the listener is interested.[16]

Like Maxwell's method, Casey envisions a preaching style that will be more interesting and motivational to the degree that it is more

[14] Rod Casey, "A Church for a Guy Like Me: Making the Case for Less Assumptive Preaching," *Preaching* 26, 1 (July/August 2010), 17.

[15] Ibid., 17.

[16] Ibid.

relevant to what the listener is currently experiencing. Casey appears to go even further than Maxwell, however, when he encourages preachers to not merely address the current crisis of the listener, but *to make* crises in which their preaching will place the listener. "After a busy week and a relational conflict at home, the listener needs the preacher to create the 'crisis' that demands the listener's attention."[17]

When it comes to preaching doctrine, Casey says that preachers should not assume his audience is biblically literate at all. "Instead, assume that a listener may be opening the Bible for the first time." Assume that they believe the Bible as much as they believe Dr. Seuss.[18] This kind of less assumptive preaching, avers Casey, places "divine revelation on the bottom shelf so everyone can reach it."[19]

Finally, in order to preach more motivating sermons, preachers need to assume less about listener buy-in. Casey gives an example from when he was preaching on the eighth commandment. He says he was "preaching reasonable truth"; telling people to let their yes be "yes" and their no be "no," and that lying hurts trust and therefore hurts relationships. But he avers that his listeners were hearing things like, "Good advice, even biblical, but you don't live with my spouse. I can't tell her the truth; she'd blow a gasket. You don't know how angry she gets, and I can't live with that. . . . My situation is certainly an exception."[20] According to Casey preaching the truth is not enough. Unless we engage "the listener's rational and emotional barriers," we "have failed to address the part of the hearer that carries the greater weight as to whether Christian formation will happen." Here Casey appeals to Acts 26:18, saying that when we directly address these barriers "we continue the instructions of our Lord Jesus when he appointed Paul 'to open their eyes, turn them from darkness, so they may receive . . . a place among those who are

[17] Ibid.
[18] Ibid.
[19] Ibid.
[20] Ibid., 18.

sanctified by faith.'"[21] Casey concludes, "'Less assumptive' preaching works hard to engage the hearer's hurdles that keep him or her from 'buying' the sermon's content and making its application to life beyond the weekend."[22]

Thus, Casey's approach is similar, even complementary, to Maxwell's in that we must study to know our audience in order to speak about their current greatest concerns. In so doing we will be facilitating the motivation process. Casey fine-tunes Maxwell's method by instructing preachers to look for those common, universal themes with which most of the audience will be able to readily identify in order to create the crisis needed to hook them. Significantly for the purpose of my book, Casey cites Acts 26:18 as scriptural support for his method. Addressing the crisis that interests the listener is how we carry out Christ's command to "open blind eyes," and so on. One final thing to notice in Casey's citation of Acts 26:18 is the middle part of the verse which he leaves out with an ellipsis: "and from the power of Satan to God, so that they may receive forgiveness of sins and a place. . . ." The one thing that has been glaringly absent as we have begun to look at methods to preach motivating sermons is any place for the doctrines of sin, Satan, and the wrath, holiness, and fear of God. This absence fits in with what we have seen in the academic literature about internal or intrinsic motivation consisting of what is inherently "positive," producing and arising from a positive attitude, positive emotions, positive rewards, positive reinforcement, positive self-image, positive examples of faithfulness, and so on. While the more popular articles are not using the same technical language, they are saying the same thing as the academic experts. To truly motivate, be effective, capture interest, get people to follow, you must engage their feelings, relate, be relevant, care for, or connect with them. Or to say it in terms of the academic literature, in order to achieve the end

21 Ibid.

22 Ibid.

goal of internally motivating your audience, you must use the means of internally motivating them.

Preaching That Helps, Not Hurts

The next work, *Preaching Grace*, by Kennon L. Callahan, takes the goal of preaching as a means to internally motivate, that is, preaching with the aim of instilling positive attitudes, interest, and emotion, and gives it a Scriptural name. According to Callahan, pastors are to preach messages that help, not messages that hurt. Preaching that helps shares things like wisdom, hope, and encouragement. Reconciliation and forgiveness come as people realize God's love. At the same time things like anger, fear, resentment, and worry diminish.[23] Hurtful preaching does the opposite. It puts people down, gives them a low self-esteem, and is harsh and demanding. In hurtful preaching, "legalism and law pour forth. Rules and regulations abound. Grace is missing."[24] This quotation is key to understanding Callahan's distinction between helpful and hurtful preaching. Hurtful preaching commands. Helpful preaching is gracious. Grace appears to be the positive contrary of the negative, law. Callahan confirms this appearance: "Some sermons [in the churched culture of the past] were filled with collections of legalisms and laws. Shoulds, oughts, and musts were frequently present. Grace was missing."[25] Thus, preaching that has imperatives frequently present is not only legalistic and out of date, but above all it is not gracious. Callahan warns that we need to constantly guard against falling back into legalistic, commanding preaching, which tempts us with the promise of immediate results. It is a serious mistake to preach in such a way, he avers. Preachers too

[23] Kennon L. Callahan, *Preaching Grace, Possibilities for Growing Your Preaching and Touching People's Lives* (San Francisco: Jossey-Bass Inc., 1999), 1–2.

[24] Ibid., 2.

[25] Ibid., 3.

easily command and demand when they should be inviting and encouraging.[26]

Callahan's contrast between legalistic and gracious preaching is akin to the academic literature's distinction between internal and external motivation. Legalistic preaching is marked by an abundance of external commands, just as external motivation compels from outside the person. Both have the effect of forcing or inhibiting someone to action, whereas gracious preaching, like internal motivation, finds its strength in appealing to persons' desires and interests, not compelling them against their wishes, but empowering them in their wishes.

Callahan finds support for his definition of gracious as opposed to commanding sermons in the Great Commission of Matthew 28:19–20: "The invitation 'Make Disciples' is really best understood as 'Invite persons to discover the grace of God and become disciples.' It is not a command: 'MAKE.' It is an invitation: 'Help people discover what you have now discovered.'"[27] He argues that the early disciples practiced his method of preaching grace, which is how people then and now can live fulfilled Christian lives. This kind of preaching is gracious and helpful. Gracious preaching helps people to become actively, willingly involved in the transformation process. Gracious preaching does not tell people what to do.

But how do we go about writing positive, gracious sermons? Callahan instructs that there are two questions that we need to ask as we study Scripture. First we need to ask what the text says. This question "invites us to open ourselves to the grace and compassion, wisdom and hope in the text itself. We can let the text speak to us and teach us about the grace of God." Callahan's second question is to ask what the text is *not* saying, because Scripture is just as

[26] Ibid., 24. We will come back to this interesting use of the word "encouraging," in the results of our study.

[27] Ibid., 11. Callahan shockingly contradicts the imperative, μαθητεύσατε of this text!

intentional in what it leaves out as in what it includes.[28] Yet whatever we might find the text saying or not saying, the thrust of the sermon is already set by the definition of gracious preaching itself, which as we saw means using helpful invitations and avoiding hurtful imperatives. Additionally, the sermon needs to have a specific focus and thrust that will invite listeners to do some one thing to make their lives better.[29] This single focus of the sermon provides a check for how we can keep track of whether or not our preaching is gracious. His argument is that since everyone struggles with the same pursuits in life, we can evaluate the sermon's quality by how well it aids people in fulfilling those quests. He then identifies four foundational life searches that we all struggle with: "Individuality, Community, Meaning, Hope."[30] Recognizing these foundational life searches that all people wrestle with is crucial in order to write gracious sermons and to have a standard by which to measure their graciousness.

At this point Callahan's approach takes a slight twist that, at first glance, appears to be exactly the opposite of the method espoused by Maxwell and Casey, in which you are to first look at your audience as you prepare your message. In Callahan's method you must look first at yourself:

> Do not look first at your congregation. Look at yourself. Discern, consciously, which of these searches is stirring in you now. . . . As you discern which of these searches is stirring in you and in those around you, your preaching will become even more intentionally helpful.[31]

Here it becomes apparent that even though Callahan espouses the exact opposite action of looking at yourself first instead of the audience, the real difference in method between his "gracious preaching,"

[28] Ibid., 72–73.
[29] Ibid., 75.
[30] Ibid., 78–79.
[31] Ibid.

and the "connecting" of Maxwell and "assuming less" of Casey is very slight. Callahan may exhort the preacher to look first at himself, but this is merely to first internally motivate himself so that he will be better able to better internally motivate the audience. The preacher is to look first at himself, but only for the sake of better connecting with his audience. The order changes, but the principle, rationale, and goal are the same.

Directly applicable to my research, Callahan addresses head-on the concept of motivation and specifically speaks to the distinction between external and internal motivation. Callahan confirms my analysis that his method seeks to deliberately internally motivate the audience, and that internal motivation is considered to be "better" than external motivation.

> Motivation is internal, not external. Manipulation may be external, but motivation is clearly internal. Each day we draw on and experience many motivations. Some are healthy. Some are confusing. Some appeal to our lesser self. Some are hurtful and damaging to our development. In preaching, it helps to resonate with the healthy motivations that stir people to live life with grace and growth.[32]

In Callahan's view, as in some of the theorists we examined, motivation in general has become equivalent to internal motivation. It is not authentically motivating but merely manipulating unless it comes from within. Moreover, Callahan reiterates what my research has seen repeatedly with respect to positive—what Callahan calls "healthy"—motivation. Helpful preaching is healthy for the person. It taps into those motivational sources in their lives that are positive and good for them. The sermon does this as it encourages and invites, which helps people to move forward in their lives.[33]

[32] Ibid., 88.
[33] Ibid., 101.

Ministers need to preach sermons that attract people to God's grace. Such preaching is encouraging and invigorating. It promotes discipleship. It shows them they are competent. Preaching that resorts to law and command discourages and hinders people from moving forward in their lives. Instead the sermons should show people how they can contribute to God's mission using the gifts and strengths He has given to them.[34] The healthy, positive motivations draw people to God and to His grace, the unhealthy ones repel them. Callahan admits that people can be motivated with lesser motivations such as anxiety, fear, and threat, but the results will not be as strong as when we help them to be self-motivated. Gracious preaching focuses on the healthy motivations of compassion, community, challenge, reasonability, and commitment, which all encourage growth and advances lives.[35]

Here Callahan names the five healthy motivations, which he asserts are present in every person, and therefore, one or two should be the aim of every sermon.[36] Though he gives five, according to Callahan, there are two motivations that are especially effective for both the churched and unchurched: the motivations of compassion and community. The minister should seek to strengthen the spirit of compassion and community in his audience, because that is the most effective kind of preaching to audiences today.[37] Callahan argues that Jesus was using the motivations of compassion and community when he restored Peter in John 21.[38] Likewise he sees the early church using these motivations to appeal to an unchurched culture, for they understood that the unchurched most desperately need compassion and community. Accordingly, since we in the early twenty-first century find ourselves in a similar cultural situation, we too should preach compassion and community.

[34] Ibid., 88.
[35] Ibid., 100.
[36] Ibid., 88–89.
[37] Ibid., 93–94.
[38] Ibid., 95.

That is what listeners are looking for, so that is how we will reach them.[39]

In addition to deliberately incorporating one of the five healthy motivations, Callahan's method demands that in every sermon, the minister have a single goal that he is heading toward. This goal or desired outcome of the sermon should be that which the minister believes will be most helpful for them on that occasion. However, Callahan states that in his experience he has learned that four outcomes are most decisive and helpful. They are grace, wisdom, hope, and mission. Every sermon needs to drive towards one of these four outcomes in order to have the maximum effect.[40]

Preaching grace therefore, involves looking at yourself, what moves you or stirs you, and then incorporating throughout your sermon one of the five healthy motivations present in everyone, seeing it in the context of addressing one of the four foundational life searches, and finally aiming at one of the four outcomes, which are helpful in people's lives. Though the various searches, motivations, and outcomes will create different topics and emphases, all sermons should be helpful. At the beginning of his book Callahan declared that helping people in their lives through the gospel is the most important thing a sermon can do. This helpfulness is what Callahan means by *Preaching Grace*. This kind of preaching brings people to discover how generous God is to them. They see and are moved by His love and compassion, His kindness and blessing. They are made to experientially know God's grace. This realization produces love, humility, thankfulness, kindness, and generosity in them. Under this kind of preaching, people "come alive . . . live richer, fuller lives."

So by preaching grace ministers can help people know God's grace, respond to God's grace, and live God's grace. Here we should note that "grace" is not defined by Callahan as God's unmerited favor, purchased for us by the righteous life and atoning blood of

[39] Ibid., 96–98.
[40] Ibid., 145.

Jesus Christ on the cross, which has satisfied God's righteousness and wrath. Grace is defined more by what Callahan everywhere sets as its contrary: law. Where law demands and condemns, grace makes no demands and accepts. Where law comes only to reveal want and lack, grace seeks to heal hurts and fill needs.

> Grace moves beyond the rules and regulations, policies and procedures, conditions and stipulations with which we weigh life down. Grace is God's response to all the shoulds and oughts we construct as our conditions for earning our salvation. . . . Try not to live a life of legalisms. Yes, there are "boundaries" important for us to set so that we do not allow ourselves to be trampled over and so that we do not trample over others. . . . And these are boundaries of grace, not law.[41]

According to Callahan, even the boundaries are somehow set not by way of command but by invitation. Thus preaching grace is best seen by not preaching law. Gracious sermons have "the spirit of invitation, not demand; of shared experience, not challenge."[42] In Callahan's method all of the important concepts we have been seeing—positive emotion, internal motivation, connecting with and reaching people, healthy motives, meaning, experience, hope, purpose, and fullness of life, as well as avoiding laws and rules—coalesce under the umbrella of preaching grace.

As noted earlier, a sermon written with Callahan's method, while aiming at one of the four different outcomes may change its topic and direction, the gracious (positive) nature remains constant. So for example, when a minister preaches a series of sermons, all of which aim at the outcome of *Hope*, each sermon "heals emotions, stirs motivations, advances hope."[43] People will learn and discover how to live hopeful lives. They move forward and progress in growing,

[41] Ibid., 147–48.
[42] Ibid., 150.
[43] Ibid., 153.

advancing, developing and building their lives as hope motivates them. Likewise when he preaches with the outcome of *Mission* the audience will grow as they discover purpose and meaning in their lives. Encouraged by God's compassion and invitation to share in His mission, they live fuller healthier lives of purpose and mission.[44] The same could be shown for sermons having the outcomes of *Grace* and *Wisdom*. The subject and details will differ, but the positive, confidence-building, life-encouraging goal and intention of the sermon will be the same.

Callahan's *Preaching Grace* provides my book with a detailed method of preaching that explicitly addresses the topic of motivation. As I prepare to wrap up this section on what motivation is, how it should be evaluated, and how it has been promoted in the church and in sermons, I want to take a brief look at some of the most popular and influential preachers of today who have explicitly called for a certain type of motivation in preaching, looking briefly at the trends that have led to them, and then moving to a quick overview of some Reformed voices including the Westminster Standards and John Calvin. At that point we will be ready to turn to the Scriptures and find out how the inspired sermons of the Bible seek to motivate their audiences.

[44] Ibid., 157.

6

Motivational Techniques of Popular Preachers

Much of what we have seen in using sermons to motivate comes from an Arminian view of man. While correcting this erroneous view of man is outside the purview of this work, I do need to highlight a few things about how it ties in with motivational principles. The Arminian view of man denies that man is totally depraved and that apart from the sovereign, irresistible grace of God, *all* of his desires or longing for compassion, community, love, meaning, and acceptance are and will continue to be expressions of his rebellion against God. Neither can the sermon (much less the minister), by way of motivation, deliver him from this condition. Thinking that it can goes back at least to the revivalism of Charles Finney, although in Finney's day, the motivation was to be saved from hell rather than to realize how much Jesus loves one.[1] On the one hand, Finney represents almost the exact opposite of today's Arminian motivational preachers. Rather than tap into what a person is currently longing for to internally motivate, Finney sought to externally motivate a person by waking him up to the danger of going to hell. Still, like today's preaching methods do implicitly, Finney and the revivalists openly rejected the doctrine of total depravity as a "major obstacle" to inducing people to make a decision for Christ.[2] To make a man a Christian, revivalism

[1] See Ian H. Murray, *Revival and Revivalism* (Carlisle, PA: Banner of Truth, 1994), 134, 140–41, 287.

[2] Ibid., 244–45.

averred, all that the sermon had to do was to apply adequate motivation, for conversion is "effected by the simple volition of the sinner's mind through the influence of motives."[3] In Finney's doctrine the Holy Spirit's role was reduced to the great Motivator: "Did the Holy Spirit do no more than persuade men by means of motives to obey the gospel? That was what Finney believed."[4]

Arminian methods can have the outward appearance of success because telling people how to avoid their fears or gain their desires will always be appealing. Sinful man has "itching ears" for such teaching (2 Tim. 4:3). The rapid success of the Arminian Word of Faith movement of a generation ago was due in a large part to its ability to tap into motivations relevant to its audience. The gospel of the Word of Faith movement promised health and wealth, during the period when materialism was becoming rampant in the prosperity and comfortability of post–World War II America.[5] Similarly, church growth advocates of the seeker-sensitive movement of a generation ago adopted this same foundational principle of offering the correct motivations to appeal to the widest possible audience under a more attractive veneer of mere Christian terminology and moderate morality. The objective was to train current members to employ the motivations that will most successfully speak to the broader community. As Reverend Bill Hybels of Willow Creek instructs, "[Christians] won't take decisive action unless we first raise our motivation level. And one of the best ways to do that is to get God's perspective on the matter."[6] According to Hybels this perspective is that "people matter to God."[7]

Hybels claims that when Christians understand how much

[3] Charles Finney, quoted in Murray, *Revival*, 244.

[4] Murray, *Revival*, 244.

[5] D. R. McConnell, *A Different Gospel* (Peabody, MA: Hendrickson, 1995), xix; Hank Hanegraaff, *Christianity in Crisis* (Eugene, OR: Harvest House, 1993), 190.

[6] Bill Hybels and Mark Mittelberg, *Becoming a Contagious Christian* (Grand Rapids, MI: Zondervan, 1994), 13.

[7] Ibid., 14–22.

people matter to God, they will be motivated to tell people about this love. Then, when lost people hear how important they are to God and how much He loves them, they will be motivated to become Christians and in turn tell others. Getting God's perspective that one matters to Him gives one the most positive of all motives: God's love. In Hybels' system, God's love becomes a powerful force of internal motivation for believer and unbeliever alike. Hybels asserts that when Christ personally taught, the weight of God's love "crushed" sinners into the kingdom.[8] We must do likewise. Here, God's love seems to be understood in terms of His acceptance and appreciation. As Hybels explains it, that God loves me means I matter to Him. When once I understand that I matter to God, He will matter to me. God's love, as His acceptance of me, motivates me to live for Him and love Him. Moreover, since God loves everyone this same way, and since I obviously want everyone to benefit from God's love the way I have, I will begin to tell them about God's love. Thus, Hybels states: "God wants us to become contagious Christians—His agents, who will first catch His love and then urgently and infectiously offer it to all who are willing to consider it."[9]

Rick Warren's incredibly successful book, *The Purpose Driven Life*, operates on the same principle of motivating people according to what they already most need and long for. Warren declares that that need is purpose. Moreover, people can find ultimate purpose only in the purpose of God. Similar to John Maxwell's emphasis on other people, Rick Warren begins his book with the words, "It's not about you."[10] His method is built on the same principle as the others:

[8] Ibid., 19.

[9] Ibid., 23.

[10] Rick Warren, *The Purpose Driven Life* (Grand Rapids, MI: Zondervan, 2002), 17. I recognize Rick Warren claims to be a Calvinist, but the book espouses a plainly Arminian doctrine of conversion, as others have noted. See review by Michael Horton, "Judging by *The Purpose-Driven Life*, Pastor Warren's theology seems to reflect run-of-the-mill evangelical Arminianism," http://www.whitehorseinn.org/blog/2010/04/01/michael-horton-on-rick-warren-modern-reformation-and-desiring-god/.

Provide the proper motivation and people will respond to Christ. Again, in Warren's work, motivation in general means internal motivation: We motivate most effectively when we appeal to what people most desire and long for in their hearts. Warren uses all of those positive, motivating terms we have seen repeatedly: focus, meaning, purpose, community, motivation, impact, relationship, identity, simplicity, hope, and so on.[11] Practicing Warren's method by seeking to give purpose in sermons means addressing people's heart-felt need for purpose, resulting in a congregation of purpose-driven, that is, internally motivated, people.

This very brief overview of some Arminian uses of motivation in preaching is quite consistent with what I have gathered from the theoretical literature and research, in the academic, religious, and popular fields. Not surprisingly, the emphasis in Arminian works is on how the minister can use motivational techniques to preach more persuasively, particularly with the aim of converting unbelievers, or as it is more often phrased, of reaching the lost or unchurched.

[11] See Ibid., 20, 30–33.

7

Motivation and Preaching in the Reformed Tradition

Leaving the Arminian scene, the final area I need to briefly consider before we turn to the Scriptures is what the Reformed tradition has to say about motivation and preaching. I want to limit my study here to three sources: a work that is widely considered as one of today's best works on Reformed preaching, Brian Chapell's *Christ-Centered Preaching*; the father of Reformed preaching, John Calvin; and the creed of my particular branch of the Reformed tradition, the Westminster Standards. I will then conclude with a brief word from Jonathan Edwards. The point of this extremely brief overview is not to try and establish anything like a Reformed consensus or a Reformed position, but rather to give a very quick summary of how these three widely respected and well-known sources speak to the subject of motivation in preaching from a Reformed perspective. After this brief overview, we will turn to the Scriptures.

Brian Chapell: Motivation via the Cross

Providing people with proper motivation is an essential consideration in Brian Chapell's *Christ-Centered Preaching*. Chapell's method is that the preacher must seek to motivate in applying the text or else the sermon does not achieve its main function—transformation.

Interestingly, the application portion of the sermon is not for the purpose of telling people what to do, but in order to give meaning to the exposition of the text. And the way in which the sermon gives this meaning is by providing the proper motivation. Thus, meaning and motivation are closely related and both are the responsibility of the preacher, who should see his sermon as the God-ordained vehicle to move the application. Providing proper motivation essentially is giving meaning, which is the kind of application for which the preacher should aim, and every part of the sermon should be used to this end. Chapell describes the way in which a sermon ought to move its application by what he calls grace motivation.[1]

In Chapell's method, a sermon motivates by grace when it intentionally appeals to the heart of the believer in order to move it by a contemplation of what Christ did for the believer in redemption. Chapell exhorts preachers to make God's redemptive work "the content, the motive, and the power" in their preaching. The goal is for people to walk away from the message "understanding that grace motivates and enables them to serve God." Chapell claims that the result of this kind of preaching coupled with this kind of understanding is necessary to avoid works righteousness and self-centered (false) religion.[2]

Chapell instructs that the way preachers make God's redemptive work the motivation of their message is by including the cross somewhere in the sermon. Every passage contains the grace of God and the preacher's job is to make sure the sermon discloses that grace, for grace is the only way a believer can legitimately serve God; or to say it another way, grace is the only legitimate motivation for the Christian. In identifying legitimate service to God as that which flows from grace, Chapell's point is that a believer's motivation determines whether or not his obedience is acceptable to God. For the believer either serves God out of appreciation for His mercy

[1] Bryan Chapell, *Christ-Centered Preaching* (Grand Rapids, MI: Baker, 1994), 209.

[2] Ibid., 310.

as seen in the gospel—meaning his understanding of God's mercy to him motivates him to obey—or else he serves himself in works righteousness.[3] Chapell tells us why we must keep the redemptive themes of grace the main focus of every sermon, because "there is no more powerful a motivation to holiness than the love of God manifested in Christ's redemptive work. When love motivates, then the Lord, his purposes, and his glory are our aim."[4] Chapell asserts that all other motivations are, in the final analysis, an appeal to self.

Thus, the minister is to highlight the love of God that is seen in Christ's redemptive work in the application portion of every sermon. As the listener is made to understand the grace seen in Christ's work, he is motivated *rightly* (legitimately), in a godly as opposed to an ungodly way, for he is now motivated by God's love for him. Here Chapell explains that this grace motivation is not simply a matter of understanding via the intellect. To be graciously motivated, the listener must have his emotions moved by the sermon. Chapell urges preachers to carefully target the emotions of their listeners through the judicious use of sermon illustrations. He calls illustrations "powerful, biblical instruments of learning and motivation." They move beyond the intellect to motivate the whole person through "touching the heart and/or eliciting its responses. . . . Illustrations persuade, motivate, touch the heart, stir the will, and result in decisions."[5]

> Descriptions of sights, sounds, and sensations . . . vicariously involve [listeners] in that experience. . . . "Words that name colors, shapes, sounds, odors, and other tangibles help create backgrounds that evoke moods. Anything that moves you can move your listeners."[6]

[3] Ibid., 208.

[4] Ibid., 208–9 (emphasis mine).

[5] Ibid., 174 (emphasis mine).

[6] Ibid., 185, portion in quotes Chapell cites as: Webb B. Garrison, *Creative Imagination in Preaching* (Nashville: Abingdon, 1960), 96.

Chapell explicitly rejects methods that appeal merely to the intellect, emphasizing instead the important role of emotions in the moving of the application of a sermon to rightly motivate the listener. Accordingly, in the above quotation Chapell lists touching the heart and stirring the will as attainable goals of the preacher via well-placed and appropriately used sermon illustrations. Likewise in the second quotation, Chapell stresses the importance of including sensory details in illustrations in order to enable the listener to become emotionally involved to the point of evoking moods and moving them. Furthermore, the object of these illustrations must not be to simply tell some randomly moving story but rather to make more plain and attractive some aspect of God's gracious redemption through the cross of Christ. The minister, considering their intellectual understanding coupled with a stirring of their emotions, seeks to motivate listeners to obey God as he sets forth the grace of God via Christ-centered preaching.

Chapell's method unabashedly urges a conscious use of motivational tools in sermons. He exhorts the minister to use grace not merely to aid in the listener's understanding, wherein he learns right from wrong behavior, but in order for the listener to lay hold of God's love. Human righteousness is only possible when people truly grasp the love that God has shown them primarily in the cross of Christ. It seems safe to conclude that when Chapell insists that ministers must use grace, he means that sermons must highlight and illustrate some aspect of God's gracious provision in redemption in an intellectually stimulating and in an emotionally provocative way.[7] Then, the listener is able to serve God in a non-legalistic way since he is moved intellectually and emotionally by the sermon's portrayal of God's grace in His work of redemption. Thus, Christ-centered preaching *centers* on the grace of *Christ* in redemption, doing its best to set forth this grace in the most powerful way possible—expositionally, intellectually, emotionally, and so on—in

[7] Ibid., 303.

order to transform the listener by bringing about grace-motivated obedience.

> Christ-centered preaching does not abolish the normative standards of Christian conduct, but rather locates their source in the compelling power of grace.... Christ-centered preaching bears the marks of grace-motivated obedience ... grounding the source of Christian behavior in appreciation of God's provision.[8]

The focus of the minister on God's grace causes the listener to see that grace—to apprehend it, to understand it, and as much as possible to feel it—and the resulting appreciation of that grace moves the listener to obey God, in what can now be called grace-motivated obedience.

Either Grace-Motivated or Works-Righteousness Preaching

Similar in some ways to Zagzebski's divine motivation theory, in the above quote Chapell grounds the *oughtness* of Christian obedience, what he calls the normative standards of Christian conduct, not in the commanding power of the law, but in the compelling power of grace. Thus he avers the source of Christian obedience is grounded in appreciation of God's provision. Chapell's position appears to be that as the sermon helps the believer to see the greatness of God's grace and love for him, the believer will be motivated by his appreciation for that grace to obey God. Just as in divine motivation theory, in Chapell's Christ-centered preaching God's law cannot play a part in motivating the believer to obedience because to the degree that it does, the believer's obedience is not gracious but legalistic. Thus, Chapell warns, "challenges to holiness must be accompanied by a

[8] Ibid., 302.

Christ-focus or they promote only human-centered, doomed-to-fail religion."[9] God's grace in redemption must be the sole motivational aim of a sermon, and not the law, even if it is accurately expounded, for "if the message does not incorporate the motivation and enablement inherent in a proper apprehension of the work of Christ, the preacher proclaims mere pharisaism."[10]

As can be seen in several of the above quotes, Chapell's articulated position repeatedly sets forth only two alternatives for the preacher: Either we fully employ the grace-motivation of Christ-centered preaching or else we are preaching the works righteousness of the Pharisees. "Make sure that you motivate believers by grace, not guilt," for every passage of Scripture contains God's grace and it is the minister's job to present that grace in an evocative way. People taught to see the grace of redemption and the love of God throughout the Bible will not trust in their works but in God's mercy. And Chapell reminds us, "God's mercy . . . is *the only legitimate source* of our service."[11]

Calvin's view of how ministers are to incorporate motivation in sermons can be largely set forth by looking more closely at a particular quotation of Calvin given by Chapell in *Christ-Centered Preaching*. Chapell references Calvin in order to argue for the importance of including application in sermons. However, when we look at the larger context of the quotation, we find that Calvin is actually setting forth his own view of how a sermon ought to motivate. Here is the full statement of Calvin with the portion quoted by Chapell in italics:

> And again Saint Paul shows you it is not enough to preach the Law of God, and the promises and what else so ever is contained in the holy Scripture, as though a man should teach in a school: but we must, "improve, threaten, and

[9] Ibid., 285.
[10] Ibid., 12.
[11] Ibid., 208 (emphasis mine).

> exhort." As if he said, *if we leave it to men's choice to follow that that is taught them, they will never move one foot. Therefore the doctrine of itself can profit nothing at all*, unless it be confirmed by exhortations, and by threats, unless there be spurs to prick men withal: for beasts that are so wild and fierce, if they should be let alone to lie growling in their slothfulness, it will be hard to make them profit in the end, and to go on in the way of salvation.[12]

As is his frequent custom, Calvin paraphrases a passage of Scripture in his own words so that we can readily see how he understands it. Clearly, like Chapell, Calvin is very interested in how a preacher should seek to motivate or move the listener. In fact, Calvin locates the distinctive element of *preaching*, as opposed to *lecturing* "in a school," precisely in its design to move the listener. Yet, as compared with Chapell, Calvin's view appears astonishing in its broadness. According to Calvin the minister "must improve, threaten, and exhort," not just the promises of God—where we see God's gracious redemption—but also "the Law of God . . . and what else so ever is contained in the holy Scripture." Calvin would have ministers use all of Scripture in order to motivate their listeners, and not just the doctrine of redemption. Moreover, Calvin avows that unless preaching is "confirmed by exhortations, and by threats, unless there be spurs to prick men" the "wild and fierce . . . beasts" that we all are by nature will continue to "lie growling in their slothfulness." Thus, according to Calvin, if sermons lack such threats and spurs directed at the congregation, "it will be hard to make them profit in the end." And so whereas Chapell argues for "motives for obedience that allow grace to replace divine threat,"[13] Calvin would have us move our listeners by means of all of the text, including the threats.

[12] *John Calvin's Sermons on the Epistles to Timothy and Titus* (Edinburgh: Banner of Truth Trust, 1983), 947; quoted in Chapell, *Christ-Centered Preaching*, 199.

[13] Chapell, *Christ-Centered Preaching*, 307.

John Calvin: Doctrine First, Motivation Second

John Calvin appears to affirm Chapell's grace-motivation when he declares that a consideration of the love of Christ (mentioned in 2 Cor. 5:14) is a "motive" that "ought to constrain our affections," "if we be not harder than iron." But going beyond Chapell, Calvin also sees fear as another valid motive to serve God: "Hence, as [Paul] had previously stated, (verse 11), that he was stirred up to duty by fear, inasmuch as an account was one day to be rendered by him, so he now brings forward another motive—that measureless love of Christ."[14] Clearly Calvin understands fear as a valid motive for service to Christ, for he calls Christ's love, not the only motive, but "another motive." Thus, it is Chapell's insistence that God's redeeming love is the *only* legitimate motive of our service that causes him to differ with Calvin at this point.

However, the differences are actually much greater. Chapell has ministers describe and illustrate God's grace and love in order to "touch the heart, stir the will, and . . . 'evoke moods.'"[15] Conversely, Calvin avers that God's love is motivating, as we *know* it, and not as we *feel* it: "'The knowledge,' I say, 'of this love, ought to constrain our affections, that they may go in no other direction then that of loving him in return."[16] Thus, Calvin interprets Paul's phrase, "the love of Christ compels us," as a love that compels us *by our knowledge* of that love, and not how we feel about that love. Calvin's position better suits the context of the whole verse, for Paul states, "For the love of Christ compels us, because we judge thus: that if One died for all, then all died" (2 Cor. 5:14). The love of Christ compels us, says the

[14] *Calvin's Commentaries*, vol. XX, trans. William Pringle, *Commentary on the Epistles of Paul the Apostle to the Corinthians*, book 2 (Grand Rapids, MI: Baker, 2003), 230.

[15] Chapell, *Christ-Centered Preaching*, 174, 185; portion in single quotes is cited approvingly by Chapell as from Webb B. Garrison, *Creative Imagination in Preaching* (Nashville: Abingdon, 1960), 96.

[16] *Calvin's Commentaries*, XX, 230. Most scholars agree with Calvin that "the love of Christ" is His love for us.

apostle, because we *judge*, not because we *feel*. In other words, the knowledge of Christ's love that a believer possesses when he judges that Christ died for all, ought to compel him to live for Christ. But this knowledge of Christ's love will only compel him if, by the sovereign grace of the Holy Spirit, he believes that it is true. Therefore, Christ's love of the believer ultimately compels him through his faith, and not through his heart being touched by his appreciation of that love.

Furthermore, Calvin grounds the need for motivation in preaching on account of man's sinfulness. Thus, Calvin comments on Paul's triple command to Timothy in 2 Timothy 4:1–2:

> *Reprove, rebuke, exhort.* By these words he means, that we have need of many excitements to urge us to advance in the right course; for if we were as teachable as we ought to be, a minister of Christ would draw us along by the slightest expression of his will. But now, not even moderate exhortations, to say nothing of sound advices, are sufficient for shaking off our sluggishness, if there be not increased vehemence of reproofs and threatenings.[17]

Surprisingly, Calvin then goes on to mention "solid doctrine" as being the necessary foundation for effectively motivating listeners in a sermon and not vice versa.

> [F]or reproofs either fall through their own violence, or vanish into smoke, if they do not rest on *doctrine*. Both exhortations and reproofs are merely aids to doctrine, and, therefore, have little weight without it. We see instances of this in those who have merely a large measure of zeal and bitterness, and are not furnished with solid doctrine. Such

[17] *Calvin's Commentaries*, vol. XXI, trans. William Pringle, *Commentary on the Epistles of Timothy, Titus, and Philemon*, book 3 (Grand Rapids, MI: Baker, 2003), 253.

> men toil very hard, utter loud cries, make a great noise, and all to no purpose, because they build without a foundation. . . . In short, Paul means that reproofs are founded on doctrine, in order that they may not be justly despised as frivolous.[18]

Placing doctrine, which is to say the content of a message, as the foundation for emotion and motivation is opposite to what we have seen thus far. In the other methods, both secular and religious, emotion and/or motivation come first in order to establish the message and cause it to be accepted, meaningfully understood, and acted upon by the listener. In Calvin's position, the doctrine goes first and then proper motivation is able to find root in that solid ground. Otherwise, all that the minister may do to move the sermon *ought to be* rejected, for Calvin calls motivation not flowing out of sound doctrine "frivolous," which is "justly despised."

We can see an excellent example of how Calvin would have sound doctrine serve as the ground for motivation when we consider his famous third use of the Law of God. The following is Calvin's third use of the Law from *The Institutes*:

> The third use of the Law (being also the principal use, and more closely connected with its proper end) has respect to believers. . . . For it is the best instrument for enabling them daily to learn with greater truth and certainty what that will of the Lord is which they aspire to follow, and to confirm them in this knowledge . . . the servant of God will derive this further advantage from the Law: by frequently meditating upon it, he will be excited to obedience and confirmed in it, and so drawn away from the slippery paths of sin. . . . The object of the Psalmist [in Psalm 119] is to celebrate the advantages which the Lord, by means of his

[18] Ibid., 253–54.

> law, bestows on those whom he inwardly inspires with a love of obedience.[19]

This brief quote from Calvin reveals a view of the Law of God that speaks directly to the way doctrine serves as the foundation for proper motivation. Notice how Calvin states that the law of God "is the best instrument for enabling" the believer to know God's will and to be confirmed in that knowledge. Then, with this sound doctrinal foundation going first, Calvin boldly asserts that "frequently meditating" on the law will "excite" and "confirm" the believer in sincere obedience. Thus motivated by the Law, the believer will be "drawn away" from toying with sin. Calvin then concludes that this greater obedience and less sin are "advantages which the Lord, by means of His law, bestows" on faithful believers. Notice how, according to Calvin, law and love are not polar opposites, but the Spirit "inwardly inspires" believers with "a love of obedience." Here, it seems Calvin is simply echoing our Lord when He said, "If you love Me, keep My commandments" (John 14:15; see also 14:21).

Westminster Standards: An Emphasis on Sovereignty

As we turn to the Westminster Standards, we find a helpful emphasis on the necessity of the *Holy Spirit* to sovereignly and effectually apply the *truth* of the preached word through the *faith* of the believer, even when the minister and listeners are faithfully preaching and hearing that Word. The Westminster Standards teach that "The Spirit of God maketh . . . the preaching of the word an effectual means of convincing and converting sinners, and of building them up in holiness and comfort, through faith, unto salvation."[20] God's Spirit convinces, converts, and builds up through

[19] John Calvin, *Institutes of the Christian Religion*, trans. Henry Beveridge (Grand Rapids, MI: Eerdmans, 1989), 2.7.12, 309.

[20] WSC 89. Thus also the emphasis on "sound doctrine" (truth) as the very first part of the answer to Q. 159 of the Larger Catechism, "How is the word

the faith that He sovereignly gives and strengthens. So as we consider the role of motivation in preaching we must not forget that ultimately only God can cause a sermon to bear fruit. Even if we were to preach perfectly, as Jesus Christ always did when He was on earth, if God does not stretch out His hand to make if effectual it will be rejected and even hated by our listeners. Consider the reaction to our Lord's message in John 6:66: "From that time many of His disciples went back and walked with Him no more." Here Christ obviously did not fail to carefully include elements of proper motivation or right doctrine in His sermon! Yet, because it was not the will of God to convert many of the Jews, only His elect few remained with Him.

Therefore, we shall examine the Standards for their teaching on our responsibility in the motivating process, while we affirm the necessity of, and attribute all to, the sovereignty of the Spirit of God, who works as He pleases in motivating and moving His people according to His good pleasure. We can readily see both emphases of God's sovereignty and our responsibility in being moved or motivated in the Standards' repeated use of the notion "to stir up," as it sets forth the doctrine of sanctification in various places. Thus in Larger Catechism question 75, the Spirit "stir[s] up, increase[s] and strengthen[s]" those "saving graces" which He "put[s] into [believers'] hearts" so "that they more and more die unto sin, and rise unto newness of life." Yet, the Confession affirms that believers are still responsible to work with the Spirit, for it states that even though believers' "ability to do good works is not at all of themselves, but wholly from the Spirit of Christ," yet it insists that these same believers "ought to be diligent in stirring up the grace of God that is in them" (16.3). In the same way, in their partaking of the Lord's Supper, believers are responsible to "affectionately meditate on [Christ's] death and sufferings, and thereby stir up themselves to a vigorous exercise of their graces" (WLC 174). Yet for any benefit

---

of God to be preached by those that are called thereunto?"

they receive they are to "bless God for it" (WLC 175). Furthermore, the benefit does not come through their feelings but through their faith: "by faith they receive and apply unto themselves Christ crucified, and all the benefits of his death" (WLC 170).

We find the same stress on God's sovereignty and our responsibility in the Standards' teaching of prayer. Thus, the Spirit helps us to pray by "working and quickening in our hearts (although not in all persons, nor at all times, in the same measure) those apprehensions, affections, and graces which are requisite for the right performance of that duty" (WLC 182). Yet, in answering the question "How are we to pray?" the Catechism instructs that believers are responsible "to pray with an awful apprehension of the majesty of God, and deep sense of our own unworthiness, necessities, and sins; with penitent, thankful, and enlarged hearts; with understanding, faith, sincerity, fervency, love, and perseverance, waiting upon him, with humble submission to his will" (WLC 185).

When we list the relevant portions of the Westminster Larger Catechism on preaching, we find the following emphasis on the sovereignty of God in making the preached Word effectual (WLC 154, 155), and also on the responsibility of the preacher and the listener in accurately setting forth and diligently receiving the Word preached (WLC 159, 160):

1. Christ makes the Word of God an effectual means of communicating to us the benefits of His mediation.
2. The Spirit of God makes especially the preaching of the Word an effectual means of:
    a. Enlightening.
    b. Convincing.
    c. Humbling.
    d. Driving sinners out of themselves and drawing them to Christ.
    e. Conforming them to His image.
    f. Subduing them to His will.

g. Strengthening them against temptations and corruptions.
h. Building them up in faith.
i. Establishing their hearts in holiness and comfort through faith unto salvation.

3. Preachers are to preach:
    a. Sound doctrine.
    b. Diligently.
    c. In season and out of season.
    d. Plainly.
    e. Not in the enticing words of man's wisdom.
    f. But in demonstration of the Spirit and power.
    g. Faithfully.
    h. The whole counsel of God.
    i. Wisely.
    j. Applying themselves to the necessities and capacities of their hearers.
    k. Zealously.
    l. With fervent love to God.
    m. With fervent love to the souls of His people.
    n. Sincerely.
    o. Aiming at His glory.
    p. Aiming at their conversion.
    q. Aiming at their edification.
    r. Aiming at their salvation.
4. Listeners are to hear sermons:
    a. With diligence.
    b. With preparation.
    c. With prayer.
    d. By examining what they hear with Scriptures.
    e. Receiving the truth with faith.
    f. Receiving the truth with love.
    g. Receiving the truth with meekness.
    h. With readiness of mind.

i. As the Word of God.
j. With meditation.
k. Discussing what they heard with other Christians.
l. Hiding it in their hearts.
m. Bringing forth the fruit of it in their lives.

Thus, if we take the Westminster Larger Catechism as a faithful guide, preachers and hearers should prayerfully ask God to make His preached Word effectual in their hearts even as they seek to give and receive such motivation which will strengthen their faith in the truth of God's Word, through which they will grow in their obedience. The individual's responsibility to be properly prepared and adequately reverent is readily apparent in the above list, as are the constant goals of God's glory and man's sanctification, and the bearing of love toward God and man throughout. However, though many motives can be deduced and argued for from the list, it appears that the Catechism's instruction on preaching does not explicitly address the question of *how* a minister should seek to motivate his listeners in a sermon.

Westminster Confession on Motivation

Similar to Calvin's third use of the law, the Westminster Confession does speak more directly to the subject of motivation when it declares the "great use" of the law for believers. The law of God functions for believers

> as a rule of life, informing them of the will of God and their duty, it directs and binds them to walk accordingly; discovering also the sinful pollutions of their nature, hearts, and lives; so as, examining themselves thereby, they may come to further conviction of, humiliation for, and hatred against sin; together with a clearer sight of the need they have of Christ, and the perfection of His obedience. It is likewise of use to

> the regenerate, to restrain their corruptions, in that it forbids sin; and the threatenings of it serve to show what even their sins deserve, and what afflictions in this life they may expect for them, although freed from the curse thereof threatened in the law. The promises of it, in like manner, show them God's approbation of obedience, and what blessings they may expect upon the performance thereof, although not as due to them by the law as a covenant of works: so as, a man's doing good, and refraining from evil because the law encourageth to the one, and deterreth from the other, is no evidence of his being under the law, and not under grace. (WCF 19.6)

Notice all through this quotation how it is the Law over and over again that is credited with supplying the motivating force of believers' obedience. The Law of God "directs and binds," it "discover[s]" our "sinful pollutions," so that by "examining" ourselves by the Law, we may grow in sanctification. As we saw earlier in Calvin, the Confession even has a sanctifying, and therefore rightly motivating, use for the "threatenings" of the law *for the believer*. Additionally, the Confession here asserts there are "promises" *of the law*. Moreover, it declares God's approval (approbation) "of obedience," and that God even blesses our obedience!

Finally, in the last section quoted above, the Confession attributes to the Law, and not to the gospel, the "encourag[ing]" of "doing good" and the "deterr[ing]" "from evil." In fact, notice how directly the Confession attributes these sanctifying motivations to the Law of God. If we emphasize the relevant terms, the Confession says that "a man's doing good, and refraining from evil *because the law* encourageth to the one, and deterreth from the other *is no evidence* of his being under the law, and not under grace." In other words when a Christian pursues holiness, that is, when he serves and obeys God by means of the law—because he is motivated by the law's commands and not by emotion, or even his appreciation of God's love or grace in redemption or anything else—the Confession says such a believer is *not* back in a covenant of works trying to earn his salvation, but he remains under grace!

The next section of the Confession confirms this proper motivation of the Law of God, stating: "Neither are the formentioned uses of the law contrary to the grace of the Gospel, but do sweetly comply with it; the Spirit of Christ subduing and enabling the will of man to do that freely and cheerfully, which the will of God revealed in the law requireth to be done" (WCF 19.7). Thus, the Confession does not limit a Christian's proper motivation to the gospel, but by the Spirit, the believer can be motivated by the Law and that motivation is not "contrary to the grace of the Gospel, but do[th] sweetly comply with it." Here the Confession cites Galatians 3:21 (ESV): "Is the law then contrary to the promises of God? Certainly not!"; and Hebrews 8:10: "For this *is* the covenant that I will make with the house of Israel after those days, says the LORD: I will put My laws in their mind and write them on their hearts; and I will be their God, and they shall be My people." Thus, the Confession, in these two sections, is teaching that when the Spirit writes the Law of God on the heart of the believer, he can be motivated by that law in such a way that he is not wrongly putting himself back in the covenant of works and—contrary to the grace of the gospel—trying to earn his salvation by his works, but in fact he is making a faithful use of the means of grace, as the motivating power of the Law compliments the motivating force of the gospel *in the believer*. Moreover, when the Confession does speak of God's love and grace as motivating factors, it attributes the motivation to the faith and not to the feelings of the believer.

Jonathan Edwards on Motivation and Emotion

The preaching method of the great American theologian, Jonathan Edwards, embodied this approach. When he preached, Edwards earnestly sought to apply the text of Scripture to the people of God in order to move them, by the truth received through their faith, toward godliness. Thus, in his "A Farewell Sermon" Edwards summarized his entire ministry at the Northampton Church as an exercise in motivation: "I have diligently endeavored to find out and use the most powerful motives to persuade you to take care for your own welfare and salvation."[21] Edwards saw the sermon as the vehicle through which the Holy Spirit of God would, as He pleased, give a spiritual taste for the things of God. As Edwards argued in *Religious Affections*, emotions of all sorts may be present or absent. Nothing definite can be proved by them alone. For the affections to be truly religious, doctrine must come first.

> Holy affections are not heat without light; but evermore arise from some information of the understanding, some spiritual instruction that the mind receives, some light or actual knowledge. The child of God is graciously affected, because . . . either he receives some new understanding of divine things, or has his former knowledge renewed. . . . Knowledge is the key that first opens the hard heart, enlarges the affections, and opens the way for men into the kingdom of heaven . . . affections which do not arise from any light in the understanding . . . is a sure evidence that these affections are not spiritual, let them be ever so high.[22]

Furthermore the person rightly motivated by divine doctrine must be convinced that it is true.

> *Truly gracious affections are attended with a conviction of the reality and certainty of divine things.* . . . All gracious persons

[21] Jonathan Edwards, "A Farewell Sermon," quoted in Dane Ortlund, *A New Inner Relish: Christian Motivation in the Thought of Jonathan Edwards* (Ross-shire, Scotland, UK: Christian Focus, 2008), 36.

[22] Jonathan Edwards, "A Treatise Concerning Religious Affections," in *The Works of Jonathan Edwards*, vol. 1 (Edinburgh: Banner of Truth, 1995), 281–82.

> have a solid, full, thorough, and effectual conviction of the truth of the great things of the gospel. They no longer halt between two opinions.[23]

The mark of divine and therefore truly Christian affections is genuine desire for God and His righteousness. God alone, as He sovereignly pleases, gives that affection. But He only gives it where His Word is believed as true. To this end Edwards sought to make full use of all of the motives of Scripture by presenting and demonstrating each doctrine as true, even as he looked entirely to God to bring the conviction of each truth home to the sinner. Thus, Edwards lists as true motives to holiness such things as: faith, love, trust, heavenly-mindedness, love of righteousness, fear of God, thankfulness, humility, and repentance.[24] Christians will grow in godliness as they are convicted of the truth of these things, for it is the nature of a man to act out of what he believes and embraces as true.

> He that has true faith is convinced of the reality and certainty of the great things of religion; and he that is convinced of the reality of these things will be influenced by them, and they will govern his actions and behavior . . . for we know the nature of man is such, that he will govern his actions by what he believes and is convinced of. . . . Their practice will be according to their convictions. The very nature of man forbids that it should be otherwise.[25]

[23] Ibid., 288, emphasis in original.

[24] Jonathan Edwards, *Charity and Its Fruits* (Edinburgh: Banner of Truth, 2005), 230–41.

[25] Ibid., 230–32.

8

Motivation in New Testament Sermons: Selecting the Texts

We now turn to the Scriptures in order to search for and examine the elements of motivation that we can find in those passages of the New Testament that are most similar to modern-day church sermons. Our goal will be to ascertain how, in each passage, the speaker is seeking to motivate his audience. Our aim is to identify and set forth those elements of motivation from the inspired sermons of Scripture, in order that today's preachers can incorporate them in their sermons. We need to look at enough examples to establish clear patterns meant to be repeated, while noting possible exceptions that are probably not to be emulated. At the same time we need to choose only those pericopes that are clearly analogous to modern-day preaching contexts. This, then, will be our criteria: We will consider those passages (1) where a public exposition of biblical truth is audibly proclaimed at some length; (2) by a person of recognized leadership in the church; (3) to a present and attentive audience; and (4) where the design of the speaker is to move his listeners to certain attitudes and actions in conformity with the proclaimed truth. Furthermore, passages will not be chosen where the speaker is: (1) disputing with or addressing opponents (Acts 4–5; 7; 15; 22; 26); (2) answering specific questions, or testifying of oneself (Acts 11; 14; 20); or (3) praying (John 17; Acts 4; 11); as these contexts are too far removed from modern preaching contexts.

Additionally, those exceptional passages, where the speaker is doing something that is clearly not to be repeated, will not be included in the sample. Thus, I will not be including Christ's discourse of parables in Matthew 13. Although the parables are often claimed as a proof text for sermon illustrations, Jesus explicitly stated that He spoke parables to Israel not to illumine His teaching but to obscure it, so that Isaiah's prophecy of Israel's judgment upon the wicked hypocrites would come to pass. (See Matt. 13:10–16.) Clearly, the ordinary minister is not called to prophetically bring God's judgment to pass by his sermons. Finally, Christ's sermons will not be considered, as we will focus on the proclamation that Christ gave to the church to preach until His return. Christ did not allow the disciples to proclaim these things before His death, neither did they understand them until He opened their minds after His resurrection (Matt. 16:20; 17:9; Mark 9:9–10; Luke 9:45; 24:45; John 12:16). Likewise, the epistles, as written letters, do not qualify under these criteria, even if some were written out sermons as has been theorized of the book of Hebrews, for this has not been established.

Thus, having set forth my criteria, the following five orations can be considered as more or less analogous to today's preaching contexts and will be examined for motivational elements:

1. Peter's Pentecost sermon: Acts 2:14–40
2. Peter's temple sermon: Acts 3:12–26
3. Peter's sermon to the Gentiles in Caesarea: Acts 10:34–44
4. Paul's synagogue sermon: Acts 13:16–41
5. Paul's Mars Hill address: Acts 17:22–32[1]

Plainly these passages contain summaries of each of the

[1] Derek Thomas counts fifteen "sermons" recorded in the Book of Acts: eight by Peter; five by Paul, in addition to four "defense speeches"; and one each by Stephen and James. See Derek Thomas, *Acts* (Phillipsburg, NJ: P&R, 2011), 40.

sermons, so we know right from the start that we are not getting everything that Peter or Paul preached, not by a long shot. Additionally, we know that sermons three and five are cut short; by the Holy Spirit in sermon three, and by mockers in sermon five. However, these facts do not take anything away from the ability of this analysis to achieve its goal. Sermons three and five are sufficiently developed to see the message and reaction to the sermon. Moreover, since all five sermons are Holy Spirit–inspired summaries, we can be confident that we are getting an accurate, and in fact, infallible portrayal of the doctrinal content, tone, and approach of the minister, and of the audience reaction for each sermon. The texts themselves give us minute, concrete details that prove this to be the case. For example, Peter stands up and raises his voice (Acts 2:14); he comments on how the audience is looking at him (Acts 3:12); Paul stands up and motions with his hand (Acts 13:16); he quotes Greek poets (Acts 17:28). Plus, in every sermon there is specific audience and speaker interaction, before, during, or after the sermon that can only occur if the summaries are giving us an accurate portrayal of what was preached. These clues and others like them assure us that we are getting a thoroughly precise, though summarized account, of each sermonic event.

9

Theological Position Statement

Because this paper is written by a Reformed minister, already convinced from Scripture that Reformed theology is true, the following doctrines are assumed in my analysis:

1. That the Bible is the inspired, inerrant Word of God.
2. That God inspired certain men called apostles with new revelation that would in time become part of the New Testament canon. Accordingly, when they *speak* words about Jesus Christ, which might not yet be part of a *written* document, I have understood them as proclaiming the Word of God.
3. That the covenant of grace was first proclaimed in the garden of Eden (Gen. 3:15), and that the ministers of God have only been authorized to proclaim that covenant from then on. The differences in the administration of the covenant from Old Testament to New are due to the amount of revelation given under type and anticipation versus reality and fulfillment. Thus, I embrace covenant theology as expounded in the Westminster Standards and I disagree with any theory or doctrine that seeks to in any way establish or recapitulate any form of a covenant of works on Mount Sinai (WCF 7.5–6; 27.5–6; WLC 31–36).
4. That the believer's relationship to the gospel of salvation and to the moral law of God has not changed from the moment

Adam and Eve were redeemed by faith. Thus, I reject any system of thought that would see the preaching of Moses, Jeremiah, Jesus, Peter, or Paul as being different in substance from one another, or from what preachers ought to be doing in church contexts today. God's people have always been justified by faith alone, and they have always been commanded to live their lives in obedience to the moral law.

5. Accordingly, I believe that the message that Peter preaches at Pentecost, at the temple, and later at the house of Cornelius, and that Paul declares in the synagogue and at Mars Hill, is the same in substance to what preachers are called to proclaim today. In these examples we can see many differences in the doctrines chosen to be expounded, in the way they are explained, in which ones are emphasized, and in how they are applied as the ministers, their audiences, and the speaking occasions differ. Such variety accentuates the beauty of the Scriptures, the wisdom of the Spirit, and the richness of our faith, but it does not at all deviate from the truth of the Bible or its universal applicability to all men at all times. In each oration the substance of the call to repent from sin, to believe in Jesus, and to live out that faith is unchanged, for it is the same gospel to the same church for the same reasons. I believe this same message is still what the church has been commanded, privileged, and entrusted to preach until Christ returns.
6. Thus extreme dispensational views that assert fundamental differences in the aim, substance, and makeup of the sermons and audiences found in Scripture from the sermons and audiences of today are rejected. It is my view that the people who needed to hear of Christ for the first time in Acts 2, 3, 10, 13, and 17 are essentially the same as the people who need to hear of Christ for the ten thousandth time in our pews today. The same Word by the same Spirit is being proclaimed to the same kind of people who need

the same grace in their hearts to believe and to do the same things according to His good pleasure. It is axiomatic to this book that we can and should learn how to preach from the inspired sermons of Scripture, as well as from the didactic portions. The sermons are not "exceptions" to the rule because they are Scripture. As we are called to go and preach and these are examples of preaching, the burden of proof is on those who would discount these sermonic examples as being exceptional rather than normative.[1]

[1] Thomas describes the Pentecost sermon as "an example of how to bring an Old Testament text that is rooted in a redemptive historical setting into the present. . . . The summary sermon is expositional, Christological, and evangelistic . . . this is news driven home to the hearts of men and women insisting that what is at stake is a matter of life and death. There is a sense of urgency. Something needs to be done and done right away!" Derek Thomas, *Acts* (Phillipsburg, NJ: P&R, 2011), 41.

10

Defining Terms and Describing Methodology

Now that we know what passages of Scripture we will be examining, we need to set forth our definition of motivation and state the criteria we will be using to discover elements of motivation in a given text. In our brief overview of academic and religious literature, we have seen a variety of meanings attached to the concept of motivation. Some kinds of motivation have been described as external, and are usually viewed negatively, as constraint. Internal motivation is very often viewed as more positive or authentic, with many proponents asserting that there can be no other kind. In some cases internal motivation is indistinguishable from emotion or feelings of fulfillment and satisfaction. In others an emotion or feeling is not considered to be a motive until it moves the subject to some action. Usually, only those emotions that are considered to be positive, that is, pleasurable or desirable as determined by the self, are awarded with the title of motive or motivation. Thus, motivation as a whole is looked at as a highly subjective phenomenon. What may serve as a motive to me may not be very moving to you, and vice versa. Yet, it is almost universally agreed that to be motivated is a desirable thing, and that the motivated person is more effective at everything!

Before we develop a working definition of motivation, we need to compare what we have learned about the subject from modern studies and preaching texts with what we find in the dictionary. Webster states the following about motivation:

1. Motivate *verb* (1885): to provide with a motive: IMPEL.
2. Motivation *noun* (1873) 1a: the act or process of motivating. b: the condition of being motivated. 2: a motivating force, stimulus, or influence : INCENTIVE, DRIVE.
3. Motive *noun* [Middle English, from Middle French *motif*, from *motif*, adj., moving, from Medieval Latin *motivus*, from Latin *motus*, pp. of *movere* to move] (15c) 1: something (as a need or desire) that causes a person to act. 2: a recurrent phrase or figure that is developed through the course of a musical composition. 3: MOTIF.
4. Motive *adjective* [Middle French or Medieval Latin; Middle French *motif*, from Medieval Latin *motivus*] (1502) 1: moving or tending to move to action. 2: of or relating to motion or the causing of motion (~ energy).
5. Motive *verb* (ca. 1650): motivate.
6. Synonym: MOTIVE, IMPULSE, INCENTIVE, INDUCEMENT, SPUR, GOAD, mean a stimulus to action. MOTIVE implies an emotion or desire operating on the will and causing it to act (a *motive* for the crime). IMPULSE suggests a driving power arising from personal temperament or constitution (buying on *impulse*). INCENTIVE applies to an external influence (as an expected reward) inciting to action (a bonus was offered as an *incentive*). INDUCEMENT suggests a motive prompted by the deliberate enticements or allurements of another (offered a watch as an *inducement* to subscribe). SPUR applies to a motive that stimulates the faculties or increases energy or ardor (fear was a *spur* to action). GOAD suggests a motive that keeps one going against one's will or desire (thought insecurity a *goad* to worker efficiency).[1]

[1] *Merriam-Webster's Collegiate Dictionary*, Tenth Edition (Springfield, MA: Merriam-Webster, 1994), s.v. "motivate," "motivation," "motive," 759–60.

From the above we see that the words motivation, motivate, and even motive are relatively new words that did not exist before the late middle ages. Consequently we find no word for "motivation" in the Greek text of Scripture. Moreover, of the Latin words mentioned above, the original Vulgate does not contain the words *motivus*, or *movere*. Other similar words occur only in the context of literal movement. However, of the six times that *motus* appears in the Vulgate's New Testament, on three occasions it means to move figuratively, in the heart (Luke 7:13; 10:33; 15:20). All of these verses use *motus* to translate the Greek word σπλαγχνίζομαι. Kittel's *Theological Dictionary* contains the following about this Greek word:

A. Greek Usage . . . It originally denotes the "inward parts" of a sacrifice, and specifically the nobler parts as distinct from the ἑτέρα, ἔγκατα, i.e., the heart, liver, lungs, and kidneys . . . from the 5th cent. It is used anthropologically for the "inward parts" of a man . . . the σπλάγχνων are seen as the seat of "impulsive passions" such as anger . . . "anxious desire" . . . "love" [footnote states: as "in a conjuration in love magic"]. . . the word finally comes to mean much the same as "heart" in its transf. sense as the centre of personal "feeling" and "sensibility." . . . In distinction from καρδία, which is more the seat of nobler affections like love and hate, courage and fear, joy and sorrow, σπλάγχνα is either more comprehensive or it is often a more blunt, forceful and unequivocal term.

B. LXX: sometimes the σπλάγχνων are also the "seat of feeling" . . . 2 Macc. 9:5f . . . "unbearable sorrow came upon him in his inward parts." . . . In this connection cf. also Prv. 26:22: "Flattering speech goes down to the inmost parts of the σπλάγχνων"; Sir. 30:7: "At the slightest cry of the spoilt child the father's σπλάγχνων are moved." . . . There are at least hints of a more specific use in two verses in Prv . . . 12:10 presupposes that the σπλάγχνα might be regarded as the seat of the positive stirring of pity . . . "to be merciful" at Prv. 17:5.[2]

BDAG says of its New Testament usage:

A. σπλαγχνίζομαι (6771)—have pity, feel sympathy, perh[aps] τινός with or for someone . . . Mt 18:27
B. σπλάγχνων (6772)—
   1. The inward parts of a body, including esp. the viscera, inward parts, entrails, lit . . . Ac 1:18.
   2. As often in the ancient world, inner body parts served as referents for psychological aspects (s. καρδία): of the seat of the emotions, in our usage a transference is made to the rendering heart, fig. (Aeschyl. et al.; Pr 12:10; Sir 30:7; PsSol 2:14; TestAbrA; TestLevi 4:4, al. in Test-12Patr; JosAs 6:1; Jos., Bell. 4, 263.—On Engl. 'bowels' in this sense s. OED s.v. bowel sb. 3), in our lit. mostly as the seat and source of love (so Herodas 1, 57; Theocr. 7, 99; Dionys. Hal. 11, 35, 4), sympathy, and mercy. . . σπλάγχνα ἐλέους *the merciful heart* (qualitative gen.; TestZeb 7:3; 8:2) Lk 1:78. Also σπλάγχνα οἰκτιρμοῦ Col 3:12. σπλάγχνα καὶ οἰκτιρμοί *affection and sympathy* Phil 2:1. . . τὰ σπλ. αὐτοῦ εἰς ὑμᾶς ἐστιν *his heart goes out to you* 2 Cor 7:15. ἐν τοῖς σπλ. ὑμῶν *in your own hearts* 6:12. σπλάγχνα ἔχειν ἐπί τινα *have compassion for someone* 1 Cl 23:1. κλείειν τὰ σπλάγχνα αὐτοῦ ἀπό τινος *close one's heart to someone* in need 1J 3:17.
   3. Of the feeling itself, pl. love, affection. . . long for someone with the affection of Christ Jesus Phil 1:8. . . αὐτόν, τοῦτ᾽ ἔστιν τὰ ἐμὰ σπλ. him, my beloved Phlm 12.[3]

[2] *Theological Dictionary of the New Testament*, vol. VII, eds. Gerhard Kittel and Gerhard Friedrich (Grand Rapids, MI: Eerdmans, 2006), 548–51.

[3] Walter Bauer, *A Greek-English Lexicon of the New Testament and Other Early Christian Literature*, edited by Frederick W. Danker, 3rd ed. (Chicago:

Clearly, although this word *family* can be used to express strong emotion, it is not equivalent to *motive* or *motivate* in the modern sense of the word. Moreover, it does not occur in any of our preaching texts. It appears that we will not be able to gather motivations directly from the grammar of any texts, but we will have to infer them from the meaning and intention of passages. Our procedure as to how we will do this will be presented below.

As noted above, the dictionary definitions for *motive*, *motivate*, and *motivation* all stress motion. The etymology and synonyms all have to do with moving. Motive, to motivate, and motivation moves people. In the same way, we saw, as we surveyed the different literature on preaching, perhaps the one thing that liberals and conservatives, Arminians and Reformed agreed on was that preaching was for the end of getting people to do something. Even those who scoff at Christianity know this when they angrily reply to someone who dares to tell them something to do or not do, "Don't preach to me!" Similarly, the secular and academic works on motivation also measured and argued for their systems and theories based upon the results. The motivated person was in some fashion moved or else the motivation was deemed insufficient. It may have just been in the way he felt about himself, but motion was the goal and the measure. Now we also saw that these studies always noted the role of emotions, but there was much disagreement as to their ultimate contribution to motivation. Yet, the one thing that is everywhere affirmed, in every study and in every method, is that motivation moves people. Whether it was better grades or higher self-esteem, motivation affected people. It changed them. And where it did not, it was not considered to be motivation, but at best, weak emotion.

Additionally, many of the academic works, all but the earliest ones, increasingly saw external or extrinsic motivation negatively and internal or intrinsic positively. How the person was moved with respect to his personal wants, desires, feelings, and especially his

---

University of Chicago Press, 2000; BibleWorks 9).

self-image became the most important thing. The unspoken and perhaps even unnoticed assumption here is that the goalposts seem to have been moved. Motivation was originally a means to an end, a tool to achieve more work or better grades. Somewhere along the line, especially in the more liberal works, the means replaced the end. Systems of motivation were not measured by test scores or productivity—such objective, external measurements were eschewed and even openly disdained by some studies. No, the goal of motivation somehow became the motivation itself. If test subjects felt better about themselves, more positive, more confident, the motivation technique was considered successful, regardless of any objective, quantifiable results. Consequently, as it has come to be more and more refined, *internal motivation* has become almost entirely subjective, individualistic, and feelings-based. It is either equated to, or closely identified with, emotion, feelings, self-esteem, or personal satisfaction. As such, internal motivation has become hard to identify, apart from people showing heightened interest or filling out self-evaluations saying they were more motivated or felt better about themselves under certain conditions. One study even openly admitted it did not know what motivation was; in other words, no one can tell *you* what motivation is. You must discover what motivates you and then get all you can of it, for it is the most important thing!

This book will do no one any good whatsoever if all it does is describe ways individuals or groups were subjectively "motivated" during isolated preaching events two thousand years ago. Plus, without specific descriptions of what and how people were feeling there is no conclusive way to determine the emotions or self-image of the preacher or the listeners during a preaching event. Neither is there any basis to postulate that by simply repeating previous circumstances we will be able to achieve the same highly subjective results today. Therefore, seeing that preaching is meant to move people to action, coupled with the fact that the original definitions and synonyms of the words motive, motivate, and motivation were consistently defined also as that which moves someone to action, we will look for the movement that the speaker is seeking to produce in his listeners by identifying the purpose or aim behind his words. Why does he say what he says? What is he trying to accomplish? To answer these questions we will examine the reasons the speaker gives, the incentives he offers (if any), and the appeals that he makes to his audience. Specifically, we will study each passage to determine:

1. Any reasons given explicitly in the text to obey a command or trust a promise or adopt a specific attitude or emotion.
2. Any reasons that are necessarily implied by the text to the same ends.
3. Any specific incentives for action explicitly given in a text, whether promised rewards or threatened punishments.
4. Any incentives that can be deduced by good and necessary consequence from the text.
5. Any appeals to put on Christian virtues or attitudes, or to avoid evil ones.
6. Any appeals to imitate Christ or other good examples, or to eschew bad ones.
7. Any appeals to faith, pleasing God, or loving the brethren, or to avoid doubt, displeasing God, or harming others.

Whatever reasons, incentives, and appeals that we can find in the speaker's words, we will use in order to determine his purpose. Likewise, if we can identify certain emotions in the text that are exemplified, commanded, or recommended to the audience, we will do so, whether or not we can conclusively link them with some particular motivation. Furthermore, we will especially focus on any call to action, whether through command, wish, or suggestion, and we will seek to identify the reason the call is made along with any promises or threats that serve to impel one toward heeding it. In order to objectively search each biblical sermon for the preceding reasons, incentives, and appeals, the following questions should be helpful:

1. Why is the speaker saying this? What is his expressed or implied point?
2. What does he desire from the listener in saying it?
3. What reasons does he offer in order to bring about the desired action?
4. What end result does he aim at?
5. What consequences does he promise or threaten if the desired action is or is not taken?
6. What response does his audience make to his message?
7. How is this response viewed?

In addition to consulting trusted Reformed and evangelical commentaries, my analysis continually applies these questions in order to allow us to see the speaker's reasons, incentives, and appeals, and therefore his purpose and aim in speaking. Knowing the speaker's purpose, in turn, reveals the specific motivations he presents to his audience, which is the goal of this project. Once we believe we have identified the purposes and motivations that the speaker is giving, we will test them with Scripture to make sure they are biblically attested to elsewhere. Then we will see if we can compile a list of common motives and motivations throughout the five public addresses in order that preachers can seek to communicate them in their sermons.

11

Possible Grammatical Indicators of Motivation as Defined by Study

In order to more accurately and objectively identify and set forth the motivational intentions of the speakers to their audiences, it is crucial that we rightly determine them from the texts. There are certain words that can indicate purpose, reason, or cause that will help us in this endeavor. The most common of these words, with the relevant portions of their definitions, are included below, from the BDAG lexicon:

εἰς

4. Marker of goals involving affective/abstract/suitability aspects
    a. Of entry into a state of being w. verbs of going, coming, leading, and so on.
    b. Of change from one state to another w. verbs of changing.
    c. Of actions or feelings directed in someone's direction in hostile or friendly sense.
    d. W. the vocation, use, or end indicated *for*, *as*.
    e. W. the result of an action or condition indicated into, to, so that.
    f. To denote purpose in order to, to . . . for which purpose . . . with this in view . . . for this reason . . . εἰς τοῦτο for this reason or purpose.

διὰ

with genitive:

3. Marker of instrumentality or circumstance whereby someth[ing] is accomplished or effected, *by*, *via*, *through*.
    - d. Of efficient cause *via, through*.

With accusative:

2. Marker of someth. constituting cause.
    - a. The reason why someth. happens, results exists: *because of, for the sake of.*
    - c. διά foll. by inf. or acc. w. inf., representing a causal clause, *because*.
    - d. Instead of διά w. gen. to denote efficient cause we may have διά, *by*

ἵνα

1. Marker to denote purpose, aim, or goal, *in order that, that*.
2. Marker of objective, *that*.

ὅπως

2. As a conj. marker expressing purpose for an event or state, (*in order*) *that*.
    - a. With numerous types of verbs (*in order*) *that*,
        - 2. ὅπως with the subjunctive . . . to denote what one wishes to be done.[1]

γὰρ

1. Marker of cause or reason, *for*.
2. Marker of clarification, *for*, *you see*.
3. Marker of inference, *certainly*, *by all means*, *so*, *then*.

[1] Second definition of "ὅπως" taken from *A Greek-English Lexicon of the New Testament*, translated, revised, and enlarged by Joseph Henry Thayer, D.D., 1889, copyright © 1998–2000 by International Bible Translators (IBT), Inc.

ὅτι

2. Marker of explanatory clauses, that.
4. Marker of causality.
    a. Subordinating, *because*, *since* . . . Used w. demonstr. and interrog. pronouns διὰ τοῦτο . . . ὅτι *for this reason* . . ., (namely) *that*.

ὥστε

1. Introducing independent clauses *for this reason*, *therefore*, *so*.
2. Introducing dependent clauses.
    a. Of the actual result *so that*.
    b. Of the intended result, scarcely to be distinguished in mng. fr. ἵνα . . . *for the purpose of*, *with a view to*, *in order that*.

ἀπὸ

5. To indicate cause, means or outcome.
    a. Gener., to show the reason for someth. *because of*, *as a result of*, *for*.
    b. To indicate means *with the help of*, *with*.
    c. To indicate motive or reason *for*, *from*, *with*.

ἐκ

3. Marker denoting origin, cause, motive, reason, *from*, *of*.
    a. The effective cause *by*, *because of*, (cp. The "perfectivizing" force of ἐκ).
    b. Of the reason which is a presupposition for someth.: *by reason of*, *as a result of*, *because of*.
    c. Sim. ἐκ can introduce the means which one uses for a definite purpose, *with*, *by means of*.

οὖν

1. Inferential, denoting that what it introduces is the result

of or an inference fr. what precedes, *so*, *therefore*, *consequently*, *accordingly*, *then*.

a. In declarative sentences.
b. In commands and invitations, with intensive force.

μετὰ

3. Marker of attendant circumstances of someth. that takes place, *with*.
   a. Of moods, emotions, wishes, feelings, excitement, states of mind or body.

When these words, or similar ones are present in a text we will examine the constructions carefully to see if purpose, cause, rationale, and thus ultimately motive is being grammatically indicated. When these words or others like them appear to be grammatically significant to our analysis, we will call attention to them.

12

Defense of Methodology

I recognize that those who restrict authentic motivation into exclusively internal, subjective, and personal well-being and feelings-based categories will reject this procedure out of hand, but I simply do not see any reason to do a study on the kind of preaching that makes an individual feel good. By definition, such preaching is subjective and changes with the desires and longings of each listener, and it does not do any ultimate good to anyone beyond satisfying their current cravings. Accordingly, it cannot have as its first design to please and glorify God, but its main focus by definition must be to please men, and that not even the best of man, but his most consuming passion of the moment. The naïveté of such an approach, in consideration of the sinful, God-hating heart of the fallen nature of every man, is stunning. It seems to me the admonitions of Paul and Jeremiah need to be considered by those who teach or seek for such motivation in preaching:

> Preach the word! Be ready in season and out of season. Convince, rebuke, exhort, with all longsuffering and teaching. For the time will come when they will not endure sound doctrine, but according to their own desires, because they have itching ears, they will heap up for themselves teachers; and they will turn their ears away from the truth, and be turned aside to fables. (2 Tim. 4:2–4)

> Thus says the LORD of hosts: "Do not listen to the words of the prophets who prophesy to you. They make you worthless; they speak a vision of their own heart, not from the mouth of the LORD. They continually say to those who despise Me, 'The LORD has said, "You shall have peace"'; and to everyone who walks according to the dictates of his own heart, they say, 'No evil shall come upon you.'. . . I have not sent these prophets, yet they ran. I have not spoken to them, yet they prophesied. But if they had stood in My counsel, and had caused My people to hear My words, then they would have turned them from their evil way and from the evil of their doings. . . . Behold, I am against those who prophesy false dreams," says the LORD, "and tell them, and cause My people to err by their lies and by their recklessness. Yet I did not send them or command them; therefore they shall not profit this people at all," says the LORD. (Jer. 23:16–17, 21–22, 32)

I'm sure the false prophets in Jeremiah's day who continually preached peace to the people and did not turn them from their evil ways would have scored very high marks in how well they internally motivated their listeners. Yet, God was not so pleased with them! Likewise, the apostle Paul admonishes Timothy to persevere in faithful preaching *with longsuffering*, indicating it will not be easy. Due to man's sinful heart, man will not naturally endure sound doctrine (which then must needs to be endured), but will seek for preachers who will satisfy his desires or, which is nearly the same thing, who will *internally motivate* him, according to the modern understanding of that phrase. In fact, they will heap up such teachers. And they do this with the design of doing themselves good. Preachers who seek to motivate people according to their desires no doubt believe they are doing them much good. Yet, as the last line of the passage from Jeremiah above declares, such preachers, who encourage a man to walk "according to the dictates of his own heart," do not do the people of God any true good at all.

The problem with viewing internal motivation as superior to external is the lack of a timeless moral standard that allows us to judge when satisfying feelings and desires is actually a bad and detrimental thing to the ultimate well-being of the person. A cocaine addict may be wonderfully internally motivated to participate in a recovery system that promises him free cocaine for meeting the program's objectives. However, I assume that even the strongest advocates of internal motivation would not endorse such a practice. Though he does not like it, and though his heart may be totally against it, most would agree that to compel the addict with external force to stop him from taking cocaine will be better for him in the long (and short) run.[1]

What our motivation experts do not acknowledge is that due to the noetic effects of sin, the desires and longings of a man's heart, apart from the grace of God, are only evil continually. Therefore, spiritually speaking, we are all cocaine addicts and the remaining sinful nature will always be internally motivated to evil: "And this is the condemnation, that the light has come into the world, and men loved darkness rather than light, because their deeds were evil" (John 3:19). Only the moral law of God reveals right and wrong and allows us to determine when it is right to act in accord with our desires, that is, when they are the regenerated desires of the new man. Therefore, sometimes it will be right to appeal to the desires of the regenerated heart, and sometimes it will be necessary to warn and buffet (1 Cor. 9:27) the old nature. Accordingly, we will accept all motivations, whether internal and agreeable to one's will and affections or external and coercive to them, just so long as we find them affirmed by Scripture, for this alone makes them desirable and good.

[1] I am not asserting that the best drug treatment is always "cold turkey," but that strong desire can be harmful.

13

Exegetical Approach: Identifying Motivation in Scripture

Each public address will be briefly described in terms of speaker, audience, location, and occasion of sermon. The exegetical procedure will be to make use of those questions and elements listed above, as they appear applicable to each particular text. This examination should result in the identification of various motives intentionally sought by the speaker to be communicated to the listener. These motivations will be identified and described as stated below. As we go through each text my intention is twofold. First, the exposition of Scripture undertaken in this analysis has the sole aim of identifying the elements of motivation that the speaker intends to convey by means of his words. Thus, all matters of textual issues, doctrinal questions, and theological implications will not be addressed except to the degree that answering them is necessary in order to shed light on discovering the motivations present in the text. At the same time that the motivations communicated in the sermonic portions of Scripture are set forth, I will also provide a summary and generalization of them for use in modern preaching contexts at the end of each section. Thus, I intend this analysis to be both descriptive and practical, for it will not only be identifying motivational examples of the texts, but it will be exhorting to "Go and motivate/be motivated likewise."

As this book is intended to be used for the preaching and

hearing of sermons, we are primarily interested in the motivation communicated and intended by the speaker, and not so much in the subjective experience of the listener. Thus, the increasingly narrowly defined concept of "internal motivation," which has become more and more indistinguishable from personal satisfaction and desire gratification, will not be pursued by this analysis. On the contrary, we will be looking at motivation as objectively present in the speech of the speaker, which will sometimes also be confirmed by the response of the listener. Therefore, my analysis considers the following as conclusive: The speaker gives motivation in his speech when he seeks to move the listener to action. The reasons, stated or implied, that the speaker gives in order to move the listener, is the motivation of the text. Additionally, here it may be helpful to further delineate our definition into the traditional categories of internal and external motivation.

Internal motivation would be all appeals to the listener to act where the speaker is seeking to stimulate him from within; from his own attitude, beliefs, commitments, and affections. Those conditions that the speaker is appealing to may already be in the listener's heart and the speaker is hoping to stir them up, or they may be wrought in his heart for the first time through the means of the words of the speaker. Of course we attribute all stirring up of and creating of right motives in the heart to the sovereign work of the Holy Spirit as He pleases.

Internal Motivation in Psalm 147:1

An example of what could be called internal motivation can be seen in the command to praise the Lord in Psalm 147:1: "Praise the Lord! For it is good to sing praises to our God; for it is pleasant, and praise is beautiful." Here the psalmist commands praise, then communicates what praising the Lord is in order to motivate the people of God to do it. The psalmist commands the people of God to praise the Lord for three reasons, which are clearly indicated by the two words, "for" and "and." The first motivation he provides is internal. When he declares that it is good to sing praises to our God, he is seeking to move God's people to praise Him, on the basis of their love of the good thing of praising God. This love of what is good is already present in their hearts, for by definition God's people love the good. Thus, the psalmist's syllogism would look like this:

> Premise A: Praising the LORD is good.
> Premise B: God's people want to do (love) what is good.
> Conclusion: God's people will want to praise the LORD.

The second two reasons that praise is pleasant and beautiful could be drawn up the same way, showing internal motivation, though here it is also possible that the psalmist is seeking to externally motivate the people of God by proclaiming to them how praising the LORD *will be good for them*. Thus, he could be appealing to the listener to praise the Lord, with the promise that if they do praise Him, they will enjoy it. Here, pleasantness and being beautiful are held out as rewards to enjoy if the condition of praising the LORD is met. The syllogism would look as follows:

> Premise A: To praise the LORD is pleasant and beautiful.
> Premise B: Pleasantness and beauty are desirable things.
> Conclusion: God's people should praise the LORD in order to experience the pleasantness and beauty that accompanies such activity.

As we can see from this example, it may not always be possible to determine if the motivation present is internal or external, and we will rarely attempt to do so here. I only give these examples to further describe how I am understanding the motivation process. Consequently, as stated above, my approach does not a priori judge external motivation as inherently bad, undesirable, or even less authentic, than the internal kind; rather, all motivation will be considered good or evil solely according to the judgment of Scripture. Thus, being unable to distinguish between internal and external motivation is ultimately irrelevant to this analysis. Our goal is to identify and then seek to emulate the motivations of Scripture. If successful here, we will not be concerned with assigning the correct labels.

External Motivation in Revelation 2:4–7

In those areas where we *can* tell the difference, external motivation will be used to describe appeals to the listener to act based upon external incentives set before him as things to seek out or things to avoid. Thus external motivations can include promised rewards or threatened punishments. An example of both kinds of external motivation can be found in Jesus' letters to the seven churches in the book of Revelation. To the church at Ephesus, Jesus commanded:

> Nevertheless I have this against you, that you have left your first love. Remember therefore from where you have fallen; repent and do the first works, or else I will come to you quickly and remove your lampstand from its place—unless you repent. But this you have, that you hate the deeds of the Nicolaitans, which I also hate. He who has an ear, let him hear what the Spirit says to the churches. To him who overcomes I will give to eat from the tree of life, which is in the midst of the Paradise of God. (Rev. 2:4–7)

Here, there are three commands given to the church: remember, repent, and do. And there are two very clear and strong external incentives given. They come as consequences of obeying or disobeying the commands. The first is the consequence of disobedience, and it comes as a warning: I will remove your lampstand. In other words, you will no longer be a church if you do not repent. It is hard to think of a more sober warning. As mentioned earlier, some try to find a way to tone down the promised rewards or threatened judgments of Scripture as they mistakenly think such things teach works righteousness. Yet, we recognize when this is the clear meaning of the text, rightly understood, such warnings do not contradict salvation by grace. Thus, this passage, which threatens the dissolution of a church for unrepentance, does not contradict the doctrine of perseverance but is only directed against antinomianism. The elect will persevere, but the elect will also repent. There is no such thing as an elect *and* unrepentant Christian, even as there is no such thing as a true *but* unrepentant church. Jesus' warning does not weaken the objective truth of God's promise but it calls upon individual Christians to test themselves and see if they be in the faith (2 Cor. 13:5) and to examine themselves in order to make their calling and election sure (2 Peter 1:10). Throughout Scripture God uses such warnings to graciously turn His people back to Him.

The fact is that while the elect will persevere, I cannot consider myself to be a believer if I do not live a life of repentance. So this warning of Christ's is good and necessary to sinners on this side of glory, where we are still working out our salvation with fear and trembling (Phil. 2:12). Also we notice that in giving this church such a sharp warning, Christ is quick to give them some comfort in verse six. He reminds them that in the midst of needing to repent, they are doing one thing right: They hate certain things that God also hates. So here we see an encouragement in existing obedience as an additional incentive to correct what is currently disobedient.

After threatening punishment, Christ promises reward in the second external motivation: Overcomers will eat from the Tree of Life in the paradise of God. Here is a promised reward every bit as desirable as the punishment was undesirable. Once again this promise does not compromise the truth of justification by faith alone but simply echoes the uniform teaching of Scripture that our judgment will be by our works (2 Cor. 5:10). Our rewards will be rewards of grace to be sure, as no one has ever made God their debtor, yet God shows His great beneficence in assuring us that even a cup of cold water given in His name will be rewarded (Matt. 10:42). It is a great temptation to think that God will not reward our works, especially knowing that because of our sinful natures, good works are never perfect and often come only after great struggle on our part. So God repeatedly exhorts us to do good works by promising to reward us, and we lose a great source of strength to God's people when we fail to give them this encouragement: "And let us not grow weary while doing good, for in due season we shall reap if we do not lose heart" (Gal. 6:9). The syllogism for this passage from Revelation would look as follows:

Context: The church of Ephesus is reprimanded by God for having fallen away from doing the good works they used to do.
Premise A: Failure to repent is bad and will be judged by God.
Premise B: To hate what God hates is good and is commended by God.
Premise C: Overcoming (repenting) will be rewarded with fruit from the Tree of Life.
Conclusion: The church of Ephesus should repent to receive the reward and avoid the punishment. They should be encouraged to repent by God's (external) praise of the good they are doing (hating what God hates).

Thus, we have two forms of external motivation, strengthened with an external encouragement of praise.

A final set of motivations can be implied from the approach that this particular passage takes. In the first verse Christ reprimands the church by saying "I have this against you." God's people do not want their Lord to have things against them. Therefore, by saying these words, Christ is giving His people a reason. He is communicating a motivation to them, to change these things so that He will no longer have anything against them. So also, the form of verse six, when Christ says in the midst of a rebuke "But this you have," is by definition an encouragement to continue their obedience in this area. For again, God's people want Him to say to them "this you have going for you" or "this is in your favor." And so the motivation of pleasing God and avoiding displeasing God can be drawn by implication from this text. We would categorize these as internal motivations, since the speaker is appealing to what believers ought to desire in their hearts with respect to their Lord, in order to stimulate them from within. These final syllogisms would appear as follows.

Premise A: Christ has something against His church.
Implied Premise B: Christ's people do not want Him to have something against them.
Conclusion: Christ's people should do what He says out of hatred of displeasing Him.

Premise A: Christ has something that He likes in His church.
Implied Premise B: Christ's people want Him to approve of their works.
Conclusion: Christ's people should continue to perform this work, and they should find in this desire of approval an incentive to stimulate them to other works.

As can be seen in these examples, motivation can be found in the content and in the form; it can be stated or implied. With these examples in mind, we are now ready to begin our study of Scripture.

14

Applying the Approach: Identifying Motivation in Our Texts

We will go through each of the passages verse by verse, in order to identify why the speaker said what he said. As a faithful minister of the gospel of Jesus Christ, each speaker unquestionably chose certain words for certain reasons. He intended to reach a certain goal. Vitally important to identifying the intention is to discern the goal the speaker desired to bring about in his audience. We have already noticed that preaching seeks to move people. Movement is the ultimate goal. The speaker speaks certain words because he believes those words are sufficient (in the sovereign grace of God) to achieve some desired movement. Thus, the speaker's words and his desired movement or goal in speaking those words, gives us his intention or purpose.

There is a certain movement that the speaker seeks to bring about in his listener by means of his speech. He chooses certain words to bring about that movement based upon underlying assumptions. An underlying assumption is the stated or implied reason *why* the speaker thought that his words would bring about his intended movement or goal. Consider the following example: A policeman sees a robber running out of a bank and yells, "Stop or I'll shoot!" Here the policeman's intention is to get the robber to stop. His goal is not to shoot but to capture the robber. His underlying assumption is that threatening to shoot will get the robber to stop so he can capture him. Stopping is the desired movement that the policeman hopes to produce in the robber. In this example the motivation given by the policeman is in the form of a threat, and the words he uses to give that motivation are, "Stop or I'll shoot!"

Discerning the desired movement or goal helps to give us the speaker's intention or purpose in speaking. Once we know the speaker's purpose in saying what he said, we then look to see the stated or implied reasons why the speaker believes his words are sufficient to bring about the intention. The motivation is the reason, stated or implied, that the speaker gives to the listener in order to move him to the speaker's desired goal. Whether or not the listener receives that motivation does not alter the fact that motivation has been given. As has been said already, we know that only the Holy Spirit can move a sinner to believe and obey the gospel.

15

Exegesis of Sermon Texts with Preaching Application Summary

Peter's Pentecost Sermon: Acts 2:14–40

Speaker:	The apostle Peter (v. 14)
Audience:	1. "Jews, devout men, from every nation under heaven . . . Parthians and Medes and Elamites, those dwelling in Mesopotamia, Judea and Cappadocia, Pontus and Asia, Phrygia and Pamphylia, Egypt and the parts of Libya adjoining Cyrene, visitors from Rome, both Jews and proselytes, Cretans and Arabs" (vv. 5, 9–11). 2. The eleven apostles (see v. 14). 3. Probably about one hundred and twenty of Jesus' disciples, including Mary, His mother (see 1:14–15; 2:1).
Location:	A house in Jerusalem (see 2:2, 5).
Occasion:	1. The Jewish feast of Pentecost (see 2:1). 2. A crowd gathered in response to the miraculous sound (see 2:2, 6) 3. The crowd was confused at the miraculous speaking in tongues by the disciples, they were asking what it meant, others slanderously mocked the Christians as being drunk (see 2:6–7, 12–13).

Verse 14

"Men of Judea and all who dwell in Jerusalem, let this be known to you and heed my words" (Acts 2:14).

Ἄνδρες Ἰουδαῖοι καὶ οἱ κατοικοῦντες Ἰερουσαλὴμ πάντες, τοῦτο ὑμῖν γνωστὸν ἔστω καὶ ἐνωτίσασθε τὰ ῥήματά μου

1. Peter speaks to answer their question of "Whatever could this mean?" of v. 12, and to clarify their confusion, and refute the mockers who slandered them as being drunk in v. 13.
2. He identifies and speaks directly and respectfully to the audience.[1]
3. Peter's appeal at this point is to the premise that godly people must seek out, judge by, and live by what they know to be true. His conclusion is that since they do not know the truth and he does, they ought to listen to him.
4. Peter is moved by false claims to appeal to the virtue of truth in his audience.
5. Underlying assumption: Godly people will want to hear and live by the truth.
6. Scriptural support: "Pilate therefore said to Him, 'Are You a king then?' Jesus answered, 'You say rightly that I am a king. For this cause I was born, and for this cause I have come into the world, that I should bear witness to the truth. Everyone who is of the truth hears My voice'" (John 18:37).

Verse 15

"For these are not drunk, as you suppose, since it is only the third hour of the day" (Acts 2:15).

οὐ γὰρ ὡς ὑμεῖς ὑπολαμβάνετε οὗτοι μεθύουσιν, ἔστιν γὰρ ὥρα τρίτη τῆς ἡμέρας

[1] "Ἰερουσαλὴμ: The tone of St. Peter throughout is that of a man who

1. Here is the reason why they should listen, as indicated by the first γὰρ.
2. Peter's point is to refute the slander of the mockers.
3. His argument is since the disciples are not drunk, the crowd needs to consider and understand what is really going on, for *it is* something to be amazed at.
4. Peter implies that their response to gather and take note was correct, but states that their understanding of the miracle of speaking in tongues was incorrect.
5. Peter seeks to prove and teach the truth to his audience. "And whereas he upbraideth the fault of a few unto all, he doth it not to this end, that he may make them all guilty of the same fault; but because a fit occasion was offered by their mocking to teach them altogether."[2]
6. The second γὰρ gives us the reason Peter offers to get his listeners to believe that the disciples are not drunk: It is only the third hour of the day.
7. This argument depends upon the generally known truth that drunken parties occur at night: "This refutation consisteth upon a probable argument; because men use not to be drunk betimes in the morning."[3]
8. Conclusion for godly people: Generally known truth should be persuasive unless proven to be false by concrete evidence. The mockers had no evidence. Therefore their comments are slander and must be rejected. Second conclusion: Godly people should not listen to mockers who give no evidence for their claims.

---

would win and not repulse his hearers, cf. v. 29." R. J. Knowling, "The Acts of the Apostles," in *Apostles, Romans, First Corinthians*, vol. 2 of *The Expositor's Greek Testament*, ed. W. Robertson Nicoll (Peabody, MA: Hendrickson, 2002), 81.

[2] *Calvin's Commentaries*, vol. XVIII, trans. William Pringle, *John 12–21; Acts 1–13*, book 2, (Grand Rapids, MI: Baker, 2003), 83.

[3] Ibid., 82.

9. Implied conclusion: Preachers should refute mockers with the truth.

Verse 16

"But this is what was spoken by the prophet Joel" (Acts 2:16).

ἀλλὰ τοῦτό ἐστιν τὸ εἰρημένον διὰ τοῦ προφήτου Ἰωήλ

1. Peter adduces a text of Scripture to prove that what is happening is significant.
2. He expects his audience to heed the Word of God.
3. Peter's purpose: an appeal to Scripture: Godly people will understand things by and obey the Word of God.
4. Scriptural support: "Your word is a lamp to my feet and a light to my path" (Ps. 119:105).

Verses 17–21

Peter paraphrases Joel 2:28–32, a passage that speaks of supernatural signs accompanying God's pouring out of His Spirit on all His people, that is itself a precursor for divine judgment. Peter ends the quotation with Joel's promise: "And it shall come to pass that whoever calls upon the name of the Lord will be saved" (Acts 2:21).

καὶ ἔσται πᾶς ὃς ἂν ἐπικαλέσηται τὸ ὄνομα κυρίου σωθήσεται.

1. With the undeniable evidence of the miracle before their eyes and in their ears, Peter declares that the first part of the prophecy of Joel has come to pass.[4] His argument is that the second half of wrath and judgment will as well.

[4] Peter explained the miracle from the prophecy of Joel before he preached the gospel because "he wants people to know that with the outpouring of the Holy Spirit the messianic era has arrived." Simon J. Kistemaker, *Exposition of the Acts of the Apostles* (Grand Rapids, MI: Baker, 2004), 92.

2. He desires the listener to rightly judge the miracle so that he will believe the prophecy and heed the promise of calling upon the Lord, in order to be saved. Here we cannot reproduce motivations given from the immediately witnessed supernatural fulfillment of Scripture. However, we can appeal to the supernatural witness preserved in Scripture. Also, the principle of heeding God's Word to avoid God's wrath still applies.
3. Peter is appealing to the people to believe in God's Word and be saved from God's judgment. His proof that the time is now is the miracle of speaking in tongues that they are currently observing through their senses. This appeal depends upon the assumption that God's people should believe and accept as true miraculous attestation that they witness through their senses. Throughout the sermon Peter's emphasis is on the truth of his teaching.[5]
4. It is implied to the audience that they too will receive God's Spirit if they heed Peter's words.[6] The negative consequence of God's wrath is strongly implied, as is the positive consequences of being saved and receiving God's Spirit. These are three external motivations: one punishment and two rewards.
5. Calvin argues that the awfulness of the threatened wrath only makes the salvation proclaimed that much sweeter to God's elect: "God doth prick us forward like sluggish asses, with threatenings and terrors to seek salvation, so . . . doth he show a means whereby salvation may shine before our eyes."[7]

[5] "Peter calls the audience to witness that his statements are true concerning 'Jesus the Nazarene.'" A. T. Robertson, *Word Pictures in the New Testament* vol. 3, *The Acts of the Apostles* (Nashville, TN: Broadman Press, 1960), 28.

[6] "And in these words Peter inviteth the Jews, unto whom he speaketh, to be partakers of the same grace." Calvin, *Commentaries*, vol. XVIII, 87–88.

[7] Ibid., 91.

6. Peter is appealing to the people on the basis of the miraculous event of speaking in tongues. His reason for quoting the prophecy of Joel is to give meaning to the miracle. The miracle in turn supernaturally, and therefore, undeniably confirms the prophecy is true and being fulfilled now.
7. Peter's purpose is that his audience will believe the Word of God from Joel, since it has partially come to pass before their eyes, so that they will believe that God's wrath is also surely coming—the second part of Joel's prophecy will come to pass: καὶ ἔσται—so that they will heed God's promise to save all who call upon His name.
8. The sensory proof provided by the miracle of tongues is an incentive that strengthens the three external motivations to call upon the Lord, to receive God's Spirit, and to be saved from God's wrath. It strengthens these motivations by proving the truth of them.
9. Scriptural support: Already given by Peter. See also 1 Thessalonians 1:10: "and to wait for His Son from heaven, whom He raised from the dead, even Jesus who delivers us from the wrath to come."

Preaching Purpose and Motivation of Verses 14–21

Preaching purpose: Peter desires that his audience reject the mockers and listen to him, as he declares from the Scriptures the true meaning of the miracle of tongues and its spiritual significance.

Motivation for use today: The miracle of tongues has ceased, but its recorded fact in Scripture still proves that the last days of Joel are upon us, so God's people must call upon the name of the Lord, to receive God's Spirit, and to be saved from the coming wrath. Preachers should seek to motivate God's people to affirm and do these things by proclaiming how God supernaturally fulfilled His word through the miracle of tongues which proved, once and for all, that these are the last days of Joel. In presenting the truth of these things preachers should vocally refute any mockers.

Ministers can do this as they remember that all of God's people, by the Holy Spirit, will have a love for what is true and a hatred for what is false.

Peter seeks to motivate God's people:	The way in which Peter seeks to move them:
1. To give attention to God's Word.	1. He speaks directly and respectfully to them.
2. To be saved.	2. Proving his claims from the miracle.
3. To receive God's Spirit.	3. Proving his claims from Scripture.
4. To avoid God's wrath.	4. By showing it is certain to come; proven by the partially fulfilled prophecy.

Verse 22

"Men of Israel hear these words: Jesus of Nazareth, a Man attested by God to you by miracles, wonders, and signs which God did through Him in your midst, as you yourselves also know" (Acts 2:22).

Ἄνδρες Ἰσραηλῖται, ἀκούσατε τοὺς λόγους τούτους: Ἰησοῦν τὸν Ναζωραῖον, ἄνδρα ἀπὸ τοῦ θεοῦ ἀποδεδειγμένον εἰς ὑμᾶς δυνάμεσιν καὶ τέρασι καὶ σημείοις οἷς ἐποίησεν δι' αὐτοῦ ὁ θεὸς ἐν μέσῳ ὑμῶν, καθὼς αὐτοὶ οἴδατε

1. The prophecy and the miracle of tongues should have their attention. Still Peter's now-repeated command to hear him argues for the great importance of what he is about to say.
2. Peter reminds his audience that they are Israelites—the people who are promised salvation by the Lord. This implies that Peter's coming appeal will be in harmony with what faithful Israelites should do.

3. Jesus of Nazareth—Peter clearly names Jesus in a way that leaves no doubt whom he is talking about. It has only been fifty days since Jesus' crucifixion.
4. Peter reminds the Jews of Jesus' many miracles. He knows they all remember them. The miracles were done in their midst, and they know it. Three times he stresses the truth and reality of the miracles Jesus did:
   a. "Which God did through Him"
   b. "In your midst"
   c. "Which you yourselves know."[8]
5. He explains the significance of Jesus' miracles to the Jews as a matter of fact.
   a. Jesus' miracles are His undeniable attestation from God.
   b. Jesus' miracles proved that God's power was in Him.
6. Peter's method is to appeal to supernatural proof: Jesus' miracles prove He is from God. Godly people will recognize and submit to God's supernatural attestation of Christ. Unbelievers will be silenced by this argument.
7. Scriptural support: "If I do not do the works of My Father, do not believe Me; but if I do, though you do not believe Me, believe the works, that you may know and believe that the Father is in Me, and I in Him" (John 10:37–38; see also John 3:2; 9:33).

Preaching Purpose and Motivation of Verse 22

Preaching purpose: to identify Jesus as supernaturally proven to be from God.

Motivation for use today: Jesus is not here on earth, neither are any alive who saw Him, but His well-attested miracles, as recorded in Scripture, prove that He was a man sent from God. Preachers

[8] "He put in three words, to the end he might more extol Christ's miracles, and enforce the people, by his heaping and laying of words together, to consider the same." Calvin, *Commentaries*, vol. XVIII, 94.

should boldly proclaim the many, many well-attested miracles of Jesus that prove He was a man from God.

Peter seeks to motivate God's people:	The way in which Peter seeks to move them:
1. To rightly judge themselves as the people to whom God's Savior came.	1. He calls them "Men of Israel" and says "God attested to you."
2. To rightly judge Jesus by his deeds.	2. He proclaims Jesus' real life and publicly seen works.
3. To rightly judge Jesus' deeds as supernatural miracles.	3. He proclaims that God did signs, wonders, and miracles through Jesus.
4. To affirm that Jesus' many miracles prove that He is from God.	4. He teaches that God attests to His prophets with miracles.

Verse 23

"Him, being delivered by the determined purpose and foreknowledge of God, you have taken by lawless hands, have crucified, and put to death" (Acts 2:23).

τοῦτον τῇ ὡρισμένῃ βουλῇ καὶ προγνώσει τοῦ θεοῦ ἔκδοτον διὰ χειρὸς ἀνόμων προσπήξαντες ἀνείλατε

1. Sovereignty of God: Peter declares that God did not abandon Jesus or fail Him. He stresses with two words (purpose, foreknowledge) that it was God's plan for Jesus to be killed the way He was.
2. Responsibility of man: He also declares that what God did in His sovereignty does not change the fact that those who killed Jesus did so lawlessly.[9]

[9] "Note Peter's boldness now under the power of the Holy Spirit. He

3. Peter's purpose is to show God's sovereignty and man's responsibility in the victory of Jesus and the sin of man. He defends Christ's ignominious death as His successful mission, from mockers who would scoff at it.[10]
4. Scriptural support: "The Son of Man indeed goes just as it is written of Him, but woe to that man by whom the Son of Man is betrayed! It would have been good for that man if he had never been born" (Mark 14:21).
5. Implication: These Jews committed a monstrous sin, against a victorious man of God. The possibility of salvation is implied by his proclamation, though Peter does not show the balm until he lays bare the wound.[11] Peter charges his audience with lawlessly taking, crucifying, and putting to death, the one to whom God Himself had given overwhelming supernatural attestation to.
6. Since it is very unlikely that these people are the ones who literally killed Jesus, in accusing these Jews of the crime, Peter implies that a nation is responsible for what its leaders do, or else that the people of a nation are responsible when that nation commits injustice.
7. Implication: We are guilty when we allow our nation to act unjustly.
8. At this point Peter wants his audience to admit the truth

charges the people to their faces with the death of Christ." Robertson, *Word Pictures*, 29.

[10] He mentions God's determinate counsel to remove the "stumbling block" of Christ's shameful death and that it was not "by chance, or because he wanted power to deliver himself, but because it was so determined (and appointed) by God. For this knowledge alone, that the death of Christ was ordained by the eternal counsel of God, did cut off all occasion of foolish and wicked cogitations." Calvin, *Commentaries*, vol. XVIII, 95–96.

[11] "[That it was] the divine purpose, revealed through the prophets, that the Messiah should suffer . . . point[s] the way to the removal of their guilt and assurance of pardon. Peter, however, says nothing about this until his hearers are truly convicted of their sin." F. F. Bruce, *The Book of the Acts*, rev. ed. (Grand Rapids, MI: Eerdmans, 1988), 64.

about their part in killing Jesus. This appeal cannot apply to people who were not born when Jesus was crucified. Yet, by implication, it was our sins that made the crucifixion of Christ necessary. Therefore, spiritually speaking, we put Him to death.

9. Additionally, Peter's purpose in declaring their guilt cannot be to condemn them or to bring Roman justice upon them. Therefore, his purpose must be to get them to admit and own that they murdered Jesus.[12]
10. Implied purpose: Godly people need to see and admit that it was their sin that crucified Jesus.
11. Scriptural support: "Who Himself bore our sins in His own body on the tree, that we, having died to sins, might live for righteousness—by whose stripes you were healed" (1 Peter 2:24).

Preaching Purpose and Motivation of Verse 23

Preaching purpose: That Jesus accomplished God's plan in His betrayal, crucifixion, and death. Peter here declares, and later proves, that Jesus' whole passion was by the divine providence of God, yet those who betrayed and murdered Him were guilty of great sin. Peter's purpose in convicting Christ's murderers turns out to be to bring them to conviction of sin that they might repent and be saved (see v. 38).

Motivation for use today: Though no one is alive today who literally killed Christ, yet all who would be saved by Him must be charged with responsibility and guilt for His death. In order for the grace of salvation to be rightly preached, ministers must first proclaim the sovereignty of God and the wickedness of sin. Preachers should proclaim these twin truths for the purpose of moving God's people to acknowledge their guilt, to repent, and to trust entirely in God's sovereign salvation.

[12] "The same knowledge of God's providence is a step to consider the end and fruit of Christ's death." Calvin, *Commentaries*, vol. XVIII, 96.

Peter seeks to motivate God's people:	The way in which Peter seeks to move them:
1. To acknowledge that Jesus was delivered into the hands of His enemies to fulfill the sovereign plan of God.	1. He demonstrates this from Scripture (as we will see later).[13]
2. To acknowledge their guilt as the betrayers and murderers of Jesus.	2. He accuses them with Jesus' unjust murder.
3. To acknowledge that Jesus really died.	3. He declares the fact of Jesus' crucifixion and death.

Verse 24

"Whom God raised up, having loosed the pains of death, because it was not possible that He should be held by it" (Acts 2:24).

ὃν ὁ θεὸς ἀνέστησεν λύσας τὰς ὠδῖνας τοῦ θανάτου, καθότι οὐκ ἦν δυνατὸν κρατεῖσθαι αὐτὸν ὑπ' αὐτοῦ

1. Peter declares that Jesus was raised from the dead by God. He wants his audience to see that the resurrection was another sign proving Christ's approval by God.
2. With καθότι, Peter declares the reason why God raised Jesus. Death was not able, not powerful enough to hold onto Jesus, implying Jesus has power over death. Calvin sees this as implying Christ's deity.[14]
3. Peter clearly wants his audience to see that Christ's resurrection proved that God is still with Him, and that He is more powerful than death. He then goes on to show that

[13] Commenting on vv. 25–28: "Now comes an Old Testament 'testimony' confirming Peter's claim." Bruce, *Acts*, 64.

[14] "[The resurrection] is a great and wonderful token of his Divine power." Calvin, *Commentaries*, vol. XVIII, 95.

this Scripture must apply to Christ from the historical facts of David's occupied tomb and Christ's empty one (see vv. 25–32).

4. Scriptural support: "But has now been revealed by the appearing of our Savior Jesus Christ, who has abolished death and brought life and immortality to light through the gospel" (2 Tim. 1:10).
5. Preaching purpose of v. 24: To show that Jesus was resurrected from the dead by God, and necessarily so, because Jesus is more powerful than death. Peter goes on to prove Jesus' great power and stature from the following Old Testament quote.

Verses 25–28

"For David says concerning Him: 'I foresaw the Lord always before my face, for He is at my right hand, that I may not be shaken. Therefore my heart rejoiced, and my tongue was glad; moreover my flesh also will rest in hope. For You will not leave my soul in Hades, nor will You allow Your Holy One to see corruption. You have made known to me the ways of life; You will make me full of joy in Your presence'" (Acts 2:25–28).

Δαυὶδ γὰρ λέγει εἰς αὐτόν, Προορώμην τὸν κύριον ἐνώπιόν μου διὰ παντός, ὅτι ἐκ δεξιῶν μού ἐστιν ἵνα μὴ σαλευθῶ. διὰ τοῦτο ηὐφράνθη ἡ καρδία μου καὶ ἠγαλλιάσατο ἡ γλῶσσά μου, ἔτι δὲ καὶ ἡ σάρξ μου κατασκηνώσει ἐπ' ἐλπίδι: ὅτι οὐκ ἐγκαταλείψεις τὴν ψυχήν μου εἰς ἅ|δην, οὐδὲ δώσεις τὸν ὅσιόν σου ἰδεῖν διαφθοράν. ἐγνώρισάς μοι ὁδοὺς ζωῆς, πληρώσεις με εὐφροσύνης μετὰ τοῦ προσώπου σου.

1. Causal words help us to see the source of David's constancy, joy, and hope throughout this quotation of Psalm 16. Also, they allow us to see how David was motivated by the promise of the Messiah's resurrection.

2. v. 25: γὰρ identified in this instance as a marker of cause or reason (BDAG). Thus, grammatically, we can say that David's words confirm Peter's previous statement that death would not be able to hold the Lord. ὅτι ἐκ with ἵνα strengthens the source of David's hope being in the constant presence of the messiah at his right hand, his might. ἵνα here denotes purpose, aim, or goal (BDAG). "*Since from* my right hand He is, *therefore* I shall not be moved." σαλευθῶ can refer to being shaken, agitated or troubled emotionally to the point of paralysis or losing hope. Because of the Messiah's victory over death, David will not be overwhelmed with this kind of emotion.
3. v. 26: διὰ τοῦτο, on account of this, or therefore.
4. v. 27: ὅτι identifies the reason for David's unshakeable hope expressed in vv. 25–26, and that is because the Messiah's soul will not be left in Hades, nor His body to rot in the grave.
5. Peter therefore cites this extended passage from Psalm 16 as a confirmation that Jesus' bodily resurrection was not only prophesied by David, but it was also David's hope and joy.[15] David's faith in the certainty of the promise produced the emotion of joy in him. David's heart rejoiced in the assurance of the Messiah's future resurrection. David himself would die in certain hope of his own resurrection because of his faith in this prophecy.
6. Peter uses what correct understanding they retained of David—that he hoped in and wrote of the Messiah—in order to prove Christ to them.[16]

[15] "*For this my heart rejoiced.* Joy of the soul, gladness of the tongue, and quietness of all the whole body, do ensue upon sure hope and confidence; for unless men be quite past feeling, they must needs be careful and sorrowful, and so, consequently, miserably tormented, so long as they feel themselves destitute of the help of God. But that sure trust which we repose in God doth not only deliver us from carefulness, but doth also replenish our hearts with wonderful joy (and gladness)." Ibid., 105.

[16] "Without question that maxim was of force amongst [the Jews], that

7. Peter adduces this testimony about Jesus from David to show to his audience that what he was preaching was the future hope of true Israelites (embodied by David), now it has come to pass. "To be like David" in faith and in joy is thus an implied external motivation to the Jews to hope in Jesus' resurrection. In the verses following this quotation he proves that this Psalm refers to Jesus' resurrection.
8. Point: The fact of Jesus being raised from the dead makes the resurrection of those who hope in Him certain, bringing them joy. Jesus is the Holy One, who always enjoys the presence of God.
9. Scriptural support: "But now Christ is risen from the dead, and has become the firstfruits of those who have fallen asleep" (1 Cor. 15:20).
10. The preaching purpose is given by Peter in the verses that follow.
11. Peter's immediate purpose is to give another witness to Jesus' resurrection from the Old Testament.

Verses 29–31

"Men and brethren, let me speak freely to you of the patriarch David, that he is both dead and buried, and his tomb is with us to this day. Therefore, being a prophet, and knowing that God had sworn with an oath to him that of the fruit of his body, according to the flesh, He would raise up the Christ to sit on his throne, he, foreseeing this, spoke concerning the resurrection of the Christ, that His soul was not left in Hades, nor did His flesh see corruption" (Acts 2:29–31).

---

they were to hope for the restoring of things at the hands of Christ alone" and this caused them to "more readily stay themselves upon the words of Peter. . . . For they were not come to that point of impudence . . . that they durst cavil in matters which were evident. . . . They sought the Messias in the Old Testament. They knew that David was a figure of him. There was amongst them some religion and reverence of the Scriptures then." Ibid., 103

Ἄνδρες ἀδελφοί, ἐξὸν εἰπεῖν μετὰ παρρησίας πρὸς ὑμᾶς περὶ τοῦ πατριάρχου Δαυίδ, ὅτι καὶ ἐτελεύτησεν καὶ ἐτάφη καὶ τὸ μνῆμα αὐτοῦ ἔστιν ἐν ἡμῖν ἄχρι τῆς ἡμέρας ταύτης: προφήτης οὖν ὑπάρχων, καὶ εἰδὼς ὅτι ὅρκῳ ὤμοσεν αὐτῷ ὁ θεὸς ἐκ καρποῦ τῆς ὀσφύος αὐτοῦ καθίσαι ἐπὶ τὸν θρόνον αὐτοῦ, προϊδὼν ἐλάλησεν περὶ τῆς ἀναστάσεως τοῦ Χριστοῦ ὅτι οὔτε ἐγκατελείφθη εἰς ἅ|δην οὔτε ἡ σὰρξ αὐτοῦ εἶδεν διαφθοράν.

1. Peter speaks boldly in referring to David as dead and in the ground, in order to more significantly exalt Jesus by comparison.
2. Jesus is not only a man approved of by God, He is the Christ, and has divine attributes.
3. Peter adduces a historical fact that they all know is true (v. 29), before he attempts to apply this Scripture to Christ.[17]
4. Again we see Peter's heart for his audience as he identifies with them, calling directly to them vocatively not only "men" but "brothers."[18]
5. Likewise, Peter will build his own witness of Christ's empty tomb upon their own undeniable witness of David's occupied one.[19]
6. Peter wants his audience to understand that David could not possibly have written Psalm 16 about himself, since it is undeniable that David's body rotted in his grave.[20]

[17] "St. Peter will first of all state facts which cannot be denied, before he proceeds to show how the words used of David are fulfilled in 'great David's greater Son.'" *Expositor's Greek*, 86.

[18] Kistemaker, *Acts*, 98.

[19] "Peter . . . points to the evidence of David's tomb in Jerusalem, but Christ's tomb is empty because God raised him from the dead. And Peter himself can testify to this fact." Ibid., 96.

[20] "David died and was buried in Jerusalem, and his tomb remained there even to the time of the apostles. No one objects to Peter's reference, because what he says is indisputable. Everyone has visited David's tomb; therefore,

7. Here Peter takes it for granted that his audience will understand that Scripture cannot err, therefore, they must grant that David could not have said that his own body would not see corruption, since it did.
8. Peter's explanation comes with the οὖν of v. 30. David was a prophet and as such, this word was given to David concerning the Christ, the Messiah.
9. According to Calvin, that God swore with an oath is mentioned to give the promise more weight with the Jews and with us.[21]
10. Peter wants his audience to believe that the correct interpretation of this Scripture is that it was given by David of the Christ and not of David himself, and David knew this fact.
11. David therefore wrote that the Christ would conquer death and be exalted to His throne after his conquest.
12. Purpose: The greatest king of the Old Testament hoped in Jesus' conquering power and not in his own. The godly should imitate David's faith.
13. Scriptural support: "But to the Son He says: "Your throne, O God, is forever and ever; a scepter of righteousness is the scepter of Your Kingdom" (Heb. 1:8).
14. Peter's purpose is to show from undeniable facts of history that Psalm 16 was intentionally written by David about the resurrection of the Messiah as a fulfillment of God's promise to David that his seed would sit on the throne.

Verse 32

"This Jesus God has raised up, of which we are all witnesses" (Acts 2:32).

Peter can speak confidently about this historical fact. . . . David's body buried in a tomb is mute evidence to Peter and his contemporaries that this particular psalm quotation (Ps. 16:10) remains unfulfilled." Ibid., 98.

[21] Calvin, *Commentaries*, vol. XVIII, 108.

τοῦτον τὸν Ἰησοῦν ἀνέστησεν ὁ θεός, οὗ πάντες ἡμεῖς ἐσμεν μάρτυρες.

1. Peter returns to Jesus of Nazareth, last mentioned by name in v. 22. He boldly declared Jesus' resurrection in v. 24. Then he proved how David wrote of and hoped in Jesus' resurrection in vv. 25–31. And he proved that David had to have been writing of Jesus with multiple arguments that are logically irrefutable.
2. Now he adds the eyewitness testimony of himself and the eleven (see Acts 1:22), if not the whole one hundred and twenty. Thus, Peter's argument that Jesus is the Christ:
    a. God Himself supernaturally attested to Jesus via signs, wonders and miracles which God did through Him, as they all knew.
    b. David prophetically wrote of Jesus and expressed his hope in Jesus' future resurrection.
    c. David had to have written this prophecy of the Christ and not of himself, as his rotting corpse and the inerrancy of Scripture prove.
    d. Peter and the other disciples were all eyewitnesses that Jesus rose from the dead.[22]
3. Peter considers this eyewitness testimony to be conclusive.[23]
4. Peter wants his audience to acquiesce in this overwhelming witness to Jesus and believe it. His audience should believe in the bodily resurrection of Christ for it is proven to be true. "Peter asserts that the evidence for his observation is irrefutable."[24]

[22] "Peter and his colleagues were making a claim which they could confirm by their personal ocular testimony: 'of this we are all witnesses.'" Bruce, *Acts*, 66.

[23] "Peter claims the whole 120 as personal witnesses to the fact of the Resurrection of Jesus from the dead and they are all present as Peter calls them to witness on the point. . . . Thus direct evidence for the resurrection of Jesus piles up in cumulative force" Robertson, *Word Pictures*, 32.

[24] Kistemaker, *Acts*, 100.

5. Peter appeals to the fact that the godly will follow the truth once demonstrated.
6. Purpose: The multiple witnesses, which Scripture presents, of Jesus' bodily resurrection are conclusive and should be embraced by the godly.
7. Scriptural support: "And I will also be diligent that at any time after my departure you will be able to call these things to mind. For we did not follow cleverly devised tales when we made known to you the power and coming of our Lord Jesus Christ, but we were eyewitnesses of His majesty" (2 Peter 1:15–16 NASB).

Preaching Purpose and Motivation of Verses 24–32

Preaching purpose: To prove the bodily resurrection of Jesus and identify Him as the Christ, and to show His divine personage and power from Scripture, from undeniable fact, and from eyewitness testimony. Peter pleads for their consent. There is no literal call to faith as Peter assumes that godly people will assent to the truth and follow it once it has been clearly demonstrated, though he pleads with them through direct and relational terms.

Motivation for use today: Only as the people of God are convinced of the undeniable historical fact of Christ's bodily resurrection will they be able to be moved to repent, to believe in Him, and to be saved. Preachers must proclaim the historical fact of Jesus' bodily resurrection from eyewitnesses, from the Scriptures of the Old Testament, and from the undeniable facts of history. They must then show that Jesus' resurrection proves that He is the Messiah that the Old Testament saints hoped in, and that God raised Him from the dead in order that He would sit on His throne forever, in accord with the Scriptures. The proven fact of the resurrection should move the godly to joyfully believe Jesus is the Christ. Preachers should speak directly to their people and humbly and compassionately use terms to identify with them.

Peter seeks to motivate God's people:	The way in which Peter seeks to move them:*
1. To believe that God raised Jesus from the dead.	1. The apostles, David, and facts of history bear witness to the resurrection.
2. To believe that Jesus could not be held by death.	2. David wrote that due to His exalted person, He could not remain dead.
3. To believe that David wrote of Jesus' resurrection and exalted person.	3. David's body rotted in the grave; he wrote of his hope and joy in the Christ.
4. To believe that Jesus sits on David's throne as the risen Christ of the OT.	4. David saw Christ's resurrection as fulfillment of God's promise to his seed.
5. To believe that the apostles were eyewitnesses of Jesus' resurrection.	5. Peter declares that the apostles were Christ's official eyewitnesses (Acts 1:22).

* In all these things he pleads with them as brothers to accept proven truth.

Verse 33

"Therefore being exalted to the right hand of God, and having received from the Father the promise of the Holy Spirit, He poured out this which you now see and hear" (Acts 2:33).

τῇ δεξιᾷ οὖν τοῦ θεοῦ ὑψωθεὶς τήν τε ἐπαγγελίαν τοῦ πνεύματος τοῦ ἁγίου λαβὼν παρὰ τοῦ πατρὸς ἐξέχεεν τοῦτο ὃ ὑμεῖς [καὶ] βλέπετε καὶ ἀκούετε.

1. οὖν indicates Peter's conclusion from all that has gone before.[25] Therefore, since it is undeniable that Jesus rose from the dead, and that from David's prophecy we see the

[25] "οὖν: the Ascension is a necessary sequel to the Resurrection . . . or the word may mark the result of the assured and manifold testimony to the Resurrection, to which the Apostle had just appealed." *Expositor's Greek*, 88.

place where He went is to the right hand of God, which is to say the place of all power, He has received the Holy Spirit and has thus poured Him out, resulting in the miraculous prophecies in foreign languages not naturally known to the speakers.

2. Here Peter wants to see his audience understand that Jesus is at the right hand of God, that He has been given God's Spirit above measure, and that He pours out this Spirit as He pleases.[26]
3. Thus, Peter has answered their question in v. 12, "What does this mean?" referring to the miracle of tongues. Peter's answer, in effect: "It means that Jesus, the Christ, raised from the dead and ascended to heaven, is pouring out the Holy Spirit, as the Scriptures so prophesied."
4. Peter adduces again the supernatural evidence that they cannot deny: Right now you see it, right now you hear it![27] The apostles and disciples heard and saw it; these Jews heard and saw it. The miraculous sensory evidence seals the proof of Jesus as the risen Messiah of David and Scripture, and that He right now is at the right hand of God (all-powerful) and empowers His people by the Spirit of God, whom Jesus now commands.
5. He appeals to what they heard and saw. By definition we cannot appeal to the seeing and hearing of miracles, but we can appeal to their record in Scripture. Since Peter's words are Scripture, we can still be strengthened in our faith by Scripture's infallible record of the things they heard and saw.
6. Implied purpose: The godly ought to receive the eyewitness testimony of Christ's own appointed apostles.

[26] "τοῦτο: . . . St. Peter thus leads his hearers to infer that that which is poured out is by its effects nothing else than the Holy Ghost." Ibid.

[27] "Because Peter's audience had not seen Jesus in the forty-day period between his resurrection and ascension, they needed proof that what the eyewitnesses proclaimed was true." Kistemaker, *Acts*, 100.

7. Purpose: Peter's audience should understand that the miraculous speaking in foreign languages by His disciples proves that Jesus is all-powerfully fulfilling the Word of God.[28]
8. Scriptural support: "And we ourselves heard this utterance made from heaven when we were with Him on the holy mountain. So we have the prophetic word made more sure, to which you do well to pay attention as to a lamp shining in a dark place, until the day dawns and the morning star arises in your hearts" (2 Peter 1:18–19 NASB).

Verses 34–35

"For David did not ascend into the heavens, but he says himself: 'The LORD said to my Lord, "Sit at My right hand, till I make Your enemies Your footstool"'" (Acts 2:34–35).

οὐ γὰρ Δαυὶδ ἀνέβη εἰς τοὺς οὐρανούς, λέγει δὲ αὐτός, Εἶπεν [ὁ] κύριος τῷ κυρίῳ μου, Κάθου ἐκ δεξιῶν μου ἕως ἂν θῶ τοὺς ἐχθρούς σου ὑποπόδιον τῶν ποδῶν σου.

1. γὰρ cited by BDAG here as marker of cause or reason. Thus, grammatically connected to the previous verse, Peter is emphasizing that David could not be responsible for the outpouring of the Spirit because he did not ascend into heaven as he testified of the Messiah.
2. Additionally, Peter adduces David's words from Psalm 110 to confirm that David recognized the Messiah as his Lord and seated at the right hand of God.[29] It's possible many of

[28] "To meet the questions of his audience, Peter alludes to Jesus' ascension and mentions Christ's place at the right hand of God . . . from his exalted position, Jesus has fulfilled the promise that the Father would send the Holy Spirit. . . . Consequently, everyone present at the temple area in Jerusalem is able to see the evidence of the outpouring of the Spirit." Ibid., 100–101.

[29] Ibid., 101.

these Jews remembered Jesus making this very same argument to the Pharisees in Matthew 22:41–45, not even two months prior when they would have been at Jerusalem for the Passover.

3. The quotation from Psalm 110 also emphasizes Christ's all-powerful kingdom and therefore the impossibility of standing against it. The right hand of God is a well-known figure for God's omnipotent power (Luke 22:69).
4. Peter uses this Scripture to defend and strengthen his interpretation of the previous passage of Scripture.[30]
5. Peter wants his audience to know that Jesus is Lord of all.
6. The adducing of this final psalm to testify of Christ's reign appeals to the godly to submit to this king.
7. Purpose: Submit to King Jesus who right now sits with God, ruling over all!
8. Scriptural support: "I charge you therefore before God and the Lord Jesus Christ, who will judge the living and the dead at His appearing and His kingdom" (2 Tim. 4:1).

Preaching Purpose and Motivation of Verses 33–35

Preaching purpose: From their own sensory reception of the miracle and from another Scripture, Peter proves to his audience that Jesus is alive and ruling God's kingdom from His heavenly throne, where He wields all the power of God. The implication is that He is currently empowering His disciples and subduing all of His enemies. He adduces David as an example of faithful Israelites who looked forward to the day of Jesus' exaltation.

Motivation for use today: Preachers are to proclaim Jesus' session at the right hand of God and call upon all men to submit to His current rule and bow before Him. The testimony of Scripture and

[30] See Bruce, *Acts*, 67; "'St. Peter does not demand belief upon his own assertion, but he again appeals to the Scriptures, and to the words which could not have received a fulfillment in the case of David,' (Knowling)" *Expositors Greek*, 88; see also Robertson, *Word Pictures*, 33.

the miracle of tongues at Pentecost prove the fact that His reign has begun. The continued presence and power of the Holy Spirit in the lives of believers, though no longer miraculous, should, by implication, be pointed to as a proof of Christ's ongoing all-powerful reign. Proving these truths is the motivation.

Peter seeks to motivate God's people:	The way in which Peter seeks to move them:
1. To believe that Jesus is exalted to the right hand of God.	1. Scripture says the Christ would be exalted to God's right hand.
2. To believe that Jesus pours out God's Holy Spirit.	2. He points to the miracle that they can see and hear.
3. To believe that David wrote of Christ's ascension and session.	3. He points to the fact that David did not ascend into heaven.

Verse 36

"Therefore let all the house of Israel know assuredly that God has made this Jesus, whom you crucified, both Lord and Christ" (Acts 2:36).

ἀσφαλῶς οὖν γινωσκέτω πᾶς οἶκος Ἰσραὴλ ὅτι καὶ κύριον αὐτὸν καὶ Χριστὸν ἐποίησεν ὁ θεός, τοῦτον τὸν Ἰησοῦν ὃν ὑμεῖς ἐσταυρώσατε.

1. οὖν as an inferential conjunction.[31] Peter makes a powerful conclusion to his whole argument: "Therefore, without slipping (ἀσφαλῶς),[32] I command the whole house of Israel

[31] Robertson, *Word Pictures*, 34.

[32] "And he saith ἀσφαλῶς, or for a surety, not only that they may repose their sure confidence and trust in Christ, but that he may take away all occasion of doubting." Calvin, *Commentaries*, vol. XVIII, 114. "ἀσφαλῶς: used here emphatically; the Apostle would emphasize the conclusion which he is about

to know, that Lord and Christ himself, God has made, this Jesus, whom you crucified!"[33]

2. He commands the whole nation to know this. Peter wants his audience to know that God's mission with Jesus has been fully successful. He commands them to know this without possibility of it being wrong. It has been so overwhelmingly confirmed from every possible corner: Scripture, eyewitnesses, miracles, historical events.[34]
3. Peter brings conviction of sin.[35] He directly charges them with the unjust murder of the one he has now proven is Messiah and more than Messiah!
4. Peter calls Jesus plainly "the Christ." What Jesus did not permit them to proclaim before the time, they are now shouting to the whole nation. Peter wants all the people of God to know that Jesus is the Messiah, and more than the Messiah. He is Lord of all, sitting on God's throne with God's power, the possessor and sender of God's Spirit. Peter strongly implies Christ's deity in his very first public sermon.[36]
5. This message also proclaims to the people of God, in no

to draw from his three texts." *Expositor's Greek*, 89. "ἀσφαλῶς . . . used figuratively, the adverb means 'beyond a doubt.' It stands first in the sentence for emphasis." Kistemaker, *Acts*, 103.

[33] "Peter draws a powerfully pungent conclusion by the use of the adverb ἀσφαλῶς and the inferential conjunction οὖν. Peter's closing sentence drives home the point of his sermon. . . . (note ὑμεῖς, strongly emphatic *ye*)." Robertson, *Word Pictures*, 34.

[34] "On the day of Pentecost the Jewish audience must have full assurance of the truth of the gospel." Kistemaker, *Acts*, 36. "The attested facts point to one conclusion: God has made the crucified Jesus both Lord and Messiah." Bruce, *Acts*, 67–68.

[35] "The stinging effect with which St. Peter's words would fall on the ears of his audience, many of whom may have joined in the cry, 'Crucify Him!'" *Expositor's Greek*, 90.

[36] "Throughout his sermon, Peter makes God the principal speaker and doer. . . . At the conclusion, he shifts attention to the deity of Jesus Christ, whom he places on the same level as God. . . . Peter teaches the deity of Jesus Christ and thus places Jesus next to God." Kistemaker, *Acts*, 102.

uncertain terms, that the time of the Messiah, which concerned most of the prophecies of all the Old Testament prophets, has come.

6. Peter makes certain they know exactly who the Messiah is: "This same Jesus, the one you crucified, by His resurrection and ascension has become Lord of all and fulfilled all that was prophesied of the Christ."
7. As Christ's spokesman, Peter officially proclaims and appeals to all the people of God to believe the overwhelming evidence and testimony that proves that Jesus is the Christ.
8. Purpose for today: Know for certain, from the testimony of Scripture, Christ's appointed spokesmen, miracle, and the facts of history that the long promised Messiah came, was wrongfully crucified by His own nation, rose from the dead, ascended to heaven, and is now the only Savior and Lord of all.
9. Scriptural support: "And truly Jesus did many other signs in the presence of His disciples, which are not written in this book; but these are written that you may believe that Jesus is the Christ, the Son of God, and that believing you may have life in His name" (John 20:30–31).

Verse 37

"Now when they heard this, they were cut to the heart, and said to Peter and the rest of the apostles, 'Men and brethren, what shall we do?'" (Acts 2:37).

Ἀκούσαντες δὲ κατενύγησαν τὴν καρδίαν, εἶπόν τε πρὸς τὸν Πέτρον καὶ τοὺς λοιποὺς ἀποστόλους, Τί ποιήσωμεν, ἄνδρες ἀδελφοί;

1. Clearly, from their response, they believed that they, the people of God, were responsible for crucifying the promised Messiah, and they understandably are devastated. Peter

makes them look upon the one whom they pierced, and they mourn for Him as one mourns for an only son (see Zech. 12:10).

2. They are persuaded in their minds and convicted in their consciences.[37]
3. The context conclusively shows that they responded rightly to the sermon.
4. Peter makes them plainly see their sin, telling them twice they crucified Jesus, with lawless hands they put Him to death (see vv. 23, 36). They feel it deep in their hearts, and they do not try to deny it or escape the consequences.[38]
5. Their earnest response to the sermon is seen in their personal appeal to the apostles, as Peter had first appealed to them.[39]
6. The appeal to the godly in reading this text is to be like these Jews. If even those who physically killed the Messiah are forgiven by admitting their sins and being truly sorry for them, how much more those who sin against Him from, as it were, a distance?
7. Purpose: The godly are to admit their sins without equivocation. They are to be sorry for them from the heart.
8. Scriptural support: "Now I rejoice, not that you were made sorry, but that your sorrow led to repentance. For you were made sorry in a godly manner, that you might suffer loss from us in nothing. For godly sorrow produces repentance leading to salvation, not to be regretted; but the sorrow of the world produces death" (2 Cor. 7:9–10).

[37] Bruce, *Acts*, 69.

[38] "κατενύγησαν τὴν καρδίαν: No word could better make known that the sting of the last word had begun to work." *Expositor's Greek*, 90.

[39] "ἄνδρες ἀδελφοί,: indicating respect and regard—St. Peter's address had not been in vain . . . but now the words come as a response to St. Peter's own appeal." Ibid.

Verses 38–40

"Then Peter said to them, 'Repent, and let every one of you be baptized in the name of Jesus Christ for the remission of sins; and you shall receive the gift of the Holy Spirit. For the promise is to you and to your children, and to all who are afar off, as many as the Lord our God will call.' And with many other words he testified and exhorted them, saying, 'Be saved from this perverse generation'" (Acts 2:38–40).

Πέτρος δὲ πρὸς αὐτούς, Μετανοήσατε, [φησίν,] καὶ βαπτισθήτω ἕκαστος ὑμῶν ἐπὶ τῷ ὀνόματι Ἰησοῦ Χριστοῦ εἰς ἄφεσιν τῶν ἁμαρτιῶν ὑμῶν, καὶ λήμψεσθε τὴν δωρεὰν τοῦ ἁγίου πνεύματος: ὑμῖν γάρ ἐστιν ἡ ἐπαγγελία καὶ τοῖς τέκνοις ὑμῶν καὶ πᾶσιν τοῖς εἰς μακρὰν ὅσους ἂν προσκαλέσηται κύριος ὁ θεὸς ἡμῶν. ἑτέροις τε λόγοις πλείοσιν διεμαρτύρατο, καὶ παρεκάλει αὐτοὺς λέγων, Σώθητε ἀπὸ τῆς γενεᾶς τῆς σκολιᾶς ταύτης.

1. Peter answers their question "what shall we do?" In asking this question they show that they were convinced that Jesus is the Messiah, and that they ought to be condemned on account of their sins. So Peter tells them to repent and enter Christ's kingdom through the sign of baptism, and upon the authority of Jesus Christ, on His name, their sins will be forgiven.
2. I take εἰς here as denoting a purpose clause or aim, though this is controversial.[40] Thus, the thought communicated is: Be baptized unto, or for the purpose of, the remission of sins. Peter's point is not that baptism literally washes away sins, but that repentant sinners who trust in Christ will be forgiven of their sins *on the basis of His name*. Thus, the order is important: be baptized, each one of you—ἐπὶ τῷ ὀνόματι

[40] See Robertson on verse.

Ἰησοῦ Χριστοῦ—for the remission of sins. Baptism was commanded by Christ, to be administered in His name, unto all His disciples. As such it serves as a powerful sign that all who trust in Him are clean in His sight and are no longer enemies but citizens of His heavenly kingdom. The motivation is by way of promise, which is assured by the now proven power of the name.

3. Peter wants his listeners to understand that the promise of salvation comes to those who believe Jesus Christ is the living Messiah, reigning on the heavenly throne, only as they live out that faith by obeying Him. You must turn away from your old way of life and live for Him. You must enter His kingdom and submit to His ordinances. Salvation is the motivation.
4. Peter urges them to respond—not just for themselves but for their children's sake, which was no manipulating sentimentalism; it was true.[41]
5. Peter wants them to know the way in which we will be able to live the Christian life—the gift of the Holy Spirit—which they had seen supernaturally displayed in the speaking in tongues in accordance with the fulfillment of Joel's prophecy, would come to them if they repented and were baptized.[42]
6. γάρ in v. 39 is an encouragement to convicted sinners. Peter is assuring his listeners that they who truly submit to Christ as Lord and live for Him, trusting in His name for

[41] "The deliverance of which Joel had spoken was to be enjoyed by a remnant of the whole people; so now Peter urged his hearers to make sure, by a repentant calling on the Lord, that they belonged to this remnant and saved themselves from that perverse generation [that did not believe Jesus' message: Luke 9:41; 11:29]. The new community is viewed, in fact, as the believing remnant of the old Israel and the nucleus of the new." Bruce, *Acts*, 72.

[42] "*Ye shall receive the gift of the Spirit*. . . . Because they were touched with wondering when they saw the apostles suddenly begin to speak with strange tongues, Peter saith that they shall be partakers of the same gift if they will pass over unto Christ." Calvin, *Commentaries*, vol. XVIII, 121.

the forgiveness of sins, will most certainly receive the Holy Spirit. Everyone, whether near or far, meaning—though it would take the Jewish church a while to see this—whether Jew or Gentile, who takes the Messiah's call to heart, will receive the Holy Spirit.[43]

7. The underlying assumption is that Jews understood that those who had God's Holy Spirit were empowered for ministry and had God's favor rest upon them (see Isa. 63:10–11; Num. 11:25–29).
8. In sum, Peter appeals to the godly to repent from their sins, to be baptized, to trust in the name of Jesus for forgiveness, in order receive and then walk in and rely upon the strength of the Holy Spirit, living as a member of God's kingdom in this world.
9. Whether for the first time or not, this call, command, and promise of the gospel ought to encourage the believer in his faith and holiness.
10. In v. 40 Peter continues to solemnly bear witness.[44] His official testimony and many words indicate his great desire that they would believe. Here we see that encouragement, biblically speaking, includes warning against sin.[45] Thus, Peter

[43] These Jews could not know that these promises extended also to them and thereby claim them by faith unless or until the apostles proclaimed this truth. "Finally, this is the rule of a true faith, when I am thus persuaded that salvation is mine, because that promise appertaineth unto me which offerth the same." Ibid., 121–22. A strong and necessary incentive to assure convicted sinners that salvation is offered to them.

[44] "He *testified* (διεμαρτύρατο) . . . old verb, to make solemn attestation or call to witness. . . . Page insists that here it should be translated 'protested solemnly' to the Jews." Robertson, *Word Pictures*, 36–37. "διεμαρτύρετο: "'Testified,' both in A. and R. V., hardly gives the full form of the word. Its frequent use in the LXX in the sense of protesting solemnly . . . seems more in accordance with St. Peter's words, who here as elsewhere . . . was not simply acting as a witness μαρτυρειν, but was also protesting against the false views of those he was addressing." *Expositor's Greek*, 92.

[45] Peter warns them that if "they entangle themselves in their wicked and

παρεκάλει exhorted/urged/encouraged them to be saved from the wickedness and the crookedness that was their own generation.[46]

11. Here we learn that biblical encouragement means not to be made to feel accepted no matter what, or to never be subjected to moral judgment, but biblical encouragement means to be strengthened in what is right even as you consider the coming wrath of God on the wicked.
12. Peter points us to the Word of the gospel throughout his message:
    a. Listen to my words (v. 14).
    b. Hear the words of Joel (vv. 16–21).
    c. Listen to my words about Jesus (vv. 22–24).
    d. Consider David's words about Jesus (vv. 25–28).
    e. Consider my explanation of David's words (vv. 29–31).
    f. Listen to our testimony of Jesus (vv. 32–33).
    g. Consider another testimony of David about this Jesus (vv. 34–35).
    h. Listen to my concluding word and know what all this means (v. 36).
    i. Even the call to repent and be baptized is heeded by believing the words (vv. 38–39).
    j. Then Peter gave more testimony to them in many more words (v. 40).
13. Purpose: Repent and grow in your repentance! Be baptized and improve your baptism! Receive the Holy Spirit and seek to walk closer with the Spirit! Jesus gives new life to all who

---

pestiferous fellowship . . . they shall surely perish. . . . And this point of doctrine is not to be neglected. For it were not sufficient to have Christ set before us, unless we were also taught to flee those things which do lead us away from him. And it is the duty of a good shepherd to defend his sheep from the wolves." Calvin, *Commentaries*, vol. XVIII, 124–25.

[46] "Peter did not use doctrine only, but did add pricks of exhortations. And he expresseth plainly that he stood much hereupon. Whereas he saith, that he did exhort and beseech, he noteth therein his earnestness." Ibid., 124.

come to Him! You will be saved if you take Him at His Word and follow Him from the heart, submitting to His order and ordinances, trusting in His remission, relying on His Spirit. Do all of these things out of faith in Jesus.

14. Scriptural support: "And Jesus came and spoke to them, saying, 'All authority has been given to Me in heaven and on earth. Go therefore and make disciples of all the nations, baptizing them in the name of the Father and of the Son and of the Holy Spirit, teaching them to observe all things that I have commanded you; and lo, I am with you always, even to the end of the age.' Amen" (Matt. 28:18–20).

Preaching Purpose and Motivation in Verses 36–40

Preaching purpose: To officially proclaim to all Israel that the Jesus they murdered has been exalted as the Messiah and the Lord God. To command convicted sinners to repent and submit to Christ's initiating ordinance of baptism, and thereby become one of His disciples. To promise those who do that they will receive God's Spirit. To assure listeners that the promise of salvation is to them and to their children.

Motivation for use today: Preachers must proclaim that the Jesus of the Bible truly is God, the only Savior of sinners. They must proclaim this authoritatively as Christ's approved spokesmen. They must proclaim that their listeners truly are guilty before this Christ. They do this in order to convict their listeners that there is no other way to escape condemnation but through receiving this salvation. As they command repentance and baptism into Christ's church, they must promise forgiveness of sins and the gift of the Holy Spirit, assuring all who sincerely respond that this salvation is truly offered to them and through them to their children. They should continue to officially exhort their listeners to be saved. We notice here that tender and affectionate addresses like "brothers" are appropriate for ministers to use in sermons. So also is formal and official language ("house of Israel," "testified and exhorted"). Both are used as the subject warrants, for our God is both immanent and transcendent.

Peter seeks to motivate God's people:	The way in which Peter seeks to move them:
1. To know that the crucified Jesus of the Bible is the living Lord and Christ.	1. By proclaiming this truth from Scripture, credible witnesses, and known facts.
2. To know that they are convicted and condemned sinners before Him.	2. By directly and personally proclaiming their responsibility in Christ's murder.
3. To repent and be baptized into Christ, trusting in His name for forgiveness.	3. By commanding these saving responses and promising God's Spirit.
4. To know that the promise of the Holy Spirit and salvation is for their family.	4. By assuring them that salvation is truly offered to them and to their children.
5. To be saved out of a sinful people.	5. By continuing to officially witness to these things exhorting them to be saved.

Peter's Temple Sermon: Acts 3:11–26

Speaker:	The apostle Peter (v. 12)
Audience:	Israelite worshippers (v. 12)
Location:	The temple in Jerusalem
Occasion:	1. A crowd formed around Peter and John at the temple when they saw the lame man, who always was laid at the temple to beg, leaping and walking, and praising God (vv. 8–10). 2. The crowd was greatly amazed at the miracle and were looking in wonder at Peter and John (vv. 11–12).

Verse 12

"So when Peter saw it, he responded to the people: 'Men of Israel, why do you marvel at this? Or why look so intently at us, as though by our own power or godliness we had made this man walk?'" (Acts 3:12).

ἰδὼν δὲ ὁ Πέτρος ἀπεκρίνατο πρὸς τὸν λαόν, Ἄνδρες Ἰσραηλῖται, τί θαυμάζετε ἐπὶ τούτῳ, ἢ ἡμῖν τί ἀτενίζετε ὡς ἰδίᾳ δυνάμει ἢ εὐσεβείᾳ πεποιηκόσιν τοῦ περιπατεῖν αὐτόν;

1. Here Peter begins to speak, as in chapter 2, to correct a misconception communicated—nonverbally, by their intense staring—that Peter and John inherently had the ability to heal.[47]
2. Peter's intent is clearly to correct that misconception and to give the glory and honor for the healing to Jesus Christ.
3. The grammar helps us to identify Peter's purpose as once again answering an erroneous judgment of the crowd: "ὡς . . . πεποιηκόσιν τοῦ περιπατεῖν: this use of the infinitive with the genitive of the article, instead of the simple infinitive with or without ὥςτε, to express a purpose, or result as here . . . may be illustrated from the LXX."[48]

Verses 13–15

"The God of Abraham, Isaac, and Jacob, the God of our fathers, glorified His Servant Jesus, whom you delivered up and denied in the presence of Pilate, when he was determined to let Him go. But you denied the Holy One and the Just, and asked for a murderer to be granted to you, and killed the Prince of life, whom God raised from the dead, of which we are witnesses."

[47] "As in his Pentecost sermon, Peter first explains the circumstances of the miracle, then acquaints his hearers with the death and resurrection of Jesus Christ, and last calls them to repentance and faith." Kistemaker, *Acts*, 127.

[48] *Expositor's Greek*, 109.

ὁ θεὸς Ἀβραὰμ καὶ Ἰσαὰκ καὶ Ἰακώβ, ὁ θεὸς τῶν πατέρων ἡμῶν, ἐδόξασεν τὸν παῖδα αὐτοῦ Ἰησοῦν, ὃν ὑμεῖς μὲν παρεδώκατε καὶ ἠρνήσασθε κατὰ πρόσωπον Πιλάτου, κρίναντος ἐκείνου ἀπολύειν: ὑμεῖς δὲ τὸν ἅγιον καὶ δίκαιον ἠρνήσασθε, καὶ ᾐτήσασθε ἄνδρα φονέα χαρισθῆναι ὑμῖν, τὸν δὲ ἀρχηγὸν τῆς ζωῆς ἀπεκτείνατε, ὃν ὁ θεὸς ἤγειρεν ἐκ νεκρῶν, οὗ ἡμεῖς μάρτυρές ἐσμεν.

1. Peter clearly identifies the Jewish God of the Old Testament and calls Jesus "His Servant." His purpose is to show that Jesus was from God in fulfillment of all His promises to Israel from the beginning until now.[49]
2. Calvin notes that both the manner and order of Peter's teaching is important.[50]
3. Peter contrasts Jesus' faithfulness with his audience's unfaithfulness.[51]
    a. Jesus was God's servant (child).
    b. Jesus was God's Holy One, the Just.
    c. Jesus was the Prince of Life.[52]
4. Peter magnifies the sin of his audience in showing how their actions were evil and opposed to God.[53] He plainly

[49] "ὁ θεὸς Ἀβραὰμ καὶ Ἰσαὰκ καὶ Ἰακώβ . . . the words were wisely chosen, not only to gain attention and to show that the speaker identified himself with the nation and hope of Israel, but also because in Jesus St. Peter saw the fulfillment of the promise made to Abraham," Ibid; "the record [of this sermon] clearly shows that Peter appeals to the religious motives of his audience. . . . The words [of the title 'I am the God of A, I, J'] are hallowed by reverential use. . . . Peter deliberately calls Jesus 'servant' to remind his listeners of Isaiah's prophecy concerning the suffering and the glory of the Lord's servant (Isa. 52:13–53:12)." Kistemaker, *Acts*, 128; see also Calvin, *Commentaries*, vol. XVIII, 144–45.

[50] Calvin, *Commentaries*, vol. XVIII, 144.

[51] "Again it is clear how the Apostolic preaching in Acts loves to emphasize the contrast between men's treatment of Jesus and God's." Bruce, *Acts*, 82.

[52] These were well-known titles of the Messiah; see Kistemaker, *Acts*, 129.

[53] "He emphasizes the denial (ἠρνήσασθε twice) and its baseness. . . .

calls out their sin while using exalted titles for Jesus, showing all of their evils to be increased to the degree that Jesus was exalted.[54]

   a. God glorified Jesus, whereas they denied and delivered Him to Pilate.
   b. Even Pilate was determined to release Jesus, but they would not allow him to. Instead they asked for a murderer to be set free and they denied the Holy One, the Just One.
   c. In killing Jesus they killed the prince, that is, ruler or author (ESV, NIV) of life. Here again God so opposed their action that He raised up Jesus from the dead.

5. By magnifying their sin and guilt, Peter gives strong internal motivation to any true Israelites; those whose hope is in the Messiah; to be sorry and repent.
6. Peter declares the fact of the resurrection and the apostles to be eyewitnesses of it. Under Jewish law they could have been condemned if they bore false witness to God for having done something He did not do.
7. Peter's purpose is to show the evil of their sin and the goodness and greatness of Jesus, in order that he can make the case that Jesus is the one who healed the lame man.

St. Chrys. writes: 'Peter shows the great aggravation of the act. As he has them under his hand, he strikes hard; while they were hardened he refrained from such language, but when their minds are most moved then he strikes home, now that they are in a condition to feel it,' (*Hom., ix*)." *Expositor's Greek*, 110–11.

[54] "He puts the burden of guilt where it belongs. The Jews are responsible for the death of God's servant. . . . 'You killed the Prince of life.' Peter's denunciation is directly aimed at the conscience of his audience." Kistemaker, *Acts*, 128; "*Whom ye have delivered.* He mingleth with doctrine a most sharp chiding, according as the matter did require; for it was impossible to bring them truly unto God, unless they were first brought to the knowledge of their sins." And in comparing them with Pilate: "Men must be so stricken, that being brought to know their guiltiness, they may earnestly fly unto the remedy of pardon." Calvin, *Commentaries*, vol. XVIII, 146.

8. Scriptural support: "My little children, these things I write to you, so that you may not sin. And if anyone sins, we have an Advocate with the Father, Jesus Christ the righteous" (1 John 2:1).

Verse 16

"And His name, through faith in His name, has made this man strong, whom you see and know. Yes, the faith which comes through Him has given him this perfect soundness in the presence of you all" (Acts 3:16).

καὶ ἐπὶ τῇ πίστει τοῦ ὀνόματος αὐτοῦ τοῦτον ὃν θεωρεῖτε καὶ οἴδατε ἐστερέωσεν τὸ ὄνομα αὐτοῦ, καὶ ἡ πίστις ἡ δι' αὐτοῦ ἔδωκεν αὐτῷ τὴν ὁλοκληρίαν ταύτην ἀπέναντι πάντων ὑμῶν.

1. Peter identifies where the power to make lame men walk comes from: the name of Jesus. Thus, the NASB translates: "it is the name of Jesus which has strengthened this man."[55]
2. Peter wants his audience to know that because of the power of His name, faith in Jesus can make a lame man walk.
3. Peter magnifies Jesus, emphasizes faith, and stresses the reality of the miracle that is before their eyes.
4. Peter's purpose is to show the miraculously confirmed power of faith in Jesus' name in order to prove that Jesus is Messiah and His offer of salvation is infallible.
5. The point is that if faith in Jesus' word to be healed brings even supernatural healing that can be seen, so faith in His word to forgive sins, to give the Holy Spirit, and to give eternal life will likewise receive these things though they cannot be seen. Thus the miracles are called *signs*; they visibly point us to an invisible, spiritual truth.

[55] "Peter's emphasis [is] on the name of Jesus, which he repeatedly mentions and even personifies." Kistemaker, *Acts*, 131.

6. Scriptural support: "And when He had come into the house, the blind men came to Him. And Jesus said to them, 'Do you believe that I am able to do this?' They said to Him, 'Yes, Lord.' Then He touched their eyes, saying, 'According to your faith let it be to you'" (Matt. 9:28–29).
7. Calvin again notes that the form is part of Peter's persuasion: "Let us, therefore, remember that Peter did use such variety and plenty of words, to the end he might stay us in Christ."[56]

Verses 17–18

"Yet now, brethren, I know that you did it in ignorance, as did also your rulers. But those things which God foretold by the mouth of all His prophets, that the Christ would suffer, He has thus fulfilled" (Acts 3:17–18).

καὶ νῦν, ἀδελφοί, οἶδα ὅτι κατὰ ἄγνοιαν ἐπράξατε, ὥσπερ καὶ οἱ ἄρχοντες ὑμῶν: ὁ δὲ θεὸς ἃ προκατήγγειλεν διὰ στόματος πάντων τῶν προφητῶν παθεῖν τὸν Χριστὸν αὐτοῦ ἐπλήρωσεν οὕτως.

1. Peter ameliorates their guilt somewhat.[57]
2. Calvin speaks elegantly to the motivating force of Peter's words:

   Because it was to be doubted, lest, being cast down with despair, they should refuse his doctrine, he doth a little lift them up. We must so temper our sermons that they may profit hearers, for unless there be some hope of pardon left, the terror and fear of punishment doth harden men's hearts with stubbornness; for that of David is true [Ps. 130:4],

[56] Calvin, *Commentaries*, vol. XVIII, 147.

[57] "Affectionate and conciliatory, *cf*, ver. 12, where he speaks more formally because more by way of reproof." *Expositor's Greek*, 117.

That we fear the Lord when we perceive that he is unto us favorable.[58]

3. He identifies with them as brothers.[59] They killed the Messiah, who is the Holy One and Author of life, not knowing who He was. They clearly should have known, as he has already shown them, even Pilate knew enough to oppose them, yet their guilt does not rise to the level of consciously seeking to overthrow God—this fact is also true for their rulers.
4. The sovereignty of God over evil: Even in their evil actions, God accomplished His good purposes for the Christ and fulfilled all that He was sent to do. Again Calvin notes the motivation: "[W]hen he telleth them that God hath accomplished those things which he had foretold, he doth so touch their offense in the death of Christ, that it turneth to their salvation."[60]
5. Peter declares that all the Old Testament prophets wrote about Jesus, and in particular, His suffering.
6. Peter's purpose is to cause them to see not only their failure to stop the Messiah, but also how He was victorious even through their evil actions.
7. The implication of these words is that you still have an opportunity to repent, but since that becomes explicit in the next verse, we will develop it there.
8. Scriptural support: "Of this salvation the prophets have inquired and searched carefully, who prophesied of the grace that would come to you, searching what, or what manner of time, the Spirit of Christ who was in them was indicating

[58] Calvin, *Commentaries*, vol. XVIII, 148.

[59] "Peter has uncovered the miserable plight of his listeners, who now see their guilt before God. . . . Peter addresses them with gentle words spoken with pastoral interest and concern. He places himself on their level and speaks words of comfort." Kistemaker, *Acts*, 132.

[60] Calvin, *Commentaries*, vol. XVIII, 149.

when He testified beforehand the sufferings of Christ and the glories that would follow" (1 Peter 1:10–11).

Verses 19–21

"Repent therefore and be converted, that your sins may be blotted out, so that times of refreshing may come from the presence of the Lord, and that He may send Jesus Christ, who was preached to you before ["the Christ appointed for you" NASB], whom heaven must receive until the times of restoration of all things, which God has spoken by the mouth of all His holy prophets since the world began" (Acts 3:19–21).

μετανοήσατε οὖν καὶ ἐπιστρέψατε εἰς τὸ ἐξαλειφθῆναι ὑμῶν τὰς ἁμαρτίας, ὅπως ἂν ἔλθωσιν καιροὶ ἀναψύξεως ἀπὸ προσώπου τοῦ κυρίου καὶ ἀποστείλῃ τὸν προκεχειρισμένον ὑμῖν Χριστόν, Ἰησοῦν, ὃν δεῖ οὐρανὸν μὲν δέξασθαι ἄχρι χρόνων ἀποκαταστάσεως πάντων ὧν ἐλάλησεν ὁ θεὸς διὰ στόματος τῶν ἁγίων ἀπ' αἰῶνος αὐτοῦ προφητῶν.

1. Two commands and three reasons to obey them clearly given.
2. Two strong indications of purpose in the grammar:
    a. εἰς τὸ with the infinitive indicates purpose, *so that* (BDAG).
    b. ὅπως ἂν with the subjunctive denotes purpose, *in order that* (BDAG).[61]
3. Peter's gives his audience three external motivations why they should repent and be converted:

[61] "ὅπως ἂν: This type of clause has "a relative or conditional force." Ernest De Witt Burton, *Syntax of the Moods and Tenses in New Testament Greek*, 195 (Grand Rapids, MI: Kregel, 1994), 85. This type of clause has also been categorized as one of the "final clauses . . . ways of expressing *purpose*." C. F. D. Moule, *An Idiom Book of New Testament Greek*, 2nd ed. (New York: Cambridge University Press, 1998), 138, emphasis in original.

   a. In order that your sins may be blotted out.
   b. So that times of refreshing may come from the presence of the Lord.
   c. So that Jesus would be sent to you, even as He was appointed for you.
4. Repenting and being converted takes care of my sins of the past.
5. Repenting and being converted will bring me the grace to live today.[62]
6. Repenting and being converted will secure my future in the kingdom.
7. Peter declares plainly that Jesus is the Christ (see vv. 18, 20). That Jesus is the one "appointed" (προκεχειρισμένον) to them adds trustworthiness.
8. Calvin notices positive and negative motivation: "There is a double prick, wherewith the faithful are pricked forward . . . so Peter mixeth in this place threatenings with promises, partly to the end he may allure the Jews unto Christ, and partly that he may prick them forward with fear."[63]
9. Christ is in heaven now, though we can enjoy His presence now also.
10. Christ will not literally return until the prophetic time of restoration has come.
11. In once again noticing the positive and negative motivation of this sermon, Calvin sees a model for ministers to imitate in terrifying and alluring:

[62] "Times of refreshment and joy which the prophets had described as features of the new age would be sent to them by God." Bruce, *Acts*, 84. "Times of refreshing . . . signifies periodic seasons in which the forgiven and restored believer experience the refreshing nearness of the Lord." Kistemaker, *Acts*, 135. "Seasons of refreshment. . . . The bright and smiling presence of God to one seeking comfort." *Expositor's Greek*, 115.

[63] Calvin, *Commentaries*, vol. XVIII, 151.

> He signifieth that the grace of the covenant was appointed principally for them. . . . And so as he pricked them forward to obey the gospel, by terrifying them with the terror of punishment, so he allureth them now again to receive the grace which is offered them in Christ; so that we see how that God omitteth nothing whereby he may bring us unto himself. And it is the duty of a wise minister so to prick forward the sluggish and slow bellies, that he do lead those gently which are apt to be taught.[64]

12. That all the prophets foretold of Christ's restoring of all things commends the gospel to this audience, since it is the same promise of salvation from the beginning.[65]
13. Scriptural support: "Therefore lay aside all filthiness and overflow of wickedness, and receive with meekness the implanted word, which is able to save your souls. But be doers of the word, and not hearers only, deceiving yourselves" (James 1:21–22).

Preaching Purpose and Motivation of Verses 12–21

Preaching purpose: To correct the error of those Jews who thought the apostles had miraculous powers. To explain that miracles are done through faith in Jesus' name, in order to show His power to do all His will. To declare that Jesus is the hope of the whole Old Testament and has been glorified by God as the highest one, and their sin has shown them to be the worst. To show that God sovereignly fulfilled His purposes even through their sins, for which they remain responsible. To call them to repentance and to turn back being through which they can be forgiven and blessed. To promise them Jesus' presence now, even though He will be in heaven until the end foretold in Scripture when all things will be restored.

[64] Ibid., 158.
[65] Ibid., 153.

Motivation for use today: Preachers must proclaim that the miracles of healing in Jesus' name proved once and for all that Christ's promise to save all those who believe in Him is infallible. They must directly convict their hearers of sin and show how evil that sin is, seeing it is against the Messiah who is the author of life, though they must do so in a way that they still give hope of salvation. In this, ministers should personally address and identify with their audiences. Ministers must show God's sovereignty and human responsibility in the drama of the salvation purchased by Christ, in order to magnify both God's power and our sin. They must show how Jesus is the hope of salvation of the whole Old Testament. Having done these things, ministers must command repentance and faith in Jesus' name and promise His presence, blessing, and forgiveness to all who do. They must declare that Jesus will return again to restore all things.

Peter seeks to motivate God's people to:	The way in which Peter seeks to move them:
1. Not to attribute Christ's miraculous power and glory to any other.	1. By showing that Jesus has been exalted to the highest place.
2. To see that Jesus is the hope of Abraham and the fathers.	2. By giving Jesus messianic and exalted titles, and the witness of the prophets.
3. To see the heinousness of their sins against Jesus.	3. By reminding them how they sought Jesus' death even when Pilate didn't and that they willingly chose a murderer over the Author of life.
4. To believe the miraculously-proven power of faith in Jesus' name.	4. By attributing the undeniable miracle to faith in Jesus' name.
5. To give hope of salvation to the vilest sinners if they but admit it.	5. By calling them brothers and telling them that they did not fully realize what they were doing. (So also did Paul; 1 Tim. 1:13.)

6. To see God's sovereign plan for Jesus accomplished even through their sin.	6. By declaring that Jesus' suffering was foretold by the prophets, and referring to Jesus under the name "Servant," which is from those passages (see Isa. 52–53).
7. To repent and be converted.	7. By commanding them, and promising them forgiveness, refreshing, and God's presence.
8. To believe that Jesus can be with them and bless them if they do.	8. By declaring that God will send Jesus to those who repent and believe.
9. To believe that Jesus will remain in heaven till He comes to restore all things.	9. By proclaiming the restoration to be accomplished by Christ as being told by all the prophets since the beginning of the world.

Verses 22–24

"For Moses truly said to the fathers, 'The Lord your God will raise up for you a Prophet like me from your brethren. Him you shall hear in all things, whatever He says to you. And it shall be that every soul who will not hear that Prophet shall be utterly destroyed from among the people.' Yes, and all the prophets, from Samuel and those who follow, as many as have spoken, have also foretold these days" (Acts 3:22–24).

Μωϋσῆς μὲν εἶπεν ὅτι Προφήτην ὑμῖν ἀναστήσει κύριος ὁ θεὸς ὑμῶν ἐκ τῶν ἀδελφῶν ὑμῶν ὡς ἐμέ: αὐτοῦ ἀκούσεσθε κατὰ πάντα ὅσα ἂν λαλήσῃ πρὸς ὑμᾶς. ἔσται δὲ πᾶσα ψυχὴ ἥτις ἐὰν μὴ ἀκούσῃ τοῦ προφήτου ἐκείνου ἐξολεθρευθήσεται ἐκ τοῦ λαοῦ. καὶ πάντες δὲ οἱ προφῆται ἀπὸ Σαμουὴλ καὶ τῶν καθεξῆς ὅσοι ἐλάλησαν καὶ κατήγγειλαν τὰς ἡμέρας ταύτας.

1. γὰρ (not in critical text) indicates purpose, μὲν calls attention to the truth of what Peter is about to say. Thus the NKJV's "For . . . truly"

2. Having asserted that all the holy prophets had spoken of Jesus, Peter now adduces proof by citing the greatest prophet, Moses.
3. Peter's purpose was to move their wills to choose Christ by convincing them that Jesus is the Prophet. Citing Moses is for the purpose of calling them by the authority of his doctrine "and this was the best way to bring the Jews to be Christ's disciples. . . . This is therefore the thing which Peter aimeth at, to bring them to hear Christ willingly, as the master whom God hath appointed to teach them."[66]
4. From Moses' testimony, Peter calls the people to obey Jesus.
5. Peter provides the external threatening incentive that if you do not completely obey the words of Jesus, you will be cut off from God's people, and thus from God.
6. Peter concludes this section by asserting that all the prophets following Moses also bear witness to these messianic days that had now begun. Peter is using the whole heritage of the Jews, and all the prophets as an overwhelming witness to prove Jesus is the Christ, to motivate them to come to Him.[67]
7. Peter's purpose is to make as clear as possible the choice before those who would claim to be God's people: obey Jesus' call to faith and repentance or be destroyed.
8. He calls on Samuel and all the prophets to strengthen his interpretation of Moses. Peter knows that multiple Scriptures strengthen one's argument.
9. He provides more incentives in adducing the testimony of Moses, Samuel, and all the prophets. To not heed Jesus is to reject their heritage, their Scriptures, their promises, all of it.
10. Scriptural support: "He who believes in the Son has eternal life; but he who does not obey the Son shall not see life, but the wrath of God abides on him" (John 3:36 NASB).

[66] Ibid., 154.

[67] "And all . . . this maketh much for the certainty of the gospel, that all the prophets, for a long time . . . testify altogether that men ought to hope for a certain, better, and more perfect thing." Ibid., 157.

Verses 25–26

"You are sons of the prophets, and of the covenant which God made with our fathers, saying to Abraham, 'And in your seed all the families of the earth shall be blessed.' To you first, God, having raised up His Servant Jesus, sent Him to bless you, in turning away every one of you from your iniquities" (Acts 3:25–26).

Ὑμεῖς ἐστε υἱοὶ τῶν προφητῶν, καὶ τῆς διαθήκης ἧς διέθετο ὁ θεὸς πρὸς τοὺς πατέρας ἡμῶν, λέγων πρὸς Ἀβραάμ, Καὶ ἐν τῷ σπέρματί σου ἐνευλογηθήσονται πᾶσαι αἱ πατριαὶ τῆς γῆς. Ὑμῖν πρῶτον ὁ θεός, ἀναστήσας τὸν παῖδα αὐτοῦ Ἰησοῦν, ἀπέστειλεν αὐτὸν εὐλογοῦντα ὑμᾶς, ἐν τῷ ἀποστρέφειν ἕκαστον ἀπὸ τῶν πονηριῶν ὑμῶν.

1. Peter reminds his audience that everything that he has been talking about is their unique heritage as the seed of Abraham.
2. He uses a direct covenantal title to motivate them to Jesus.[68]
3. Past blessings are cited to motivate them to come to Christ, the source of all blessing: Come to Christ and claim your inheritance![69]
4. This favored position has resulted in their being honored with the first opportunity to receive Jesus.
5. These first two points are by definition unique to this first-century audience. Once Jesus was proclaimed to the Gentiles, the first proclamation privilege had been fulfilled.
6. Peter again declares the resurrection of Jesus and asserts to them that in the preaching of the gospel God has sent Jesus to them.

[68] "Peter telleth the Jews, that Christ is promised unto them after this sort, to the end they may more willingly embrace him." Ibid., 158.

[69] "In these verses Peter reminds his audience of the covenant blessings which they have inherited through Abraham, their spiritual father. Now, through Jesus Christ, God continues to bless his people." Kistemaker, *Acts*, 139, 140.

7. The purpose for which Jesus has come to them in the preaching of the gospel is to bless them by turning them away from their iniquities. Again Peter emphasizes repentance at the end of a sermon. Here it is not a command but a work of God, which Peter calls a blessing, and attributes it to the ministry of "His Servant Jesus."[70]
8. Scriptural support: "How shall we escape if we neglect so great a salvation, which at the first began to be spoken by the Lord, and was confirmed to us by those who heard Him, God also bearing witness both with signs and wonders, with various miracles, and gifts of the Holy Spirit, according to His own will?" (Heb. 2:3–4).

Preaching Purpose and Motivation of Verses 22–26

Preaching purpose: To show Moses as another witness to Jesus, and that they must listen to Him or be cursed. To show that all the prophets after Moses are also witnesses to Jesus. To remind his audience of their privileged heritage of the oracles of God and the covenants (this purpose was limited to first-century Jews). To present Jesus as a blessing from God in turning them away from sin.

Motivation for use today: Preachers should proclaim Moses, Samuel, and all the prophets as witnesses to Jesus in order to establish the certain truth of His life and reign. They should cite specific Scriptures, as Peter does. They should show how the Scriptures teach that one's response to Jesus determines whether or not you are in God's kingdom. They should seek to allure God's people by assuring them that the promises of the gospel are for them. Again they should cite specific Scriptures to certify this offer. They should teach that Jesus suffered to bless them with the blessing of turning them from their sins.

[70] "*Whilst that he turneth.* He doth again commend the doctrine of repentance, to the end we may learn to conclude under the blessing of Christ newness of life." Calvin, *Commentaries*, vol. XVIII, 163.

Peter seeks to motivate God's people to:	The way in which Peter seeks to move them:
1. Heed Moses' witness and listen to Jesus in everything.	1. He quotes from a passage of Moses commanding us to listen to Jesus.
2. Heed Moses' witness and fear the curse if you do not listen to Jesus.	2. He quotes from a passage of Moses threatening judgment.
3. Heed Samuel and all the prophets' witness to the life and reign of Jesus.	3. He declares that Samuel and all the prophets are Jesus' witnesses.
4. Come to Jesus and be blessed.	4. He uses familial and biblical language to assure them the promise is to them.
5. Desire Jesus' blessing of turning us from our iniquities.	5. He declares that God sent Jesus to them for this purpose of blessing.

Peter's Sermon to the Gentiles: Acts 10:34–48

Speaker:	The apostle Peter (v. 34)
Audience:	Gentile God-fearers (v. 2) Cornelius' worship was accepted by God (vv. 4, 31). These are believers who have not yet been called by the gospel of Christ.[71]
Location:	Cornelius' house in Caesarea
Occasion:	1. Cornelius had a heavenly vision directing him to send for Peter "who will tell you words by which you and all your household will be saved" (Acts 11:14). 2. Peter has a heavenly vision wherein he is taught not to call anything unclean that God has cleansed. 3. Peter is told by the Holy Spirit to go to Cornelius' house and not to doubt him. 4. Cornelius tells Peter his vision and that he and his house are present "to hear all the things commanded you by God" (Acts 10:33).

[71] "Cornelius possessed a genuine faith in Israel's God." Kistemaker, *Acts*,

Verses 34–35

"Then Peter opened his mouth and said: 'In truth I perceive that God shows no partiality. But in every nation whoever fears Him and works righteousness is accepted by Him. But in every nation whoever fears Him and works righteousness is accepted by Him'" (Acts 10:34–35).

Ἀνοίξας δὲ Πέτρος τὸ στόμα εἶπεν, 'Επ' ἀληθείας καταλαμβάνομαι ὅτι οὐκ ἔστιν προσωπολήμπτης ὁ θεός ἀλλ' ἐν παντὶ ἔθνει ὁ φοβούμενος αὐτὸν καὶ ἐργαζόμενος δικαιοσύνην δεκτὸς αὐτῷ ἐστιν.

1. Peter speaks this preamble to set the stage for his sermon.
2. Rather than a personal address to these strangers, he protests his truthfulness in a way befitting the occasion.[72]
3. He is telling the Gentiles that, contrary to what they had heard and seen from Jews previously and even what he himself had believed, God does not favor Jews over Gentiles.[73] This acknowledgment motivates them by assuring them that they can be saved.
4. National status is not recognized by God, but he accepts those who fear Him and do good works.[74] Here Peter says nothing new.

---

371. "Cornelius must be put in the catalogue of the old fathers, who hoped for salvation of the Redeemer before he was revealed. . . . Cornelius could not pray unless he had faith." Calvin, *Commentaries*, vol. XVIII, 414.

[72] "επ' ἀληθείας. . . . It introduces a solemn statement" says it is Luke's transliteration of ἀμὴν, ἀμὴν. Kistemaker, *Acts*, 398.

[73] προσωπολήμπτη "the noun and the adj. always imply favoritism." *Expositor's Greek*, 259. "The idea is to pay regard to one's looks or circumstances rather than to his intrinsic character. The Jews had come to feel that they were the favorites of God. . . . John the Baptist rebuked them for this fallacy." Robertson, *Word Pictures*, 143.

[74] "The early prophets . . . insisted that God's choice of Israel was an act of grace, not of partiality, and that it called for a response of obedience service, not of careless complacency." Bruce, *Acts*, 212.

5. The fear of God is the hallmark of believers from the garden on:
    a. "And He said, 'Do not lay your hand on the lad, or do anything to him; for now I know that you fear God, since you have not withheld your son, your only son, from Me'" (Gen. 22:12).
    b. "Then a voice came from the throne, saying, 'Praise our God, all you His servants and those who fear Him, both small and great!'"(Rev. 19:5).[75]
6. By the fruit of their faith, Peter judges these Gentiles as God's people.[76]
7. The word acceptable, δεκτός, is used extensively in Leviticus in the LXX to describe sacrifices acceptable to God. So also Paul: "Indeed I have all and abound. I am full, having received from Epaphroditus the things sent from you, a sweet-smelling aroma, an *acceptable* sacrifice, well pleasing to God" (Phil. 4:18).
8. Peter is calling the Gentiles clean in the most holy setting of worship. Having ordinarily been excluded from

[75] "*He which feareth God, and doth righteousness.* In these two members is comprehended the integrity of all the whole life. For the fear of God is nothing else but godliness and religion; and righteousness is that equity which men use among themselves, taking heed lest they hurt any man, and studying to do good to all men." Calvin, *Commentaries*, vol. XVIII, 439. "By the feare of God, the Hebrews understand the whole service of God whereby we perceive that Cornelius was not void of faith, no more than they were which lived before Christ's time; and therefore they deal foolishly, which build preparative works and free will upon this place." *1599 Geneva Bible* (White Hall, WV: Tolle Lege, 2010), Acts 10:35n1, 1108.

[76] "καταλαμβάνεσθαι is to apprehend, or to gather by reasons, signs, and conjectures. Cornelius was a Gentile born, yet God heareth his prayers; he vouchsafeth to show him the light of the gospel; he appointed and sendeth an angel to him particularly; thereby doth Peter know, that, without respect of persons, those do please God which live godly and innocently. . . . By which example, we are taught how greatly we ought to beware of prejudices, which make us oftentimes judge amiss." Calvin, *Commentaries*, vol. XVIII, 437.

Jewish worship, the Gentile God-fearers would be intimately acquainted with this word (see Acts 10:28, "You know . . .").

9. Peter is not preaching a gospel of works righteousness but only the truth of James 1:22: "But be doers of the word, and not hearers only, deceiving yourselves." Only those who bear the fruit of faith are acceptable to God.
10. Purpose: to show these Gentiles that God accepts sincere believers who work righteousness, which is the fruit of true faith and repentance.
11. Scriptural support: "Therefore bear fruits worthy of repentance, and do not begin to say to yourselves, 'We have Abraham as our father.' For I say to you that God is able to raise up children to Abraham from these stones" (Luke 3:8).

Verses 36–38

"The word which God sent to the children of Israel, preaching peace through Jesus Christ—He is Lord of all—that word you know, which was proclaimed throughout all Judea, and began from Galilee after the baptism which John preached: how God anointed Jesus of Nazareth with the Holy Spirit and with power, who went about doing good and healing all who were oppressed by the devil, for God was with Him" (Acts 10:36–38).

Τὸν λόγον ὃν ἀπέστειλεν τοῖς υἱοῖς 'Ισραήλ, εὐαγγελιζόμενος εἰρήνην διὰ 'Ιησοῦ χριστοῦ- οὗτός ἐστιν πάντων κύριος- ὑμεῖς οἴδατε, τὸ γενόμενον ῥῆμα καθ' ὅλης τῆς 'Ιουδαίας, ἀρξάμενον ἀπὸ τῆς Γαλιλαίας, μετὰ τὸ βάπτισμα ὃ ἐκήρυξεν 'Ιωάννης•

'Ιησοῦν τὸν ἀπὸ Ναζαρέτ, ὡς ἔχρισεν αὐτὸν ὁ θεὸς πνεύματι ἁγίῳ καὶ δυνάμει, ὃς διῆλθεν εὐεργετῶν καὶ ἰώμενος πάντας τοὺς καταδυναστευομένους ὑπὸ τοῦ διαβόλου, ὅτι ὁ θεὸς ἦν μετ' αὐτοῦ.

1. The word God sent to Israel is the same word Peter is bringing to Gentiles.
2. The word is sent to them both by preaching.
3. The content of the proclamation is peace through Jesus, who is the Christ.
4. This peace is more certain because Jesus the Christ is also the Lord of all.
5. It began to be proclaimed by John the Baptist, and Peter emphasizes they were familiar with the content of the message.[77]
6. John preached repentance to Israel (see Mark 1:4), now Peter to the Gentiles.
7. Peter gives more attestation (proof) to his gospel when he declares that he is preaching nothing new, but the same gospel they had heard.[78]
8. Thus this peace is reconciliation with God in the forgiveness of sins through repentance and faith in Jesus (see v. 43).[79] The message, "peace," is also the motivation.
9. His purpose is to proclaim this peace to the Gentiles that they would receive it, and he first begins with a factual summary of Jesus' life.[80]
10. It is implied that this peace is received as one receives Jesus

[77] "*Ye know* (ὑμεῖς οἴδατε). Peter reminds his Gentile audience that the main facts concerning Jesus and the gospel were known to them. Note emphatic expression of ὑμεῖς (you)." Robertson, *Word Pictures*, 144.

[78] "To the end Peter may purchase greater credit, he saith that he will speak of no new or unknown thing, but of the restoring of the Church, which did depend upon the eternal covenant of God, and which was now manifestly showed." Calvin, *Commentaries*, vol. XVIII, 441.

[79] "Peter here presents an objective statement of the life, death, and resurrection of Jesus with proof from the Scriptures that he is the Messiah. It is a skilful presentation." Robertson, *Word Pictures*, 145.

[80] "Christ cannot otherwise be set before us to salvation, than if we first know [what he has done in history]. Again, lest the knowledge of the history be unprofitable and cold, we must also show the end why he came down from his heavenly glory." Calvin, *Commentaries*, vol. XVIII, 442.

Christ. Thus, the summary of the proclamation: "peace through Jesus Christ."

11. Scriptural support: "How then shall they call on Him in whom they have not believed? And how shall they believe in Him of whom they have not heard? And how shall they hear without a preacher? And how shall they preach unless they are sent? As it is written: 'How beautiful are the feet of those who preach the gospel of peace, who bring glad tidings of good things!'" (Rom. 10:14–15).
12. That Jesus is "Lord of all" is an incentive to the Gentiles that He is for them.
13. God anointed Him with the Holy Spirit, as the Messiah, and with power, as a miracle worker.[81]
14. Jesus was good; He lived a life of obedience. He did miracles. He even supernaturally freed people from the power of the evil one, the most difficult of miracles, since in these He must overcome the resistance of Satan.[82]
15. Jesus was able to do these things, for, ὅτι, God was with Him.[83]
16. Christ is once again proven to be from God by miracle. Calvin's testimony of the attestation of Christ's miracles is worth pondering:

> *Because God was with him*. Peter noteth briefly to what end those powers did tend which were showed by the hand of Christ, to wit, that he might purchase credit among men,

[81] "Jesus' works of mercy and power." Bruce, *Acts*, 214. "God enabled Jesus to perform miracles and signs, because of the Father's presence in his Son." Kistemaker, *Acts*, 394. "Peter saith immediately after, that this power appeared in miracles." Calvin, *Commentaries*, vol. XVIII, 443.

[82] "*Those which were holden of devils*. This also was a more manifest token of God's power in Christ, that he did not only heal men of common diseases, but did also cure desperate evils." Ibid., 444.

[83] "God enabled Jesus to perform miracles and signs, because of the Father's presence in his Son." Kistemaker, *Acts*, 394.

who did behold God as it were present; and this was the true use of miracles, as we have said already elsewhere, and as we shall see again . . . powers [miracles] did plainly prove that Christ descended from heaven.[84]

17. Scriptural support: "This man came to Jesus by night and said to Him, 'Rabbi, we know that You are a teacher come from God; for no one can do these signs that You do unless God is with him'" (John 3:2).

Preaching Purpose and Motivation of Verses 34–38

Preaching purpose: To correct the pride of the Jews that kept Gentiles out of the kingdom of God. To show that everyone, and only those ones, who fear God and work righteousness are acceptable to Him. To declare the same word of peace with God through repentance and faith in Jesus that was preached to Israel beginning with John, because Jesus is Lord not just of Israel but of all. To remind his hearers that they know this word and can check what Peter says with what they have heard. To declare that Jesus is the Messiah because God anointed Him with the Holy Spirit and power, and Jesus lived a life of good works and miracles, proving God was with Him.

Motivation for use today: Preachers should declare that God has no bias or favorites of any kind. The only way to be acceptable to God is to truly fear Him and live a life of obedience to His commandments, which is nothing else but the fruit of living faith. Preachers should assure their audiences that they are preaching the same gospel that was preached by John the Baptist, Jesus, Peter, and all the apostles, in order to better commend the truth of their words. Preachers should offer peace with God to all through Jesus Christ, which is possible because Jesus is Lord of all. They should teach about Jesus' life, especially His righteousness and mercy, and the many miracles He did, even those which required Him to overcome

[84] Calvin, *Commentaries*, vol. XVIII, 444–45.

the power of Satan. They should proclaim that Jesus was able to do these works because God was with Him. And, consequently, these miracles proved that He was anointed by God with the fullness of the Holy Spirit and with power.

Peter seeks to motivate God's people:	The way in which Peter seeks to move them:
1. To know that God shows no favorites or biases.	1. By his own example of accepting and treating all alike, and by solemn testifying to this teaching about God.
2. To fear God and do works of righteousness to be accepted by Him.	2. By promising acceptance with God to all who do these things.
3. That peace with God is by the preaching of Jesus Christ.	3. By reminding them that this gospel was the one preached in Israel by John.
4. To know that this peace is offered to them and it is certain.	4. By declaring that Jesus is Lord of all, and God sent this word of peace.
5. To know that God appointed Jesus and gave Him His Spirit and power.	5. By declaring Jesus' good works and his mightiest miracles.

Verses 39–41

"And we are witnesses of all things which He did both in the land of the Jews and in Jerusalem, whom they killed by hanging on a tree. Him God raised up on the third day, and showed Him openly, not to all the people, but to witnesses chosen before by God, even to us who ate and drank with Him after He arose from the dead" (Acts 10:39–41).

Καὶ ἡμεῖς ἐσμεν μάρτυρες πάντων ὧν ἐποίησεν ἔν τε τῇ χώρᾳ τῶν Ἰουδαίων καὶ ἐν Ἱερουσαλήμ· ὃν καὶ ἀνεῖλον κρεμάσαντες ἐπὶ ξύλου. Τοῦτον ὁ θεὸς ἤγειρεν τῇ τρίτῃ ἡμέρᾳ, καὶ ἔδωκεν αὐτὸν ἐμφανῆ γενέσθαι, οὐ παντὶ τῷ λαῷ, ἀλλὰ μάρτυσιν τοῖς προκεχειροτονημένοις ὑπὸ τοῦ θεοῦ, ἡμῖν, οἵτινες συνεφάγομεν καὶ συνεπίομεν αὐτῷ μετὰ τὸ ἀναστῆναι αὐτὸν ἐκ νεκρῶν.

1. Peter summarizes Jesus' life and death.
2. The apostles' witness to Jesus' supernatural powers and good works is grammatically emphasized: "Emphatically he say that he and the rest of the apostles are eyewitnesses of all that Jesus did throughout the land of Israel."[85]
3. The Jews should have accepted the supernatural witness of Christ's many miracles, but instead they murdered Him. Peter mentions the witness now so that these Gentiles would believe.[86]
4. By implication Peter assumes that Jesus' life of good works and miracles should have caused His people to believe in Him, and since they did not, their sin was greater. God Himself is seen in Jesus' miracles.
5. Scriptural support: "If I had not done among them the works which no one else did, they would have no sin; but now they have seen and also hated both Me and My Father" (John 15:24).
6. Peter declares Jesus' resurrection on the third day.
7. The apostles were divinely chosen to be official witnesses of Christ's resurrection, making it more and not less certain. Nothing is left to chance.[87]
8. Peter has already been attested to by miracle in the

[85] Kistemaker, *Acts*, 394.

[86] "*And we be witnesses.* That he may make his words to be believed, he saith, that he and his fellows in office saw with their eyes all those things which they spake concerning Christ." Calvin, *Commentaries*, vol. XVIII, 445.

[87] "For the certainty of the resurrection was proved by many and firm testimonies, and this was profitable to exercise the faith of the godly to believe the gospel rather than their eyes." Ibid., 446.

supernatural vision given to Cornelius, commending Peter (see Acts 10:4–6).

9. The miraculously attested apostles not only saw the resurrected Jesus, but they ate and drank with Christ after He rose from the dead. He grammatically emphasizes Christ's appearance to the apostles as part of their being His chosen, official witnesses: "'ἡμῖν . . . 'is emphatic."[88]
10. He proclaims the quality of that supernatural witness. They did not merely see Him from a distance, at a glance, or in a moment, but they ate and drank with Him; they sat down with Him for hours at a time.
11. Peter's purpose is to show how the proclaimed fact of the resurrection is based upon official, God-appointed, eyewitness testimony.[89]
12. Scriptural support: "For we did not follow cleverly devised tales when we made known to you the power and coming of our Lord Jesus Christ, but we were eyewitnesses of His majesty" (2 Peter 1:16 NASB).
13. In setting forth such convincing evidence for the resurrection of Christ, by implication, we can see that Peter assumes that when God's people see the evidence for the truth of the resurrection they will believe it.
14. "For if we sin willfully after we have received the knowledge of the truth, there no longer remains a sacrifice for sins" (Heb. 10:26).

[88] Kistemaker, *Acts*, 398.

[89] "Peter proclaims the good news of Jesus' resurrection and thus introduces his apostolic office. With the other apostles, Peter is a witness of the resurrection (1:22). He is a witness to Jesus' entire ministry, but this witness culminates in testifying to his resurrection." Ibid., 395. "Therefore, let us assure ourselves of this, that the holy apostles were chosen by the holy decree of God, that by their testimony the truth of Christ's resurrection might stand . . . if we covet to have God the sure author of our faith, let us learn to be content with the witnesses whom in due time he hath brought forth, as it were, by his hand, being ordained by him before the world was made." Calvin, *Commentaries*, vol. XVIII, 446.

Verses 42–43

"And He commanded us to preach to the people, and to testify that it is He who was ordained by God to be Judge of the living and the dead. To Him all the prophets witness that, through His name, whoever believes in Him will receive remission of sins" (Acts 10:42–43).

Καὶ παρήγγειλεν ἡμῖν κηρύξαι τῷ λαῷ, καὶ διαμαρτύρασθαι ὅτι αὐτός ἐστιν ὁ ὡρισμένος ὑπὸ τοῦ θεοῦ κριτὴς ζώντων καὶ νεκρῶν. Τούτῳ πάντες οἱ προφῆται μαρτυροῦσιν, ἄφεσιν ἁμαρτιῶν λαβεῖν διὰ τοῦ ὀνόματος αὐτοῦ πάντα τὸν πιστεύοντα εἰς αὐτόν.

1. Peter declares that Jesus commanded the apostles:
    a. to preach to the people and to testify . . .
    b. that Jesus is the one ordained by God . . .
    c. to be the judge of the living and of the dead.
2. Thus the authenticity and therefore the credibility of the gospel rest upon the official testimony of the apostles.[90]
3. Peter proclaims that Jesus is also the Savior:
    a. All the prophets testify that salvation is through the name of Jesus.
    b. All the ones believing in Him are forgiven their sins.
4. Peter wants these Gentiles to see the truth of his testimony and thereby believe in the name of Jesus. They must see that Jesus has the power and the authority to deliver them from the judgment by forgiving their sins.[91]

[90] "In the word *testify* there is great weight; because, as men are naturally inclined unto unbelief, the simple preaching of the gospel should not be so effectual, unless the Lord should establish it with strong protestations." Ibid., 448.

[91] "Peter warns the members of his audience to seek forgiveness of sin through faith in Jesus Christ, so that when they appear before the God-appointed judge they may be acquitted." Kistemaker, *Acts*, 396–97.

5. There is an implied urgency: Since Jesus is the judge of the *living*, they are either to be forgiven right now or continue in the state of being condemned.[92]
6. Peter also is urging that the word of the disciples is the Word of Jesus.
7. Scriptural support: "He who believes in Him is not condemned; but he who does not believe is condemned already, because he has not believed in the name of the only begotten Son of God" (John 3:18).
8. Peter again brings in all the prophets as witnesses to Jesus for certification. In this repeated emphasis of apostolic preaching, Calvin finds a motivation that modern day preachers must imitate:

> This point is very needful to be known, that the grace which was offered at length by Christ is the same which the law and the prophets, in times past, delivered unto the fathers to be hoped for. And surely it was of great force with Cornelius and such like, who did greatly reverence the law and the prophets, that they might know that that was performed and accomplished in very deed in Christ which was testified in the oracles of the prophets. Therefore, to the end the ministers of the Church may agree with the prophets in their form of teaching, let them study by preaching to set forth Christ; let them continually testify that we must seek righteousness at his hands alone.[93]

[92] "The apostles must warn the people that God has set a judgment day and has already appointed Jesus to serve as judge . . . by having appointed Jesus as judge, God declares that Jesus is equal to himself. Both God the Father and God the Son will judge the people on the judgment day." He cites, "Gen. 18:25; Judg. 11:27; John 5:22, 27; 9:39; Rom. 2:16; 14:9–10; 2 Tim. 4:1; 1 Peter 4:5." Kistemaker, *Acts*, 396.

[93] Calvin, *Commentaries*, vol. XVIII, 450–51.

9. In verse 44, God supernaturally confirms that Peter's doctrine is correct by visiting the same miracle of tongues upon the Gentiles.[94]

Preaching Purpose and Motivation of Verses 39–44

Preaching purpose: To declare the apostolic eyewitness to Jesus' life of righteousness and good works. To declare Jesus' unjust crucifixion and death. To declare Jesus' bodily resurrection on the third day by God. To declare the official apostolic witness of Jesus' bodily resurrection as specifically chosen by Jesus Himself. To declare that the preaching of the church is Jesus' continued proclamation to the world. To officially testify that Jesus is now and will be the judge of all men. To declare that all the Bible witnesses to the forgiveness of sins that comes by faith in Jesus.

Motivation for use today: Preachers must motivate people to believe in Jesus by demonstrating the truth of His miraculous life, resurrection, and salvation. They must emphasize the eyewitness testimony to Jesus' whole life of righteousness and miracles, in order to prove that He is from God. Preachers must teach that Jesus was unjustly crucified and killed. They must declare the truth of the bodily resurrection, and show how it is established on the official eyewitness testimony of the apostles, who were attested to by supernatural miracles and visions, and chosen by Jesus Himself. Preachers must proclaim that Jesus Himself commanded the preaching of His final judgment to cause men to fearfully turn from sin. They must encourage their hearers that the way of forgiveness is by faith in Jesus, as the whole Bible teaches.

[94] Ibid., 451; ""πεπεσέν . . . By this wonderful proof St. Peter and his Jewish brethren with him saw that, uncircumcised though they were, Cornelius and his household were no longer 'common or unclean.' 'The Holy Ghost,' said the Jews, 'never fell upon a Gentile.'" *Expositor's Greek*, 262.

Peter seeks to motivate God's people:	The way in which Peter seeks to move them:
1. To believe the truth of Jesus' righteous and miraculous life, and unjust crucifixion and death.	1. By proclaiming the many witnesses to Jesus life and death.
2. To believe God raised Jesus from the dead on the third day.	2. By the official eyewitness testimony of the apostles.
3. To believe the apostolic witness.	3. By showing how they were specifically chosen by Christ as official witnesses to His bodily resurrection. And they did not just see Him at a glance; they ate and drank with Him in intimate fellowship after He rose from the dead.
4. To believe in the preached word of the gospel.	4. By testifying that Jesus commanded it to be preached, so it is ensured by His power.
5. To know that Jesus is the judge of the living and the dead.	5. By teaching that the apostles testify to Jesus being the judge by the commandment and therefore by the power of Jesus.
6. To know that by believing in Him they have remission of sins.	6. By proclaiming that all the prophets bear witness to the fact that this is the way of forgiveness.

Paul's Sermon in the Synagogue: Acts 13:16–42

Speaker:	The apostle Paul (v. 16)
Audience:	Jews and Gentile God-fearers (vv. 16, 42)
Location:	The synagogue in Antioch of Pisidia (v. 14)

Occasion:	1. The Sabbath day after the reading of the Law and Prophets (vv. 14–15) 2. The rulers of the people spoke to Paul and his companions: "Men and brethren, if you have any word of exhortation for the people, say on" (v. 15).

Verse 16

"Then Paul stood up, and motioning with his hand said, 'Men of Israel, and you who fear God, listen'" (Acts 13:16).

Ἀναστὰς δὲ Παῦλος, καὶ κατασείσας τῇ χειρί, εἶπεν, Ἄνδρες Ἰσραηλῖται, καὶ οἱ φοβούμενοι τὸν θεόν, ἀκούσατε.

1. Paul commands both Jews and Gentiles to listen, implying both have an interest in the gospel of Christ.
2. God's people should be motivated to hear God's ministers in worship!

Verses 17–22

Paul summarizes Israel's history from Abraham to David. He emphasizes God's action, and mentions Israelite privilege, "The God of this people Israel chose our fathers" (v. 17), but also their failure: "He put up with their ways" (v. 18). Paul highlights:

1. God's choice of "our" fathers from "this" people Israel.[95]
2. God's exaltation of the people of Israel in Egypt.
3. God's deliverance of them from Egypt.
4. How God "put up with their ways in the wilderness" (v. 18).
5. God's destruction of the nations in Canaan.
6. God's distributing the land to His people.

[95] "τουτου: this points back to Ἰσρ. An appeal to the national pride of the people in their theocratic privileges and names." *Expositor's Greek*, 291.

7. God gave them judges.
8. They asked for a king and God gave them Saul.
9. God removed Saul and raised up David, who was a man after God's heart and would do God's will. Paul now has their attention on the promised Christ.[96]
10. Paul's purpose in giving this summary is to lead them to Jesus Christ: "Paul . . . speaketh nothing but that which is most convenient for the present purpose. His purpose is to bring the Jews unto the faith of Christ."[97]
11. Throughout this summary, all of the actions are ascribed to God except when Israel asked for a king. The consistent emphasis seems to be on God's power and blessing upon Israel. Paul is recounting those past acts of God's salvation, which were chief in mind of the Jewish believer, as a prelude to help them better see the necessary culmination, which has now finally come in Christ's accomplishment of salvation.[98] Paul sought to motivate them by establishing this truth: The hope of Israel culminated in Christ.

Verses 23–25

"From this man's seed, according to the promise, God raised up for Israel a Savior—Jesus—after John had first preached, before His coming, the baptism of repentance to all the people of Israel. And as John was finishing his course, he said, 'Who do you think I am? I am not He. But behold, there comes One after me, the sandals of whose feet I am not worthy to loose'" (Acts 13:23–25).

Τούτου ὁ θεὸς ἀπὸ τοῦ σπέρματος κατ' ἐπαγγελίαν ἤγαγεν τῷ Ἰσραὴλ σωτηρίαν, προκηρύξαντος Ἰωάννου πρὸ προσώπου τῆς εἰσόδου αὐτοῦ βάπτισμα μετανοίας τῷ Ἰσραήλ. Ὡς δὲ

[96] Calvin, *Commentaries*, vol. XVIII, 520.

[97] Ibid., 515.

[98] "Verses 17–22 correspond to an ancient confessional summary. . . . These events, in fact, constitute an Old Testament *kerygma* which is summarized in

ἐπλήρου ὁ Ἰωάννης τὸν δρόμον, ἔλεγεν, Τίνα με ὑπονοεῖτε εἶναι; Οὐκ εἰμὶ ἐγώ. Ἀλλ' ἰδού, ἔρχεται μετ' ἐμέ, οὗ οὐκ εἰμὶ ἄξιος τὸ ὑπόδημα τῶν ποδῶν λῦσαι.

1. Paul continues to show God's faithfulness to Israel and he ties in the coming of Christ and of John the Baptist as part of that faithfulness: "[He] brought to Israel a Savior" (NASB) and "John . . . proclaimed . . . [to] Israel," (NASB) but His focus is on the seed and His exaltedness.[99]
2. Jesus is clearly raised up according to the promise of God to save by a seed of David. And he is raised up "for" or "to Israel" (ESV, NASB).
3. Jesus is the Savior, the seed of David, the fulfillment of the promised Messiah.
4. Paul also adduces John the Baptist's witness to the greatness of Jesus as a further proof of Christ. Clearly Paul's audience knew who John was, and had a high opinion of him.[100]
5. John prepared for the coming of Jesus by preaching repentance to all the people of Israel.
6. Paul's purpose is to show how Jesus is the fulfillment of the promised seed of David who is the Messiah.[101]

Paul's address as a prelude to the New Testament *kerygma*[,] . . . the inevitable sequel to God's dealings with his people." Bruce, *Acts*, 254.

[99] "Emphatic position of τουτου. Of this one from the (his) seed." Robertson, *Word Pictures*, 189; see also Kistemaker, *Acts*, 476.

[100] "Paul bringeth in [John's] testimony, that he may prove to the Jews that he preached no false Christ, but the true Christ of God, whom that most famous forerunner had before commended," for "all men almost did think [John] to be a prophet of God." Calvin, *Commentaries*, vol. XVIII, 522.

[101] "After providing a brief historical survey of the Old Testament Scriptures, Paul is going to show their fulfillment in Jesus. He is ready to point out that God has fulfilled the promise of the Messiah's coming through Jesus Christ." Kistemaker, *Acts*, 474.

Preaching Purpose and Motivation of Verses 16–25

Preaching purpose: Paul wanted the people to listen to him. He identifies and equates Israelites with God-fearers. Thus, Paul declares what really counts with God is fearing Him. He wanted them to see how the history of God's saving acts in Israel was by the power of God and that the people of Israel were helpless and sinful. Paul shows how the Old Testament bears witness to Jesus. Paul recounts this history to show that the promise of the Christ is God's ultimate salvation to Israel, to which everything else pointed. Thus, he concludes his summary of Israel's history with the coming of Jesus, the fulfillment of the promise to David. Paul wants his audience to know that God raised up Jesus even as He performed all His previous saving acts for Israel. Paul identifies Jesus' God-given office with the messianic title: Savior. Paul then adduces John the Baptist's witness to Jesus to prove that Jesus is the Christ. Paul indicates that preaching repentance prepares the way for Christ. Finally he cites John's testimony of the greatness of Jesus—John said Jesus was incomparably higher than himself, and John was the only true prophet in four hundred years!

Motivation for use today: As Paul addressed his audience with respectful and honorable titles in calling them to listen, so should ministers today. Ministers should remind their audiences that it is only those who fear God who can truly be God's people. Ministers should show how the Old Testament bears witness to Jesus, and how the history of Israel points to Jesus, and how Jesus is sent from God to save His people. They should show how Jesus came as God's official Savior, to encourage people that Jesus comes to save and is able to save. They should show how Israel did nothing to save themselves or to earn their salvation but even continually rebelled against God. They should show how God called His people back from sin through the preaching of repentance. Ministers must declare John the Baptist's witness to Jesus to prove Jesus is the Christ and greater than even the most exalted prophet.

Peter seeks to motivate God's people:	The way in which Peter seeks to move them:
1. To understand that all those and only those who fear God are acceptable to Him.	1. By equating "Men of Israel" with "you who fear God." This implies that the true Israelites are those who fear God, and those who fear God are of Israel.
2. To see how God saved Israel in spite of their impotence and unworthiness.	2. By recounting the history of God's saving acts and Israel's sins in the Bible.
3. To see how the whole Old Testament bears witness to Jesus.	3. By showing how saving history continued to build to this climax, citing particularly God's promise to raise up the seed of David as Messiah.
4. To see that Jesus is from God, the Savior to God's people.	4. By teaching that God raised up Jesus and sent Him to be the Savior for His people.
5. To know that the preaching of repentance prepared for Jesus.	5. By adducing the witness and ministry of John the Baptist, who preached repentance to prepare the way for the Lord.
6. To understand that John the Baptist identified Jesus as the Christ and that no man is worthy to serve Him in the lowest service.	6. By citing John's testimony to this effect.

Verse 26

"Men and brethren, sons of the family of Abraham, and those among you who fear God, to you the word of this salvation has been sent" (Acts 13:26).

Ἄνδρες ἀδελφοί, υἱοὶ γένους Ἀβραάμ, καὶ οἱ ἐν ὑμῖν φοβούμενοι τὸν θεόν, ὑμῖν ὁ λόγος τῆς σωτηρίας ταύτης ἀπεστάλη.

1. Paul's urging is increased as the names he addresses his audience by goes from two in v. 16, to four here in v. 26.
2. These terms are more intimate (brothers).[102] Paul more closely identifies with his audience in order that they would listen.[103]
3. Though he continues to emphasize Jewish privilege, he never ceases to include God-fearing Gentiles in his address. Paul equally includes both the sons of Abraham and the God-fearing Gentiles together in the one group: brothers.
4. Astonishingly God has sent his salvation equally to Jews and to God-fearing Gentiles: "To you the word of this salvation has been sent" (v. 26).
5. He urges the Jews to be faithful to their family and claim their inheritance, and so invokes their father Abraham to move them thereunto.[104]
6. The whole hopes and longings of the people of God from Abraham on have now come to pass—they can have all that was promised if they receive this word, for it is the word of salvation. Paul's passion for His people is genuine, and palpably expressed.[105]
7. Paul pleads with them to listen to what he is saying. Paul is confident that his argument is true and that the Israelites will be persuaded by it if they rightly consider his words with a desire to embrace what is true.
8. Paul's underlying assumption is that God will only convert them as they see the truth.
9. We notice again that fearing God is the emphasized

[102] "ανδρες αδελφοί, the address of ver. 16 is here renewed in more affectionate tones." *Expositor's Greek*, 294.

[103] "'Men and brothers' . . . Paul's tone of voice is intimate because he speaks to fellow Jews . . . and in his desire to acquaint them with Jesus Christ, he calls them 'men and brothers.'" Kistemaker, *Acts*, 477.

[104] "He calleth them *children of Abraham* . . . that they may know that they be heirs of eternal life" Calvin, *Commentaries*, vol. XVIII, 523–24.

[105] "*Men and brethren*. Paul doth again prick forward the Jews to embrace

disposition or emotion attributed to the true worshipper of God.

Verse 27

"For those who dwell in Jerusalem, and their rulers, because they did not know Him, nor even the voices of the Prophets which are read every Sabbath, have fulfilled them in condemning Him" (Acts 13:27).

Οἱ γὰρ κατοικοῦντες ἐν Ἱερουσαλὴμ καὶ οἱ ἄρχοντες αὐτῶν, τοῦτον ἀγνοήσαντες, καὶ τὰς φωνὰς τῶν προφητῶν τὰς κατὰ πᾶν σάββατον ἀναγινωσκομένας, κρίναντες ἐπλήρωσαν.

1. The reason why the word has been sent to them is that the leaders of the nation have rejected it. They rejected Jesus and the prophets.
2. Paul warns the men of Antioch not to repeat Jerusalem's apostasy and in so doing he answers the strongest possible objection to his sermon.[106] This provides a strong external motivation to not be like the unfaithful majority.
3. Paul proves their fault by showing that the reason they condemned Jesus was that they did not know him. Moreover, this ignorance was sinful, considering that they heard the prophets speak of Him every week.[107]
4. The fact that God's Word about Him was proclaimed to them every week only aggravated the evil of their sin in rejecting Him: "Thus doth Paul teach how monstrous their unbelief was, that he may make the hearers loathe it."[108]

Christ. . . he speaketh to them so fair that it might not grieve them to depart from the scribes and priests." Ibid.

[106] *Calvin's Commentary*, XVIII, *Acts*, 525.

[107] "This ignorance mitigated the degree of their guilt, but it did not remove it, for it was willing ignorance and prejudice." Robertson, *Word Pictures*, 191.

[108] Calvin, *Commentaries*, vol. XVIII, 527.

5. Paul motivates to faith by magnifying the evil of unbelief!
6. Paul's argument assumes that God's Word spoken by prophets is to be held by the common people above all human authority and to be believed.
7. Their rejection of the prophets, made manifest in their condemning of Jesus, only fulfilled them. God's sovereign will is established in and through their rebellion. Again, this commends Christ's power and successful mission.
8. Once more God's sovereignty and man's responsibility are both stressed.
9. The implication is that a faithful Jewish remnant is now being sought for outside of the land of Israel. For Antioch this news provides a double external motivation: a judgment to be feared and avoided, and an opportunity of great blessing to be seized.

Verses 28–32

"And though they found no cause for death in Him, they asked Pilate that He should be put to death. Now when they had fulfilled all that was written concerning Him, they took Him down from the tree and laid Him in a tomb. But God raised Him from the dead. He was seen for many days by those who came up with Him from Galilee to Jerusalem, who are His witnesses to the people. And we declare to you glad tidings—that promise which was made to the fathers" (Acts 13:28–32).

Καὶ μηδεμίαν αἰτίαν θανάτου εὑρόντες, ᾐτήσαντο Πιλάτον ἀναιρεθῆναι αὐτόν. Ὡς δὲ ἐτέλεσαν πάντα τὰ περὶ αὐτοῦ γεγραμμένα, καθελόντες ἀπὸ τοῦ ξύλου, ἔθηκαν εἰς μνημεῖον. Ὁ δὲ θεὸς ἤγειρεν αὐτὸν ἐκ νεκρῶν• ὃς ὤφθη ἐπὶ ἡμέρας πλείους τοῖς συναναβᾶσιν αὐτῷ ἀπὸ τῆς Γαλιλαίας εἰς Ἱερουσαλήμ, οἵτινές εἰσιν μάρτυρες αὐτοῦ πρὸς τὸν λαόν. Καὶ ἡμεῖς ὑμᾶς εὐαγγελιζόμεθα τὴν πρὸς τοὺς πατέρας ἐπαγγελίαν γενομένην

1. Paul continues to declare the wickedness of "those who dwell in Jerusalem, and their rulers" of the previous verse:
    a. They condemned a man whom they knew was innocent.
    b. They asked Pilate to put Him to death.
2. Yet God's sovereignty overruled all these things—all they did was accomplish God's plan for Jesus, and then God raised Him up.
3. Paul, point by point, proves that Jesus of Nazareth is the Messiah and that everything in His life and even in His death evidences this fact. Paul motivates his audience by proclaiming and proving the truth about Jesus.[109]
4. Christ's real death, the resurrection, and the many witnesses to it are stressed.[110]
5. Calvin notes how Paul again seeks to motivate by the truth proven: It was "Paul's drift in this place . . . to prove Christ's resurrection."[111]
6. Note the two pronouns at the beginning of v. 32: ἡμεῖς ὑμᾶς; Kistemaker asserts that they "are juxtaposed for emphasis and inclusiveness."[112]
7. The glad tidings of Jesus' victorious reign, as seen especially in his resurrection, is the promise of salvation made to David through His seed.

Preaching Purpose and Motivation of Verses 26–32

Preaching purpose: Paul passionately pleads with his audience to hear and receive the truth, multiplying phrases of respect

[109] "Paul seeks to convince the audience that Jesus of Nazareth indeed is the Messiah." Kistemaker, *Acts*, 479.

[110] "οἵτινες. . . . is not causal but emphatic . . . and means 'these very people are now witnesses.'" Ibid., 482.

[111] Calvin, *Commentaries*, vol. XVIII, 529.

[112] Kistemaker, *Acts*, 490; "Paul becomes personal with the use of the pronoun '*we*.' . . . In the Greek, the pronouns in this verse are pronounced: '*we*

(men), identification (brothers), and biblical approbation (sons of Abraham, and you who fear God). He wants them to know that God has purposely and sovereignly sent the word of salvation to them. This word is from God and for them, therefore, it has the highest commendation and they can trust it. He wants them to know that part of the reason this word of salvation has come to them now is because those most privileged to hear it have rejected it. He magnifies their sin, even as he declares their ignorance, by showing that their ignorance was culpable. He proclaims God's sovereignty and man's responsibility. He declares how Christ's execution was an unjust murder, yet God was accomplishing His will for the Christ in spite of the intentions of wicked men. He declares Christ's burial to magnify the miracle of His resurrection, which he proves by the testimony of official witnesses over many days. Paul concludes that all of these things are the fulfillment of God's promises to Israel, and hence they are most glad tidings to all true Israelites.

Motivation for use today: Preachers should speak respectfully, personally, and passionately to their audiences, identifying with them. They should commend to them biblical categories like the true sons of Abraham and people who fear God. They should assure their audiences that God has deliberately sent His word of salvation to them. They should warn them how the Israelites had this word preached to them and rejected it to the point where they became God's enemies and killed their own messiah. They should then be shown how God sovereignly accomplished His good will in and through the wicked acts of sinful men. They must declare the real death, burial, and bodily resurrection of Jesus Christ, which they must prove by the official apostolic witness that occurred over many days. They must show how this whole plan of salvation was what God promised to the fathers of Israel from Abraham on, so that they can see the good news that it is.

---

ourselves proclaim this good news *to you.*'" Ibid., 482.

Peter seeks to motivate God's people:	The way in which Peter seeks to move them:
1. To commend salvation to the true sons of Israel, that is to those who fear God.	1. By grouping "sons of Abraham" and "you who fear God" together as the intended audience for the salvation of the gospel.
2. To receive the word of salvation.	2. By passionately declaring that God Himself has sent them this word.
3. To be warned by the example of the Israelites who did not receive it and so became God's enemies and condemned the Messiah.	3. By teaching how the people of Israel misinterpreted the Scriptures and rejected their witness to Jesus' exalted person.
4. To know that God's sovereign plan for Jesus was accomplished through these evil acts.	4. By showing from the Old Testament how Jesus' passion was predicted.
5. To know that Christ's execution was an unjust murder by wicked men.	5. By declaring the testimony and admission of His killers that they had no cause to put Him to death.
6. To know that Jesus was really dead and buried.	6. By proclaiming His Roman-ordered execution, crucifixion, and entombment.
7. To believe that God raised Jesus from the dead.	7. By proclaiming the many witnesses to it over many days.
8. To believe the eyewitnesses to Jesus' resurrection.	8. By showing how Jesus appointed "His witnesses" from "those who came up with Him from Galilee" (the official apostolic witness chosen by Christ).
9. To know that these things are the fulfillment of all God's promises to Israel.	9. By showing how all the promises God made to His people in the Old Testament are fulfilled in Christ.

Verses 33–37

"God has fulfilled this for us their children, in that He has raised up Jesus. As it is also written in the second Psalm: 'You are My Son, today I have begotten You.' And that He raised Him from the dead, no more to return to corruption, He has spoken thus: 'I will give you the sure mercies of David.' Therefore He also says in another Psalm: 'You will not allow Your Holy One to see corruption.' For David, after he had served his own generation by the will of God, fell asleep, was buried with his fathers, and saw corruption; but He whom God raised up saw no corruption."

ὅτι ταύτην ὁ θεὸς ἐκπεπλήρωκεν τοῖς τέκνοις αὐτῶν ἡμῖν, ἀναστήσας Ἰησοῦν• ὡς καὶ ἐν τῷ ψαλμῷ τῷ δευτέρῳ γέγραπται, Υἱός μου εἶ σύ, ἐγὼ σήμερον γεγέννηκά σε.

Ὅτι δὲ ἀνέστησεν αὐτὸν ἐκ νεκρῶν, μηκέτι μέλλοντα ὑποστρέφειν εἰς διαφθοράν, οὕτως εἴρηκεν ὅτι Δώσω ὑμῖν τὰ ὅσια Δαυὶδ τὰ πιστά. Διὸ καὶ ἐν ἑτέρῳ λέγει, Οὐ δώσεις τὸν ὅσιόν σου ἰδεῖν διαφθοράν• Δαυὶδ μὲν γὰρ ἰδίᾳ γενεᾷ ὑπηρετήσας τῇ τοῦ θεοῦ βουλῇ ἐκοιμήθη, καὶ προσετέθη πρὸς τοὺς πατέρας αὐτοῦ, καὶ εἶδεν διαφθοράν• ὃν δὲ ὁ θεὸς ἤγειρεν, οὐκ εἶδεν διαφθοράν.

1. God has fulfilled the promise of salvation in raising up Jesus to the office of Messiah.
2. God has fulfilled this promise for us, the living Israelite children. Again a strong plea to the Israelites to receive their inheritance, not only for themselves, but for their children.
3. Your inheritance is ready for you now! The promise is now fulfilled. That is why these tidings should be so glad!
4. In Isaiah 55:3 the "sure mercies of David" include God's everlasting covenant.
5. In true Jewish fashion, Paul connects these τὰ ὅσια Δαυὶδ with τὸν ὅσιόν σου in order to solidify his case. The gift

of "the holy faithful things of David" is given in God's not allowing "Your Holy One" to see corruption. Thus, Paul uses the same Scripture-interprets-and-strengthens-Scripture technique, which we saw in Peter, to prove from Scripture that Jesus can never die.

6. The thrust of his argument is that because Jesus is alive, He infallibly gives you all these things, therefore receive them.[113]
7. Paul quotes several psalms to prove that Jesus, and not David, fulfilled these prophecies, because Jesus, not David, rose from the dead.
8. As in Peter's argument in Acts 2, having proven the resurrection of Christ has clinched the case. David's body rotted in the grave, Jesus' body did not. Therefore, these passages refer to Jesus, not David.
9. In the final verse we see God's sovereignty and David's obedience. This verse is better translated by the NASB and ESV to read, "For David, after he had served the purpose of God in his own generation, fell asleep."[114] By this rendering we see another contrast between David's temporal service which ended, and Christ's which will never come to an end.[115]
10. Paul indicates that these Jews and God-fearers should rejoice that they should be so fortunate as to be the generation that should see all these long-awaited promises come to pass. Paul stresses the truth of these things presuming that

[113] "Hilgenfeld . . . justly remarks that the speech which was intended to move the Israelites to a recognition of Jesus as the promised Saviour of the seed of David, would have been imperfect, unless it had set forth His sufferings and after-resurrection." *Expositor's Greek*, 296.

[114] "The direct object of this verse is God's desire, that is, God's purpose. For this reason, translators and interpreters favor the reading, "He served God's purpose in his own generation." Kistemaker, *Acts*, 486.

[115] "τῇ τοῦ θεοῦ βουλῃ with ἐκοιμήθη . . . the contrast drawn between David serving the counsel or purpose of God for one, or during one generation, whilst in Christ the eternal purpose of God was realized." *Expositor's Greek*, 296.

as they see the truth, the godly will be motivated to embrace it with joy.

Verses 38–39

"Therefore let it be known to you, brethren, that through this Man is preached to you the forgiveness of sins; and by Him everyone who believes is justified from all things from which you could not be justified by the law of Moses" (Acts 13:38–39).

Γνωστὸν οὖν ἔστω ὑμῖν, ἄνδρες ἀδελφοί, ὅτι διὰ τούτου ὑμῖν ἄφεσις ἁμαρτιῶν καταγγέλλεται• καὶ ἀπὸ πάντων ὧν οὐκ ἠδυνήθητε ἐν τῷ νόμῳ Μωϋσέως δικαιωθῆναι, ἐν τούτῳ πᾶς ὁ πιστεύων δικαιοῦται.

1. As if these things were not clear enough already, Paul makes it even more explicit. The grammar expresses how important Paul viewed his words.[116]
2. He appeals to them as "men, brothers" both nouns in the vocative, though for some reason only "brothers" makes it into English translations. Paul earnestly desires them to hear these things.[117]
3. "Therefore, let it be known to you"; Know this for certain, for it is true: motivation given through assurance of truth.
4. "That through this Man"; Jesus is the one brings ultimate salvation: the forgiveness of sins. Paul here declares Christ's office.[118]

[116] "Paul introduces this news first by a weighty statement, 'Therefore, . . . let it be known to you . . .' and then by the familiar address men and brothers. The statement actually means that Paul is about to proclaim something of utmost importance. Further, the repetitious address means that Paul and his listeners are on the same level in respect of finding remission of sin." Kistemaker, *Acts*, 487.

[117] "This glorious message Paul now presses home in his exhortation." Robertson, *Word Pictures*, 194.

[118] "After he hath declared the mean whereby salvation is purchased through

5. v. 39: literally: "and from all the things which you are not able in the law of Moses to be justified, in this Man every one believing is justified" (translation mine).
    a. Incredible statement of justification by faith alone apart from the works of the law![119]
    b. The graciousness of this free salvation has been so emphasized.
    c. Paul sought to humble Jewish pride in works righteousness.[120]
6. By spelling out how privileged they are to be the generation to behold these things; how clearly God has proven this salvation; how great it is; and how gracious; Paul has done much to motivate these Jews to be saved.
7. Many commentators notice the similarity between Peter and Paul. Here is one example: "So far the words represent the entire harmony between the preaching of St. Peter and St. Paul."[121]

Verses 40–41

"Beware therefore, lest what has been spoken in the prophets come upon you: 'Behold, you despisers, marvel and perish! For I work a work in your days, a work which you will by no means believe, though one were to declare it to you'" (Acts 13:40–41).

Christ, he doth now intreat of his office and power. And this is the principal point, to know what good thing we have by the coming of Christ, and what we are to hope for at his hands." Calvin, *Commentaries*, vol. XVIII, 540.

[119] "This is a characteristic Greek sentence with the principal clause at the end and Pauline to the core. . . . The climax is at the close and gives us the heart of Paul's teaching about Christ." Robertson, *Word Pictures*, 194.

[120] "Now we see Paul's drift and purpose; to wit, that he meant to draw away the Jews from the false and perverse confidence which they reposed in the law; lest being puffed up, they should think that they had no need of Christ's help." Calvin, *Commentaries*, vol. XVIII, 542.

[121] *Expositor's Greek*, 297.

Βλέπετε οὖν μὴ ἐπέλθῃ ἐφ' ὑμᾶς τὸ εἰρημένον ἐν τοῖς προφήταις, Ἴδετε, οἱ καταφρονηταί, καὶ θαυμάσατε, καὶ ἀφανίσθητε• ὅτι ἔργον ἐγὼ ἐργάζομαι ἐν ταῖς ἡμέραις ὑμῶν, ὃ οὐ μὴ πιστεύσητε, ἐάν τις ἐκδιηγῆται ὑμῖν.

1. Now Paul emphasizes the other side of the message: To spurn so great and gracious a salvation is to show horrendous contempt for God.
2. Both verses begin with an imperative "to warn the people of impending judgment if they fail to heed the warning."[122]
3. Paul quotes a passage from Habakkuk 1:5 in the LXX, which speaks to the great judgment that was coming upon Israel by the Chaldeans—a judgment they could not escape. It came though they did not believe in it.[123]
4. To not believe in this great salvation, proven truth as it is, is to be a despiser, a scoffer. To hear the truth and to reject it is to be without excuse. Such a one is liable only to judgment. Paul provides a powerful external motivation of horrific judgment as he passionately seeks to move his audience.[124] Calvin believed that modern ministers are to do the same:

    Habbakuk prophesieth of the destruction brought upon them by the Chaldeans; but the punishment whereby God

[122] Kistemaker, *Acts*, 491.

[123] "Ye despisers (οἱ καταφρονηταί,). Not in the Hebrew, but in the LXX. It is pertinent to Paul's purpose. . . . Paul has hurled a thunderbolt at the close." Robertson, *Word Pictures*, 195.

[124] "Paul first exhorts his listeners to pay attention to what the Old Testament prophets have declared. . . . Likewise, Paul warns the worshipers in Pisidian Antioch to listen to the message of salvation and to put their faith in Jesus Christ. . . . Paul instructs his audience to take a close look at what is happening. Those who scoff at the message of salvation are rejecting God himself. . . . Abruptly Paul ends his sermon to attain maximum effect. Never before had his audience heard such 'a message of encouragement' (v. 15)." Kistemaker, *Acts*, 488–89.

revenged the contempt of his gospel was more cruel, [severe]. Therefore, let us accustom ourselves to fear God and reverently embrace his word, lest some such things befall us.[125]

5. Here we see the justice of God, if they will not marvel at their salvation, they will be made to marvel at their destruction.
6. As strong of a motivation as was the goodness of the promised salvation, so also is the badness of this destruction.[126] Paul is powerfully calling on them to be saved—"for why should you die, O house of Israel?" (Ezek. 18:31)—only on account of their willful blindness.

Verses 42–43

"So when the Jews went out of the synagogue, the Gentiles begged that these words might be preached to them the next Sabbath. Now when the congregation had broken up, many of the Jews and devout proselytes followed Paul and Barnabas, who, speaking to them, persuaded them to continue in the grace of God" (Acts 13:42–43).

Ἐξιόντων δὲ ἐκ τῆς συναγωγῆς τῶν Ἰουδαίων, παρεκάλουν τὰ ἔθνη εἰς τὸ μεταξὺ σάββατον λαληθῆναι αὐτοῖς τὰ ῥήματα. Λυθείσης δὲ τῆς συναγωγῆς, ἠκολούθησαν πολλοὶ τῶν Ἰουδαίων καὶ τῶν σεβομένων προσηλύτων τῷ Παύλῳ καὶ τῷ Βαρνάβᾳ· οἵτινες προσλαλοῦντες, ἔπειθον αὐτοὺς ἐπιμένειν τῇ χάριτι τοῦ θεοῦ.

1. v. 42: Amazing that the Gentiles would respond to what was such a Jewish gospel emphasis. Paul had addressed them in his opening verse, but from then on the address was heavily Jewish, pleading with his countrymen with many Old

[125] Calvin, *Commentaries*, vol. XVIII, 546.

[126] "With true rhetorical force St. Paul concludes his speech, as at Athens, by an appeal to awaken all consciences." *Expositor's Greek*, 298.

Testament verses and allusions, although there is much manuscript evidence for the critical text's reading of "the people" rather than "the Gentiles" of the Byzantine family.

2. They begged to hear more of the right interpretation of God's Word about the salvation that is in Jesus Christ. Paul's sermon (by the sovereign grace of God) had motivated "many" (v. 43) of them.[127]
3. v. 43: Clearly, whatever the correct reading of v. 42, many of both Jews and Gentiles "followed" Paul and Barnabas, meaning here that they received their words and wanted to learn from them.
4. Sincerely following the apostles, truly receiving their words, is being in the grace of God, according to this verse.
5. Ministers are to persuade, convince, and win over believers to continue to be hearers and doers of the Word of God; they do this by speaking to them.[128]

Preaching Purpose and Motivation of Verses 33–41

Preaching purpose: Paul seeks to show his audience that in the resurrection of Jesus, God has fulfilled the promise of salvation to Israel and to their children, implying that this is the fullness and final salvation for all time. He shows that Jesus being the Messiah and even Son of God is by God's plan (raised up to His office, see v. 33). Paul proves from Old Testament passages that the resurrection of the Messiah was the plan of God all along. Like Peter, Paul proves that these passages could not apply to David by citing undeniable historical facts. David did not rise again from the dead, rather his body rotted in his grave, but Jesus was raised from the dead, thereby fulfilling this text and proving to be the promised Messiah. Paul indicates that because Jesus will never die ("no more to return

[127] "Paul's words aroused intense interest in a large part of his congregation." Bruce, *Acts*, 263.

[128] "The verb to continue indicates that the people already have put their trust in Jesus and have accepted him as their Messiah." Kistemaker, *Acts*, 492.

to corruption" v. 34), He is able to give forgiveness of sins to all who believe in Him. Paul wants his audience to know and believe that the law of Moses cannot justify them but faith in Jesus will. Upon setting forth such gracious salvation, Paul wants his audience to soberly consider the judgment of God that will come upon those who reject it, for the certainty of both the salvation of those who receive Him and the judgment of those who reject Him is established by the same prophetic witness. To not believe is to bring a frightful blinding upon yourself.

Motivation for use today: Preachers should allure people to receive the salvation of Christ by assuring them of the certainty of it. We must proclaim that God Himself has fulfilled the promises He made to all Old Testament saints in the person and work of Jesus Christ. We must declare that it was God's perfect plan to send Jesus as the Messiah and as His Son. Preachers must declare that this fulfillment is seen in the bodily resurrection of Jesus Christ. They must show how large this salvation is; that it is to them and to their children. They must prove from Old Testament passages that only Jesus fulfilled those verses prophesied of the Messiah. They must also point to undeniable historical facts, such as David's corpse decaying in his tomb, to show that Jesus alone fulfilled these prophecies. They must establish the certainty of Christ's salvation on the basis that He is still alive, can never die, and it is by His authority (through His name) that forgiveness of sins is assured to all who believe in Him. They must also show the impossibility of any works saving you; that even through perfect obedience to the law of God one cannot be forgiven of their sins. They must explain that justification is by faith alone and not by the works of the law of Moses. They must also threaten and warn their hearers that even as God did not spare His unbelieving and therefore disobedient people in the Old Testament, neither will he spare any who do not sincerely receive this message. They must declare that this terrifying judgment is just as certain as the promised salvation as it is solemnly proclaimed by the exact same prophets.

Paul seeks to motivate God's people:	The way in which Paul seeks to move them:
1. To know that God has fulfilled His promise of salvation for us and for our children.	1. By presenting Jesus as holding the office of Messiah and Son.
2. To know that He raised up Jesus to be the Messiah, and indeed His Son.	2. By showing this from the prophecies of Scripture.
3. To know that God bodily raised Jesus from the dead to live forever.	3. By showing that David wrote of Christ's bodily resurrection and incorruptibility.
4. To believe that David prophesied that Jesus would be raised from the dead.	4. By showing from undeniable facts that David could not have written about himself since he did not rise again from the dead, but rotted in the grave.
5. To know the certainty of the promise of forgiveness in Christ.	5. By understanding the necessary consequence of these passages that Jesus lives forever and has commanded this forgiveness to be preached in His name.
6. To know that for everyone (God has no favorites) forgiveness is by believing in Jesus.	6. By teaching that this is His promise, which He keeps by His authority and power.
7. To know that not even the perfect law of God (and therefore anything else) can bring forgiveness of sins, but that justification is solely by faith in Christ.	7. By teaching that the law is not able (ἠδυνήθητε) to justify sinners and that Christ, by His conquest of death and the grave, has proven that He is.
8. To know that everyone who rejects this message will suffer horrible judgment, making them hopelessly blind to the things of God.	8. By showing that God did not spare His unbelieving people in the Bible, but as they rejected His Word, they became more and more spiritually blind.

Paul's Sermon at Athens: Acts 17:22–34

Speaker:	The apostle Paul (v. 22)
Audience:	Men of Athens (v. 22), including women (v. 34); Epicurean and Stoic philosophers (vv. 18–20); certain foreigners (v. 21).
Location:	The Areopagus or court of Athens (v. 19)
Occasion:	1. Epicurean and Stoic philosophers encountered Paul in the marketplace and decided to give him an official hearing (vv. 18–19). 2. They wanted to know what Paul's doctrine meant (vv. 19–20). 3. At least some wanted to hear merely because it was "new" (v. 21).

Verses 22–23

"Then Paul stood in the midst of the Areopagus and said, 'Men of Athens, I perceive that in all things you are very religious; for as I was passing through and considering the objects of your worship, I even found an altar with this inscription: TO THE UNKNOWN GOD. Therefore, the One whom you worship without knowing, Him I proclaim to you'" (Acts 17:22–23).

Σταθεὶς δὲ ὁ Παῦλος ἐν μέσῳ τοῦ Ἀρείου πάγου ἔφη, Ἄνδρες Ἀθηναῖοι, κατὰ πάντα ὡς δεισιδαιμονεστέρους ὑμᾶς θεωρῶ. Διερχόμενος γὰρ καὶ ἀναθεωρῶν τὰ σεβάσματα ὑμῶν, εὗρον καὶ βωμὸν ἐν ᾧ ἐπεγέγραπτο, Ἀγνώστῳ θεῷ. Ὃν οὖν ἀγνοοῦντες εὐσεβεῖτε, τοῦτον ἐγὼ καταγγέλλω ὑμῖν.

1. "Men of Athens": Polite, formal address of respect and courtesy.
2. "You are very religious" (δεισιδαιμονεστέρους): "A very neutral word (from *deido*, to fear, and *daimon*, deity)."[129]

[129] Robertson, *Word Pictures*, 284.

a. I side with the early Greek and the modern commentators and translations that Paul means this statement in a good sense and not as a rebuke.[130] "[I]t is incredible that St. Paul should have commenced his remarks with a phrase calculated to offend his hearers."[131]

b. In commending their religiosity, Paul did not praise idolatry, neither did he compromise Christianity. It is not possible that Paul was just using a rhetorical flourish to, in effect, duplicitously commend them for something that he knew was wrong, and so just did it to gain their favor. That is called lying. Paul did not begin his official address to the city of Athens with a lie. Thus, I disagree with:

    i. "Paul . . . calls them with kindly ambiguity."[132]

    ii. "In the context of the speech, Paul uses the term affirmatively, because he is interested in gaining the attention of the Athenian crowd. To complete his commendation, he even adds the words *in every respect*."[133]

c. Paul is speaking to them out of real compassion for their souls, acknowledging that they were right in

[130] "Very religious"–NKJV, NASB, ESV, NIV, RSV, NET; R. C. Sproul, Derek Thomas, Kistemaker, F. F. Bruce, Jamieson, Fausset, Brown, John Gill, A. T. Robertson, Marvin Vincent; "superstitious"–KJV, GNV; Calvin, Matthew Henry. See also: "Acts 17:22 it must mean *devout, religious* (so X., Cyr. 3, 3, 58, Ages. 11, 8; Aristot, Pol. 5, 11 p. 1315a)," BDAG 1760; δεισιδαιμονεστέρους—"Since this is an introduction where Paul is trying to gain his audience, the dominant idea is probably this positive sense (BAGD 173) [*sic*]. Later, he will tell them that their religiosity is wrongheaded." Darrell L. Bock, *Acts* (Grand Rapids, MI: Baker, 2009), 564.

[131] *Expositer's Greek*, 370. A. T. Robertson refers to the negative translation as "unlikely;" akin to Paul "giv[ing] this audience a slap in the face at the very start," *Word Pictures*, 285.

[132] John Henry Thayer, trans., rev., and ed., *A Greek-English Lexicon of the New Testament* [1889] (*Bibleworks* Software), 1231.

[133] Kistemaker, *Acts*, 231.

being religious, but (as he will soon show them) correcting their idolatrous expression of religion.

d. Thus, Matthew Henry praises the sermon: "[A]n admirable discourse it is, and every way suited to his auditory and the design he had upon them."[134]

e. Paul sincerely compliments the good, which by the common grace of God, remained even in their idolatry. They recognized that they should worship a higher order of being. That was good, it admitted their purpose of existence, and at that point, they were better than many atheistic or agnostic societies today.

f. In complimenting the good he finds in them before addressing their sins, Paul reflects the usual approach Christ took with the seven churches in Revelation 2–3.

g. Paul seeks to instruct and correct in order to win them for God, not to rebuke them without first showing the reason, which would then only be a prideful assertion of his own religious superiority: Paul's purpose was "to bring the men of Athens unto the true God. For they were persuaded that there was some divinity; only their preposterous religion was to be reformed."[135]

3. v. 23, γὰρ—"Paul gives an illustration of their religiousness from his own experiences in their city."[136] Paul demonstrates why he says they are religious. They have altars to gods all over the place, even to ones they do not know. Paul's comment on them being religious was not a lie or a rhetorical device, it was true. They were religious. A blind man could have seen it. In speaking truthfully, but not for flattery or

[134] *Matthew Henry's Commentary on the Whole Bible Complete and Unabridged in One Volume* (Peabody, MA: Hendrickson, 2012), 1713.

[135] *Calvin's Commentaries*, vol. XIX, trans. William Pringle, *Acts 14–28*; *Romans 1–16*, book 1, (Grand Rapids, MI: Baker, 2003), 157.

[136] Robertson, *Word Pictures*, 285.

even to gain their attention, Paul sets the tone: He is interested in the truth, and that is what he will tell them.

4. Paul seeks to correct their ignorance, which they themselves admitted in the words inscribed on this altar.[137]
5. Paul speaking with such respect and fairness to such crass pagans would surely have been motivating to all who (by the grace of God) were interested in honest speech.
6. "I proclaim to you." Paul declares his office as an authorized herald of this unknown God.[138] Here, he motivates with right authority as a herald. As an official spokesman sent to them, they owe Paul a hearing out of rightful respect for lawful authority and out of common courtesy. The grammar indicates Paul claimed this official status.
7. Bullinger finds a *hyperbaton* in this verse, a figure of speech where words are taken out of their usual order for emphasis: "The true emphasis is here brought out by the *Hyperbaton* . . . 'What therefore, unknowing, ye reverence, this I—even I, announce to you.'"[139]
8. There is an order to motivating in sermons. Thus, it was necessary for Paul to preach the things he did, before he declared the faith of the gospel.[140]
9. Calvin sees Paul purposely arguing not from Scripture, but from nature: "He showeth by natural arguments who and what God is, and how he is rightly worshipped."[141]

[137] "Paul doth not in this place [v. 23] commend that which the men of Athens had done; but taketh from their affection, though it were corrupt, free matter for teaching." Calvin, *Commentaries*, vol. XIX, 157. "Since they acknowledged their ignorance of the divine nature, he would tell them the truth about it." Bruce, *Acts*, 336.

[138] "'I am proclaiming to you.' He speaks on behalf of God and thus his authority is divinely decreed." Kistemaker, *Acts*, 632.

[139] E. W. Bullinger, *Figures of Speech Used in the Bible* (Grand Rapids, MI: Baker, 1997), 695.

[140] Calvin, *Commentaries*, vol. XIX, 154.

[141] Ibid.

Preaching Purpose and Motivation of Verses 22–23

Preaching purpose: Paul's purpose is to teach them who God is in order to call them to the right worship of Him. His initial purpose in speaking is to do what they have asked him to do (v. 20), even though some asked him merely out of vain curiosity (v. 21). So he begins to speak in order to tell them the doctrine that he believes. As one compassionate for their souls, Paul compliments the remnant of truth that by the common grace of God remained with them, even when the expression that flowed from it was sinful. As God with the Ninevites (Jonah 4:11), Paul was truly concerned about their souls. He then cites an area where they admitted ignorance and from that accurate confession he finds his starting point to teach them who God is and how He is rightly worshipped.

Motivation for use today: Preachers need to use respectful addresses appropriate to the occasion. In speaking to people who know very little about God, preachers must begin slowly. Graciously, they should look for something right in them before they begin to show them their sin and call them to repentance. Ministers should then begin to speak about the most important things of God that their audiences have corrupted: who God is, how He is worshiped, and so on. The minister should truly learn about the people he is going to preach to, so that he can correct their sinful corruption as he does. If he can find a place where they admit ignorance or error, he should use that admission to gently begin to instruct them. The minister must not feign these things, but pray to God that he would honestly and truly care for the people he is going to speak to, so that he would want to do these things sincerely, out of love for them. He should make sure his audience knows that he is an authorized ambassador for Christianity.

Paul seeks to motivate God's people:	The way in which Paul seeks to move them:
1. To hear his words.	1. He addresses them in a respectful and appropriate way: He does not flatter them; he does not insult them.
2. To see that it is good to be religious.	2. He proclaims in a complimentary fashion that they are religious.
3. To see that Paul had examined and considered their practices in the area he was going to address.	3. He tells them how he observed their worship and their gods.
4. To give them true knowledge of who their "unknown God" is.	4. He declares that he is here to officially proclaim this God.

Verses 24–25

"The God who made the world and everything in it, being Lord of heaven and earth, does not live in temples made by man, nor is hc served by human hands, as though he needed anything, since he himself gives to all mankind life and breath and everything" (Acts 17:24–25 ESV).

Ὁ θεὸς ὁ ποιήσας τὸν κόσμον καὶ πάντα τὰ ἐν αὐτῷ, οὗτος, οὐρανοῦ καὶ γῆς κύριος ὑπάρχων, οὐκ ἐν χειροποιήτοις ναοῖς κατοικεῖ, οὐδὲ ὑπὸ χειρῶν ἀνθρώπων θεραπεύεται, προσδεόμενός τινος, αὐτὸς διδοὺς πᾶσιν ζωὴν καὶ πνοὴν κατὰ πάντα·

1. Paul begins with proclaiming God as the sole Creator of all that is.
2. He begins where he does to address the problem he has just introduced: He is here to explain the God about whom they confess their ignorance.

3. He begins where the problem was: The Athenians did not doubt the existence of the divine; they were ignorant of the true God and His rightful worship. They did not know the promise of the Christ and its recent fulfillment. Thus, he does not argue for the existence of God, when that was not the Athenian problem. Neither does He begin with proving Jesus is the Messiah, since that was a meaningless concept to them.
4. Likewise, Paul cites no Scripture since they had no knowledge of it. Instead he teaches them the doctrines of Scripture from reason. Thus, Calvin: "Furthermore, because he had to deal with profane men, he draweth proofs from nature itself; for in vain should he have cited testimonies of Scripture."[142]
5. Thus, Paul continues by extrapolating from the doctrine of creation he has just articulated to declare that God is absolute owner and ruler of all things.
6. Here we have proof that Paul was not seeking to deceitfully flatter the Athenians in his opening words, for his very first point is to teach a doctrine they all rejected (in the Greek religious tradition): the doctrine of creation.[143]
7. The argument depends upon logic, drawing conclusions from antecedents and building one upon another. The reasoning is tight:
    a. Since God created all things:
        i. He is Lord of heaven and earth.
        ii. He does not and cannot live in dwellings made by men.
        iii. He cannot be served by human hands.
            1. For this would suggest that He needed some *thing*.
            2. But He gives to all:

[142] Calvin, *Commentaries*, vol. XIX, 157–58; see also Kistemaker, *Acts*, 633.
[143] "Stoic philosophy . . . has no doctrine of creation." Kistemaker, *Acts*, 633.

   a. Life,
   b. Breath (continued life),
   c. And all things.
8. Paul's motivation in these statements is the truth, as established by the undeniable authority of rational thought.
9. Paul's underlying assumption is that the Athenians, like all men, cannot rightly deny demonstrated, logically proven truth.

Verses 26–28

"And He has made from one blood every nation of men to dwell on all the face of the earth, and has determined their preappointed times and the boundaries of their dwellings, so that they should seek the Lord, in the hope that they might grope for Him and find Him, though He is not far from each one of us; for in Him we live and move and have our being, as also some of your own poets have said, 'For we are also His offspring'" (Acts 17:26–28).

ἐποίησέν τε ἐξ ἑνὸς αἵματος πᾶν ἔθνος ἀνθρώπων, κατοικεῖν ἐπὶ πᾶν τὸ πρόσωπον τῆς γῆς, ὁρίσας προστεταγμένους καιροὺς καὶ τὰς ὁροθεσίας τῆς κατοικίας αὐτῶν• ζητεῖν τὸν κύριον, εἰ ἄρα γε ψηλαφήσειαν αὐτὸν καὶ εὕροιεν, καί γε οὐ μακρὰν ἀπὸ ἑνὸς ἑκάστου ἡμῶν ὑπάρχοντα. Ἐν αὐτῷ γὰρ ζῶμεν καὶ κινούμεθα καί ἐσμεν• ὥς καί τινες τῶν καθ' ὑμᾶς ποιητῶν εἰρήκασιν, Τοῦ γὰρ καὶ γένος ἐσμέν.

1. After declaring the sovereignty and self-sufficiency of God from the doctrine of creation, and deducing certain conclusions about God's independence from resistless logic, Paul proclaims the biblical truth, that all men are created equal, because this was the way God made man. This teaching was an affront to both Greek and Jewish superiority.[144]

[144] "Of one blood . . . the unity of the human race with a common origin . . .

2. This truth was also rationally self-evident and incontestable. All men undeniably have the same blood, that is, life.
3. Paul asserts this self-evident truth as proof of God's power and goodness.
4. Paul avers that God's sovereignty over and care of men includes where and when they live, showing not only that God rules over all, but that He notices and cares for all men.[145] God made man for the purpose of living.[146]
5. Paul teaches that this sovereign disposal and care of man is not just for his temporal wellbeing in this physical world, but that God made man to know and desire God.[147] Thus the creation declares the glory of God.
6. So Paul concludes the nearness of God to all men if they would but use the sufficient means He gave them for the purpose He intended: that they would know and fellowship with God.[148]
7. Thus it is man's privilege and duty to seek God, implying that it is due to sin when he does not seek or find Him.[149]

---

runs counter to Greek exclusiveness . . . and to Jewish pride." Robertson, *Word Pictures*, 287; see also Bruce, *Acts*, 337.

[145] ἀπὸ ἑνὸς ἑκάστου ἡμῶν "The words may well have struck a responsive chord in the hearts, not only of some in the crowd, but of some of the Stoics who were listening . . . the expression of belief in the fatherly love and goodness of God." *Expositor's Greek*, 376.

[146] "*For to dwell* (κατοικεῖν) Infinitive (present active) of purpose, so as to dwell." Robertson, *Word Pictures*, 287.

[147] After Paul speaks of the nature of God he moves to show them "that men must be very careful to know God, because they be created for this same end, and born for that purpose." Calvin, *Commentaries*, vol. XIX, 164.

[148] "The Apostle now proclaims the nearness of God, not only in creation, in its maintenance and preservation, but in the spiritual being of man . . . οὐ μακρὰν: the word implies not mere local nearness, but spiritual." *Expositor's Greek*, 375.

[149] "Paul doth give us to understand, that their own sluggishness is the cause that they cannot perceive that God is present. . . . Neither doth Paul intreat in this place of the ability of men, but he doth only show that they be without excuse, when as they be so blind in such clear light, as he saith in the first

8. The grammar emphasizes God's nearness.[150]
9. God made man for the purpose of seeking in order to find Him.[151]
10. God's demonstrated goodness, power, generosity, and care for man are all powerful motivations for the Athenians to want to be reconciled to this God.
11. Paul quotes a pagan poet again not to criticize this idolatrous expression to Zeus, nor to sinfully praise it, but to merely notice the common grace truth it expresses: In the true God we do live and move and have our being.[152] He is not afraid to illustrate his argument from pagan idolaters.[153] Thus: "He citeth half a verse out of Aratus, not so much for authority's sake, as that he may make the men of Athens ashamed; for such sayings of the poets came from no other fountain save only from nature and common reason."[154]
12. Making them ashamed in this fashion is giving an internal motivation to seek this God, to any listener who, by the grace of God, will just admit this truth and thereby seek to follow it. Paul's doctrine here is that men will be saved when they come to the knowledge of, that is sincerely embrace, the truth.
13. Scriptural support: "[God] who desires all men to be saved and to come to the knowledge of the truth" (1 Tim. 2:4); "And you shall know the truth, and the truth shall make you free" (John 8:32).

---

chapter to the Romans, (Rom. i. 20)." Calvin, *Commentaries*, vol. XIX, 166–67.

150 "The negative οὐ rather than the usual μή with the participle makes an emphatic negative. Note also the intensive particle γε" Robertson, *Word Pictures*, 289.

151 ζητεῖν τὸν κύριον: infinitive of purpose "*That they should seek God.*" Robertson, *Word Pictures*, 288.

152 "Originally ascribed to Zeus, yet Paul takes their corrupt knowledge and speaks to the truth that was in it." *Expositor's Greek*, 376.

153 Bruce, *Acts*, 338.

154 Calvin, *Commentaries*, vol. XIX, 169.

14. Again we see Paul focused on the exact error of the Athenians: They do not rightly worship God; or, which is nearly the same thing, they do not worship the right God.
15. How gently Paul exposes their sinful practices in this sermon as compared with the other sermons! The different audience called for a different tone: "There is indeed a difference of emphasis," here in Paul's speech as compared to what he wrote in Romans 1–3, Bruce writes:

    In that letter Paul writes to established Christians, while here he is trying to gain a hearing from pagans; but there is no hint in the speech that the Athenians' confessed ignorance of the divine nature was blameless. Even some of their own teachers . . . had perceived, however dimly, how near God was to those who truly sought him.[155]

16. Paul humbles himself and exalts the Athenians as having equal human dignity and worth in the eyes of God by identifying himself with them through first person plural pronouns, even as he corrects their shameful idolatry of which he had never been guilty. Here we see an astonishing act of compassion and humility on the part of the exalted and knowledgeable apostle: He uses first person plural pronouns throughout this section to identify his common humanity with these ignorant, idolatrous pagans![156]
17. The pagan poet was right when he said all men were God's offspring, even though he did not acknowledge and submit to the true God, and so Paul commends the truth of his words as a powerful motivation to come to this God, whose truth was clearly seen everywhere.

[155] Bruce, *Acts*, 338.
[156] See *Expositor's Greek*, 376.

Preaching Purpose and Motivation of Verses 24–28

Preaching purpose: To teach from nature and reason what the Scriptures reveal about who the true God is in His creation and in His sovereignty over and goodness to man, and to gently show man's sin in not pursuing this good God. To affirm that God made all things, and therefore He rules over and owns all things, and therefore He cannot possibly live in man-made dwellings. To show that this spiritual, and eternal, and all-powerful God cannot possibly be benefited or served by creatures that He made or worshipped through created things, because He Himself gave and continues to sustain the life and breath of all living things; thus, we need everything from Him and He needs nothing from us. To declare that all men are created equal and that God is totally sovereign over the lives of men, that this sovereignty is disposed to man's good, that God has created man for the high privilege and duty of knowing and seeking out God that man might dwell with Him, and that God has made this very easy since all that man does is, in a sense, in God. Paul illustrates how near God is by quoting the truth about God that some pagan Greek poets had written.

Motivation for use today: Preachers should teach from nature and from reason basic truths of the Bible, especially if their audience has no familiarity with Scripture. They should move logically from God, to creation, to show how worshipping this God through the creation is folly. Then they should proclaim God's absolute sovereignty over all things and His utter independence from His creation, and yet they should show how God cares for His creation and gives and sustains all life. They should extrapolate from these truths the equality of all man, and that it is man's greatest duty and privilege, and in fact, his responsibility to seek this God in order to fellowship with Him. Ministers should encourage their audiences as to how near God is, illustrating this point by showing how general revelation has taught unbelievers truths about God, even though they wrongly apply them. Throughout, ministers must humbly identify with sinful people in the misery of their sin, and in the glory of their creation, proclaiming that all men are equally the offspring of God.

Paul seeks to motivate God's people:	The way in which Paul seeks to move them:
1. To know who God is.	1. By declaring that God is the Creator of all things.
2. To know that God does not dwell in man-made temples.	2. By deducing from His being the Creator that He is Lord of all creation.
3. To know that God is not worshipped with men's hands.	3. By concluding that He cannot need anything from the creature for he made and sustains all things, including therefore, all men.
4. To know that God is the author and sustainer of all life.	4. By deducing this conclusion from the fact that God is sovereign over all.
5. To know that all men are created equal by God.	5. By declaring the self-evident truth that He made them all from one blood, and therefore the different races and people groups are by His will.
6. To know that God is totally sovereign over all men.	6. By declaring His predestination of the times and locations of all nations.
7. To know that men are responsible to seek and find God.	7. By declaring that God has exercised His sovereignty to the end that man would know Him, for that is man's purpose.
8. To know the nearness of God in that all that we do is in a sense in God and that we are the image of God.	8. By showing the truth of these things from the "prophets" of general revelation and common grace: illustrating how these truths about God and man's being are found even in idolaters, though they use them to suppress the truth.

Verses 29–31

"Therefore, since we are the offspring of God, we ought not to think that the Divine Nature is like gold or silver or stone, something shaped by art and man's devising. Truly, these times of ignorance God overlooked, but now commands all men everywhere to repent, because He has appointed a day on which He will judge the world in righteousness by the Man whom He has ordained. He has given assurance of this to all by raising Him from the dead" (Acts 17:29–31).

Γένος οὖν ὑπάρχοντες τοῦ θεοῦ, οὐκ ὀφείλομεν νομίζειν χρυσῷ ἢ ἀργύρῳ ἢ λίθῳ, χαράγματι τέχνης καὶ ἐνθυμήσεως ἀνθρώπου, τὸ θεῖον εἶναι ὅμοιον. Τοὺς μὲν οὖν χρόνους τῆς ἀγνοίας ὑπεριδὼν ὁ θεός, τὰ νῦν παραγγέλλει τοῖς ἀνθρώποις πᾶσιν πανταχοῦ μετανοεῖν• διότι ἔστησεν ἡμέραν, ἐν ᾗ μέλλει κρίνειν τὴν οἰκουμένην ἐν δικαιοσύνῃ, ἐν ἀνδρὶ ᾧ ὥρισεν, πίστιν παρασχὼν πᾶσιν, ἀναστήσας αὐτὸν ἐκ νεκρῶν.

1. Paul draws a conclusion from the tight, step-by-step argument that he is making, leading the pagan audience from a right understanding of God, to a right understanding of themselves, to now a right understanding of worship.[157]
2. Paul here appeals to the dignity of man that he has now established: "since we are the offspring . . . we ought not to think . . ." Man, as the image of God ought to aspire to the nobility that is his heritage. Thus, Paul proclaims man's duty.
3. Here we see that even as Paul could allure Israel to claim their covenanted heritage, so he can seek to motivate pagans to aspire to their noble heritage, not as the chosen people, but as the divine-image-bearing people. And as he identified with the Jews, so he humbly and compassionately identifies

[157] "With the adverb *therefore*, Paul indicates that he is ready to draw the conclusion and apply his message to the audience." Kistemaker, *Acts*, 638.

with these Greeks. He corrects them, but includes himself in the correction.[158]

4. It is the same incentive from a different starting point.
5. And the specific thing Paul appeals to man to do, in his God-likeness, is to not think a certain way, which is very similar to repentance.
6. People carrying God's image ought not to think that God, whom we are like, is like inanimate stone or metal or wood, shaped by creaturely man!
7. Paul's motivation appeals to their own dignity: We have been shaped by God, and it is our highest dignity to be like Him, so why would we seek to make Him so much less than ourselves? It is folly.
8. Here, as we have seen both Peter and Paul do, Paul ameliorates their guilt somewhat by showing them that though they may have thought such things in the past, today is the day to cast them off. Now they have been taught better. So, in order to get right with this God, whom we have been acting so foolishly toward, we must repent.
9. God is not going to put up with this foolishness forever; in fact, He has already appointed a day of judgment when absolute righteousness will be the bar.
10. The grammar clearly indicates that repentance is commanded because (διότι) the judgment day is established (ἔστησεν ἡμέραν).
11. So with the doctrine of coming, certain judgment, Paul urges repentance.[159] Thus, an external motivation in the form of a threat: Avoid this punishment.

[158] "St. Paul's plain and direct words were the utterances of a man who had in mind the severe and indignant protests of the Hebrew prophets, cf. Isa. 44:12— οὐκ ὀφείλομεν: at the same time the use of the first person plural again points to the conciliatory tone of the speech." *Expositor's Greek*, 377.

[159] Calvin, *Commentaries*, vol. XIX, 175; see also Kistemaker, *Acts*, 639.

12. As with creation, and a personal God, the doctrine of final judgment was offensive to the Greeks.[160]
13. Paul's purpose here is not only to show the way of salvation for man, but to defend the righteousness of God.[161]
14. Throughout his argument Paul depends upon the fact that their consciences will convict them and that they will see that the ignorance that they had, and to some degree still have, is no excuse. In fact, it reveals their blameworthiness for not removing it when it would be so easy to do.
15. Likewise, God has also appointed a certain man to be the judge, and the proof of this is this man's resurrection from the dead.
16. Here miracle proves Jesus, not as the Christ, but as the judge of all mankind, which is also how Peter proclaimed Jesus to the Gentiles at Caesarea (see Acts 10:42).
17. Paul's underlying assumption here, even to pagans, is that miracle proves the exalted nature of a person. All men inherently know that miracle is a conclusive and irrefutable divine attestation.
18. Paul does not quote a single word of Scripture but all that he teaches is entirely Scriptural.[162] Paul cites pagan poets, but the religion he teaches is entirely against paganism:

    [E]ven if the prophets are not formally quoted . . . the direct quotations from pagan poets, have their place as points of

[160] "Greek thought had no room for such an eschatological judgment as the biblical revelation announces." Bruce, *Acts*, 340–41.

[161] "And Paul (not that he might lay the fault and blame upon God, but that he might cut off occasion of curious and hurtful questions) said, that the world did err whilst God did wink." Calvin, *Commentaries*, vol. XIX, 174.

[162] "Strictly speaking, Paul's address in Athens is . . . a proclamation of the gospel . . . the basic elements of the gospel [are present:] sin, repentance, judgment, and the resurrection." Kistemaker, *Acts*, 640. To this could be added, creation, God, man, worship, providence, divine sovereignty, human responsibility, God's personal nature, monotheism, and Christ's death.

> contact with the hearers, and illustrate the argument in terms familiar to them, but they in no way commit the speaker to acquiescence in their philosophical presuppositions.[163]

19. And also:

> Paul uses these pagan features as points of contact with his audience but refuses to accommodate and compromise the gospel message. . . . Whether Paul faces a Jewish audience or a pagan assembly, he faithfully teaches the uncompromising truth of God's revelation.[164]

20. As we saw with Peter, Paul is respectful to and compassionate for his audience as he speaks. He identifies with them and pleads with them to heed his message. He is very gentle at times, yet he does not compromise the doctrines he preaches one bit. Paul plainly and unapologetically declared doctrines that he knew were almost entirely rejected and even ridiculed by the Greeks. And here in this last section he proclaims two more: the bodily resurrection and the final judgment.[165] Paul's chief concern, like Peter's, is to proclaim, defend, and establish the truth, and his desire is that men would admit and believe it.

Verses 32–34

"And when they heard of the resurrection of the dead, some mocked, while others said, 'We will hear you again on this matter.' So Paul departed from among them. However, some men joined him and

[163] Bruce, *Acts*, 342.

[164] Kistemaker, *Acts*, 641.

[165] "The idea of retribution beyond the grave would have been equally alien to the Stoic as to the Epicurean, and both Stoic and Epicurean alike would have ridiculed the idea of a resurrection of the body." *Expositor's Greek*, 380.

believed, among them Dionysius the Areopagite, a woman named Damaris, and others with them" (Acts 17:32–34).

Ἀκούσαντες δὲ ἀνάστασιν νεκρῶν, οἱ μὲν ἐχλεύαζον• οἱ δὲ εἶπον, Ἀκουσόμεθά σου πάλιν περὶ τούτου. Καὶ οὕτως ὁ Παῦλος ἐξῆλθεν ἐκ μέσου αὐτῶν. Τινὲς δὲ ἄνδρες κολληθέντες αὐτῷ, ἐπίστευσαν• ἐν οἷς καὶ Διονύσιος ὁ Ἀρεοπαγίτης, καὶ γυνὴ ὀνόματι Δάμαρις, καὶ ἕτεροι σὺν αὐτοῖς.

1. Paul's message is cut off; his bold declaration of the bodily resurrection was so absurd to them, Paul was not able to continue.[166]
2. However, we know from the response that Paul's gospel found good ground, for v. 34 notes several believers who became disciples as a result.
3. We conclude again that Paul was not seeking to flatter this pagan audience to gain a hearing. He was respectful. He was sincere. He was humble. He was compassionate for their souls. And though he spoke well, out of all of these dispositions, the one burning commitment throughout his sermon that comes through is his continual effort to bring to his audience the truth of God, man, salvation, and judgment. Paul looked for the Spirit of God to call His people from death to life, through his preaching of the truth of the gospel.

Preaching Purpose and Motivation of Verses 29–31

Preaching purpose: To show from the doctrines of man and God that the worship of false idols is shameful and degrading both

[166] "Notwithstanding, there is no cause why the ministers of the gospel should omit the preaching of the judgment which is enjoined them. Though the wicked do laugh and mock, yet this doctrine, which they go about to make of none effect, shall so gird them, that they shall at length perceive that they have striven in vain with their snare." Calvin, *Commentaries*, vol. XIX, 177.

to God and to man. To show that because of who they are, all men have a duty to no longer think wrongly about God. To declare that for a time God permitted nations to go on in this folly and reap the shameful results, but that time ended with the resurrection of Jesus Christ. God's patience is coming to an end. He is sending out a clear call to repent. All men of all places must get right with God by repenting from all of their previous wrong thinking, acting, and living. The final purpose of these verses is to urge the audience to repentance with the doctrine of a coming fixed judgment. In fact, we must show that God has already fixed the day and chosen the judge, and to give even more certainty to the truth of these things, God has proven who the judge is by raising Him from the dead. So we must preach the final judgment and the resurrection of Jesus Christ as incentives to repentance.

Motivation for use today: Preachers are to show their audiences the logical consequences of being made in the image of God. We need to live lives that reflect who we are. And we need to worship God in a way that is acceptable to Him, without any statues or pictures or anything made by man. The duty and nobility of right worship should be employed as motivations to it. Ministers should exhort idolatrous people, that while God has been patient, and they have been ignorant, the time for such things is over. Today is the day of salvation (see Heb. 3–4)! Preachers must command all men to repent as the only way to be reconciled to God and they should urge them to do so, due to the fact that a judgment day has been fixed by God and it is certain to come, and the righteousness of God will be the bar of that judgment. Preachers should also identify Jesus as the final judge, for God proved Him to be such when He raised Him from the dead. Ministers must show that Jesus is the judge by teaching the irrefutable proof of His bodily resurrection.

Paul seeks to motivate God's people:	The way in which Paul seeks to move them:
1. To think like the offspring of God about God.	1. Because it follows that this is our duty and our highest honor.
2. To not worship God through objects.	2. By reminding them that God's nature is not of created things.
3. To understand that God allowed a time of ignorance.	3. By declaring that the command to all to repent shows that time is over.
4. To repent.	4. Because judgment day is coming and righteousness is the standard.
5. To know that the judgment day has been fixed.	5. Because He has a Man ordained to be the judge.
6. To know that the Man who is to be the judge has already been appointed.	6. Because He has raised Him from the dead.
7. To know that this Man rose again from the dead.	7. By proclaiming the resurrection, and then presumably, if given the chance, Paul would have spoken of the witnesses to this event to establish it.

16

A Defense of Application

This work has sought to examine the sermons of Scripture in order to discover and record how inspired ministers of the Word endeavored to motivate their audiences in their preaching. Before we began our examination of Scripture, we looked at a brief survey of academic literature and studies, both secular and religious, to see what they had to say about motivation. We also observed the motivational methods of popular pastors, and we looked at a few examples from the Reformed tradition. We observed the definition and etymology of "motivation" and "motive." We then set forth our definition of motivation and our methodology of examination. Since ancient Greek did not have a word corresponding to "motivation," we included a study of koine Greek terms that often indicated motivation, according to how we are defining that term in this book. We were finally ready to begin our study.

To accomplish our goal we took the public speaking passages of Scripture that were the most similar to modern-day preaching situations. Five texts were clearly the best according to our criteria. We set forth a verse-by-verse exegesis of Scripture of each of those passages, solely with the aim of discovering motivation. We used grammatical reference works and lexicons, and we defended any motivational elements we claimed to find with Scripture and with citations from respected commentaries and language studies. We summarized our findings in paragraphs and numerical lists at the end of each section. The purpose of all of this detailed analysis was to enable modern-day pastors and congregants to incorporate and make use of biblical methods of motivation through sermons. What have we discovered?

Unique to Their Time?

The five passages were remarkably similar in some ways and very different in others. The similarities were chiefly doctrinal and structural, while the differences were largely in tone and emphasis.[1] Some of these similarities can be accounted for by the fact that in each scriptural sermon, the apostles were announcing to audiences, for the first time, the new epoch in the unfolding plan of salvation that had begun with the exaltation of the Messiah:

> The early apostolic preaching regularly comprises four elements (not always in the same order): (1) the announcement that the age of fulfillment has arrived; (2) an account of the ministry, death, and triumph of Jesus; (3) citation of Old Testament scriptures whose fulfillment in these events proves Jesus to be the one to whom they pointed forward; (4) a call to repentance.[2]

Thus, there was an anticipation-fulfillment context that was unique to the first proclamation of the gospel, as the Jewish people needed to be told that the new age of the Messiah had arrived. And indeed, this uniqueness can be used as the strongest objection to the method I have pursued in this book. My approach cries out for justification from the critic who asks: "How can I benefit from a motivational analysis of first-century apostolic preaching? All of your results can be said to be exceptional, since the unique

[1] See Appendices A, B.

[2] F. F. Bruce, *The Book of the Acts*, rev. ed. (Grand Rapids, MI: Eerdmans, 1988), 63.

preaching context of giving the first announcement of the coming of the Messiah will never be repeated—so what good does it do to study them?"

Doctrine and Mankind's Needs Are Unchanging

This criticism does not hold water for several reasons. First, no matter the context of proclaiming Jesus as the Messiah, whether it is for the first time or the ten-thousandth time, the doctrines of Christianity do not change; neither do the needs of sinful men. Thus, in his summary above, all four of Bruce's elements are just as important for us today, though the emphasis is different. However, this difference should not surprise us at all. It is always the case that some doctrines will be emphasized more than others, depending on the situation. During the Reformation we see Calvin and Luther stressing justification on the one hand and critiquing Romanism on the other. Yet who would claim that their unique context makes the preaching of Calvin and Luther obsolete to us today? Moreover, even within nearly identical contexts we can find a difference of emphasis. Of the five sermons examined in this book, none had a more similar context than the sermons Peter preached in Acts 2 and Acts 3. The sermons were at about the same time, in the same city, to the same nation, by the same preacher, yet their emphasis notably differs: "But whilst we may grant the common and identical aim of the two discourses, to proclaim the Messiahship of Jesus before the Jews, none can fail to see that in chap. iii., the Messianic idea becomes richer and fuller."[3]

In addition to varying degrees of emphasis, we find diverse applications in the preaching of the Bible even as we do in our sermons today. Of course there is a direct application that Peter makes to the Jews in two of his sermons; that they killed the Christ and that they saw His miracles, which we obviously cannot so directly apply

[3] R. J. Knowling, "The Acts of the Apostles," in *Apostles, Romans, First Corinthians*, vol. 2 of *The Expositor's Greek Testament*, ed. W. Robertson Nicoll (Peabody, MA: Hendrickson, 2002), 108.

to contemporary audiences. Yet, as I tried to show in my exegesis, it is still true that every believer is just as responsible for the death of Christ, insofar as Christ died for his sins. Likewise, believers today have the infallible record of all of the miracles before us, the cumulative testimony of which, Calvin says in various places, is greater than if we had seen some of them with our own eyes. They saw them directly; we see them indirectly, through the infallible Word.

Similarly, even though modern ministers cannot be witnesses of Christ and His resurrection in the way that the apostles were, who would say that they cannot then authoritatively preach His Word? Especially seeing that Christ gave not only apostles but pastors and teachers for the purpose of preaching His Word (see Acts 6:4; Eph. 4:11; 2 Tim. 4:2). The apostles witnessed to Christ directly, today's ministers do so indirectly, through His infallible Word. Thus, Kistemaker's remark about the early church could just as easily be applied to our day: "A characteristic theme that the apostles Peter and Paul express in their sermons appears in this sequence: You Jewish people killed Jesus; God raised him from the dead; and we apostles are witnesses."[4] Two thousand years later, we Christians killed Jesus by our sins; God raised Him from the dead; and we ministers bear witness through His Word.

Purpose of the Sermons Varied

Second, it simply is not true that all five of the sermons in our study had as their chief purpose the announcement of the coming of the Messiah to His people. The third sermon, in Acts 10, was preached by Peter to Gentiles. The Jewish-Messiah context could almost be seen as a hindrance in this situation. And, in fact, in this sermon Peter makes no attempt to prove that Jesus is the Christ, he simply calls Him "Jesus Christ" in his opening remarks (see Acts 10:36). Rather, to the Gentiles, Peter emphasizes Jesus as "Lord of

[4] Simon J. Kistemaker, *Exposition of the Acts of the Apostles* (Grand Rapids, MI: Baker, 2004), 129.

all," and "Judge of the living and the dead" (Acts 10:36, 42). Further, the only reference to the Jews is when Peter says "they killed him" (Acts 10:39). And in the final sermon of our study, Paul preaches to a pagan audience where he does not even mention the Scriptures, let alone the Christ! Thus, forty percent of our sample is not concerned with the announcement that the Messiah has come.

Christian Gospel Is Unchanging

Last, granting that we will never be in a situation where we will have to proclaim Christ as having just come to His people, what does that fact have to do with how we should seek to motivate in our sermons? Those who would dismiss my book as archaic must show that the motivation given by the apostles in their sermons is entirely outmoded for today. Yet, as long as the audience consists of sinners who need to believe and obey the gospel, and as long as the speaker is a minister who is called by God to proclaim that gospel, it seems safe to say that the motivation given and received will be very similar if not identical. This conclusion necessarily stands unless one can show that the apostles in Acts are not preaching the Christian gospel.

Accordingly, commentators note significant differences between the sermons of our study. "Paul's sermon at Athens" was quite different from those "which the apostles preached to the Jews." In sermons to the Jews, "their business was to lead their hearers by prophecies and miracles to the knowledge of the Redeemer, and faith in him"; in sermons to the heathen Paul sought "to lead them by the common works of providence to the knowledge of the Creator, and the worship of him."[5] Furthermore, various commentators see, in the few apostolic sermons of holy writ, an example that went well beyond the pages of Scripture, and is in fact, a model of the preaching of the early church:

[5] *Matthew Henry's Commentary on the Whole Bible Complete and Unabridged in One Volume* (Peabody, MA: Hendrickson, 2012), 1713.

> In summary form, this sermon is a type that Paul delivered throughout Asia Minor, Macedonia, and Greece.[6]

> C. H. Dodd is no doubt right in suggesting "that the speech before Cornelius represents the form of *kerygma* used by the primitive Church in its earliest approaches to a wider preaching."[7]

> If the address to Pisidian Antioch in 13:16–41 is intended to serve as a sample of Paul's preaching to a synagogue congregation, the present speech is equally well designed to serve as a sample of his preaching to pagans.[8]

My contention is that what was true for the early church period is still true today. Man, sin, and salvation have not changed. Having answered the potential criticism, we now give our analysis.

[6] Kistemaker, *Acts*, 468.

[7] Bruce, *Acts*, 212n48, citing C. H. Dodd, *The Apostolic Preaching and its Developments* (London, 1936), 56.

[8] Bruce, *Acts*, 334–35.

17

Biblical Motivation, Part One: The Substance

There is a common method of motivation seen in the sermons of Scripture. This motivation is given through the doctrine, tone, and disposition of the speaker. From our study we learned that the traditional categories of motivation are identified under content, approach, and emotion. Therefore, we will look at the doctrine as the content, the tone and compassion as the approach, and finally we will summarize our findings on the emotional motivation found in biblical sermons.

First we consider the doctrinal motivation. Each sermon contained a declaration of the glory, might, sovereignty, and goodness of God/Christ. These truths about God were taught from both special and general revelation, according to the preaching context. In every sermon the main actor was God: what God has done, what God is doing, what God will do.[1] Where man was mentioned, it was either in his helplessness or in his sin. Even in his first sermon to Gentile pagans, Paul does not hesitate to mention God's sovereignty in creation, providence, and the predestination of all things. This doctrine is pressed in all of the sermons for two reasons: (1) to show the inescapability and certainty of God's judgment, and (2) to show the goodness and power of God to save sinners.

[1] "In his gospel proclamation, Peter places the emphasis on God." Simon J. Kistemaker, *Exposition of the Acts of the Apostles* (Grand Rapids, MI: Baker, 2004), 93.

God's Judgment, Man's Sin, and the Call to Repent

We consider first God's judgment, which comes on account of man's sin. As noted above, every sermon in our study contains a declaration and conviction of man as a sinner. Consequently, those pastors who purposely avoid preaching against sin in order to "win" people entirely by "love," and "mercy," do not preach the sermons of Scripture. The preachers of Scripture preach against sin at every occasion. They personally and directly convict their audiences before the bar of God's justice as guilty sinners worthy only of condemnation before Him. Often they preach against sin in graphically personal terms: with "lawless hands," "you have delivered up and denied the Holy and Righteous One"; "You condemned Jesus even when wicked Pilate wanted to let Him go"; "You asked for a murderer to be released to you instead." The greatness of their evil is magnified as Peter charges them, "you killed the author of life." Thus, the preachers personally convict their hearers emphatically: "This Jesus whom you, you crucified (τοῦτον τὸν Ἰησοῦν ὃν ὑμεῖς ἐσταυρώσατε) is Lord."

Sometimes the conviction of sin is done with great severity and bluntness, but at other times with amazing gentleness and restraint: "I know you did it in ignorance" and "we ought not to think that the Divine Nature is like gold or silver or stone, something shaped by art and man's devising," but it is always a part of the sermon, even when it is only implied by the proclamation of baptism, remission of sins, and the coming judgment as in Acts 10. No doubt the difference in tone was due to what the context required as discerned by the preacher. So, for example, "The tone of the Areopagitica is different from that of Romans 1–3, but Paul knew the wisdom of adapting his tone and general approach to the particular audience or readership being addressed at the time."[2] Thus, Calvin taught that it was

[2] F. F. Bruce, *The Book of the Acts*, rev. ed. (Grand Rapids, MI: Eerdmans, 1988), 334.

the hardness or softness of heart in their audiences that caused the preachers of Scripture to alter their tone accordingly:

> Because he had to do with stiff-necked men, or at least there were divers in the company which were stiff-necked, (as if he meant with a hammer to soften their stubbornness,) he addeth a chiding unto doctrine. For if the Jews had been obedient and willing to obey, undoubtedly he would have sought sweetly to allure them unto Christ. But it was either their sluggishness, or else their willfulness, that caused him to be more angry. . . . He signifieth, indeed, that there is yet place left for repentance . . . yet, notwithstanding, he telleth them . . . the horrible vengeance of God is not far off.[3]

The great tragedy in not preaching against sin is that the minister does everlasting harm to the sinner even as he puts forth all his effort to make him feel good. In Jeremiah, God threatened fierce judgment against those preachers who refused to preach against sin:

> Therefore I will give their wives to others, and their fields to those who will inherit them; because from the least even to the greatest everyone is given to covetousness; from the prophet even to the priest everyone deals falsely. For they have healed the hurt of the daughter of My people slightly, saying, "Peace, peace!" When there is no peace. (Jer. 8:10–11)

The "healing" given by ministers who never preach against sin is a slight healing. It is entirely surface-oriented and feelings-based. Such preaching deals falsely; it does not deal truthfully with the

[3] *Calvin's Commentaries*, vol. XVIII, trans. William Pringle, *John 12–21; Acts 1–13*, book 2, (Grand Rapids, MI: Baker, 2003), 545.

sinner. It flows from covetousness; it desires praise and so it says words that are geared to gain praise for the speaker. These preachers claim to preach out of love, whereas in truth, they preach out of hate. However, it is precisely because they loved their audiences that the preachers of Scripture thundered against their sins: "[T]o the end he may prick their consciences with the feeling of sin, he saith that they slew him."[4] Biblical preaching seeks the true good of the listener, so that he would be motivated to repentance. Thus, "the fruit of the sermon . . . [is that] they were touched with feeling of sorrow; and secondly . . . they were obedient to Peter's counsel."[5]

The sermons of the Bible forthrightly addressed sin and thereby motivated their hearers who were moved, ultimately by God's sovereign Spirit, to confess their sin and repent in a true conversion. Thus, we recall the end result of Peter's fiery announcement at Pentecost: that "'this Jesus, whom you crucified [is] both Lord and Christ.' Now when they heard this, they were cut to the heart, and said to Peter and the rest of the apostles, 'Men and brethren, what shall we do?'" (Acts 2:36–37). Peter's direct and personal conviction brought about one of the most tender verses in all the book of Acts, as the people were savingly brought to true conviction. If man were not, from the bottom of his heart, a sinner, perhaps the method of wooing him to repentance by words exclusively of love and mercy would yield similar results. But the Bible teaches that man is a sinner, and the example of every faithful preacher from Enoch on (see Jude 1:14–15) is to preach repentance: "The call to repentance had been sounded by John and Jesus (and by Jesus' disciples in his name) in the years preceding the crucifixion, and it remained an essential element in the proclamation of the apostolic message."[6] How can it be that ministers today are doing it differently and claiming success? Either man has changed or their success is gloss.

Accordingly, every one of the sermons in our study placed a

[4] Ibid., 95.

[5] Ibid., 115.

[6] Bruce, *Acts*, 69.

strong emphasis on repentance—even in Peter's sermon at Caesarea, where the word repentance is not found. When Peter later recounted this sermon to the Jews, they described its successful reception by saying "Then God has granted to the Gentiles repentance to life" (Acts 11:18). Thus, the Scriptures' designation for the salvation of the Christian faith, "repentance to life." True repentance is sweet for it delivers from death and brings life. Consequently whenever repentance was commanded we saw that with it came the promise of "remission of sins," "receiv[ing] the . . . Holy Spirit" (2:38), "times of refreshing" (3:19), and "Jesus Christ [sent to you]" (3:20). And so God would have men motivated to repentance by the promise of salvation.

However, just as often, we saw men being motivated to repentance by the threat of God's judgment. In fact, all five of our sermons proclaimed or threatened the coming wrath and judgment of God:

> The coming of the great and awesome day of the LORD. (Acts 2:20)

> Every soul who will not hear that Prophet shall be utterly destroyed from among the people. (Acts 3:23)

> He who was ordained by God to be Judge of the living and the dead. (Acts 10:42)

> Beware therefore, lest what has been spoken in the prophets come upon you: "Behold, you despisers, marvel and perish! For I work a work in your days, a work which you will by no means believe, though one were to declare it to you." (Acts 13:40–41)

> Because He has appointed a day on which He will judge the world in righteousness by the Man whom He has ordained. (Acts 17:31)

Always this judgment is proclaimed with a view to excite or move God's people to fear God and turn from their sins. Thus Calvin comments on the motivation given in each of the passages on God's judgment found within all five of our sermon texts:

> Acts 2:19–20: [The heavenly signs] foreshow God's wrath and displeasure. . . . But this serveth greatly to the setting forth of grace, that whereas all things do threaten destruction, yet whosoever doth call upon the name of the Lord is sure to be saved.[7]

> Again, it is out of all doubt, that God meaneth by this so doleful a description, to stir up all godly men, that they may with a more fervent desire seek for salvation. And Peter citeth it to the same end, that the Jews may know that they shall be more miserable unless they receive that grace of the Spirit which is offered unto them. [Calvin asks, how these two things can go together] because men are too slow to receive Christ, they must be constrained by divers afflictions, as it were with whips. Secondly . . . we must first be tamed by many miseries that we may learn humility.[8]

> Acts 3:20–21: He setteth before them the day of judgment, to the end the former exhortation may take the greater effect. For there is nothing which doth more prick us, than when we are taught that we must once give an account.[9]

> Acts 10:42: In the word *testify* there is great weight; because, as men are naturally inclined unto unbelief, the simple

[7] Calvin, *Commentaries*, vol. XVIII, 89.
[8] Ibid., 90.
[9] Ibid., 150.

> preaching of the gospel should not be so effectual, unless the Lord should establish it with strong protestations.[10]

> Acts 13:40–41: The conclusion containeth a chiding: for he threateneth to them horrible judgment, if they refuse the author of their salvation.[11]

> Acts 17:31: He maketh mention of the last judgment, that he may awake them out of their dream. For we know how hard a matter it is for men to deny themselves. Therefore, they must be violently enforced unto repentance, which cannot be done better than when they be cited to appear before God's judgment seat, and that fearful judgment is set before them, which they may neither despise nor escape. Therefore, let us remember that the doctrine of repentance doth then take place, when men, who would naturally desire to flatter themselves, are awaked with fear of God's judgment, and that none are fit teachers of the gospel but those who are the criers or apparitors [court officials] of the highest Judge.[12]

Calvin clearly sees setting God's fearful judgment before men as the best way to "enforce unto repentance." And in fact, in every sermon in our group, the inspired preachers urge the call to repentance with the loving threatening of God's certain judgment.[13] They issue this call soberly, seriously, and without the emotional manipulation of elaborate and gruesome portrayals of the torments of hell. The emphasis of their preaching is on the certainty and inescapable

[10] Ibid., 448.

[11] Ibid., 516.

[12] Calvin, *Commentaries*, vol. XVIII, 175.

[13] Thus Calvin teaches that by giving the Jews "a good hope of pardon," Peter "doth make the day of Christ pleasant to them, to the end they may

nature of the coming wrath and on their authority as the official proclaimers of it.

The Blessing of Salvation

With the command to repent and the warning of judgment, God also motivates His people with the incomparable blessings of salvation. In the sermons in our study, these blessings are declared and promised in official and legal language. The ministers never wax poetic on how much God loves you (the word "love" does not occur in the book of Acts). They do not plead with their audiences about how much God wants a relationship with you (the word "relationship" does not occur in the whole Bible—NKJV, ESV). They are never seen giving detailed descriptions of how Jesus suffered on the cross for you, how His heart was broken for you, how He bled and died for you, and so on. What they do is matter-of-factly, officially, and passionately proclaim the certainty, goodness, and blessedness of God's salvation, and how to receive it, by faith and repentance:

> [B]e baptized in the name of Jesus Christ for the remission of sins; and you shall receive the gift of the Holy Spirit. For the promise is to you and to your children, and to all who are afar off, as many as the Lord our God will call. (Acts 2:38b–39)

> [T]hat your sins may be blotted out, so that times of refreshing may come from the presence of the Lord, and that He may send Jesus Christ, who was preached to you before.... To you first, God, having raised up His Servant Jesus, sent Him to bless you, in turning away every one of you from your iniquities. (Acts 3:19b–20, 26)

---

desire the same." Ibid., 151.

> [P]reaching peace through Jesus Christ . . . through His name, whoever believes in Him will receive remission of sins. (Acts 10:36b, 43)

> And we declare to you glad tidings—that promise which was made to the fathers . . . that through this Man is preached to you the forgiveness of sins; and by Him everyone who believes is justified from all things from which you could not be justified by the law of Moses. (Acts 13:32, 38b–39)

> So that they should seek the Lord, in the hope that they might grope for Him and find Him, though He is not far from each one of us. (Acts 17:27)

The salvation is real. It is good news. It is for you and for your children. It brings times of refreshing. It is a blessing. It turns you from your sins. It brings peace with God, peace of mind, the presence of God, the gift of the Holy Spirit, remission of sins, and justification before God. It is wide and generous to all who are far off; it is certain and sure, appointed for you; and it is easy and near, believe. These blessings are true and real, and the ministers urge their audiences to receive them. Yet, they never do so by emotional manipulation, by play-acting or performing, or by cajoling or deceiving. They proclaim, by their preaching, the beauty, truth, and certainty of these things to all who sincerely repent and believe.

Though all the sermons in our study taught these and other doctrines, with different emphases and tones, and in a variety of details, in every sermon there was a concentrated and relentless effort to communicate God's truth to the faith of the believer. This was the overwhelming thrust of the preacher every single time and throughout every doctrine and in every tone of expression: to prove the truth of his words to the audience. Moreover, the subject on which the preachers spent the most time and energy to prove was the person and work of Jesus Christ. The particular attribute that they most often demonstrated about Christ was His goodness or the goodness of God in Him; especially as it is seen in God's promising Him, sending Him, and raising Him from the dead. Thus, secondly, we consider the biblical preachers' setting forth of God's goodness, which they do primarily in Christ.

God's Goodness

As seen on the Doctrinal Similarities Chart,[14] God's goodness was the primary thrust of every sermon. When we reflect that it was out of His goodness and faithfulness that God spoke through the prophets, sent the Christ, gave Him power to do miracles, and raised Him from the dead, this fact becomes even more obvious. God's goodness is His unwavering commitment to do what is truly good to His people. Because of His goodness, God is faithful, generous, patient, and compassionate to His creation and to all living men, but especially toward His people (living or dead). Every sermon labored to set forth, in a variety of ways, the goodness of God. The preachers proclaim and defend God and His goodness. They extol Him as the faithful God, the God who remembers His covenant to Israel, His promise to Abraham, Isaac, Jacob, David, the fathers, Moses, Samuel, Joel, John the Baptist, and all the prophets. He is the God who saves His people, which includes all who fear Him, who rules over and predestines all things for their good, giving them a time and place to live, and disposing all things so that they would know Him: the greatest gift of all!

Even though, as we saw above, God, in the person of His Son, is betrayed, denied, condemned, crucified, and murdered by them, still He puts up with them, for He is a generous and magnanimous God. He gives life and breath to all things. He made man His own offspring and He remains near to every single one. Though His people are helpless and sinful, He bears them in the wilderness.

[14] See Appendix B.

He notices and overlooks their ignorance. He continually sends His word to them, through His prophets, patiently putting off the day of judgment. He proclaims salvation and peace to them, promising that without partiality he accepts all who fear Him and work righteousness before Him. When He came in the person of His Son, He did good among them and to them, healing all who were oppressed by the devil, bringing healing and strength through faith in Him. God gives believers His Spirit and presence, times of refreshing, the sure hope of life after death, and the restoration of all things. He delivers them from their iniquities and directs them away from evil. The biblical sermons of our study expounded all of these themes.

Certifying Salvation and Judgment through the Miracle of the Resurrection

However, they do more than just proclaim them, they prove them. The preachers of our study certify salvation and judgment by proving that Jesus is the Christ, the Holy and Righteous One, God's Son, the Author of Life, the Lord, the Judge of the living and the dead. And the way in which they prove these things about Jesus is primarily by proclaiming and proving His resurrection. All of the sermons in our study placed enormous emphasis on the resurrection of Jesus Christ, and on each occasion this doctrine was expounded as a motivation to believe in Him for salvation. Thus, Kistemaker comments on Acts 2:32: "Once again Peter stresses the theme of the early Christian church: the resurrection from the dead."[15] And again on Acts 17:31: "True to apostolic form, wherever Paul preaches the Good News, he teaches the resurrection of Jesus Christ. For the apostles, this doctrine is basic to the Christian faith."[16]

[15] Kistemaker, *Acts*, 100.
[16] Ibid., 640.

Jesus' resurrection is proven by the apostles to their audiences in three ways: (1) by the witness of the Scriptures and John the Baptist; (2) by the supernatural witness of Jesus' miracles and signs during His life; and (3) by their own official witness as His appointed apostles.

Witness of the Scriptures and John the Baptist

First, we consider the witness of the Scriptures. The scriptural witness to Jesus is asserted by His fulfillment of the prophecies of the Christ. Thus, in Acts 2, Peter explains the miracle of tongues as supernaturally proving that the last days of Joel's prophecy are here. Joel's prophecy ends with the promise that whoever calls on the name of the Lord will be saved. Thus, Peter transitions from this prophecy to introduce Jesus. After citing the miraculous proof of Jesus, and mentioning His rejection and murder, Peter proclaims that God raised Jesus from the dead "*because* it was not possible that He should be held by it. *For* David says concerning Him . . ." (Acts 2:24b–25, emphasis added). In other words, God had to raise Jesus from the dead because He is the exalted person that David wrote about in Psalm 16, whose body would never decay because God would resurrect Him. Furthermore, Peter then proves that this verse could not be about David because David's body did decay in the grave. Thus, Peter's correct application of this psalm to Jesus depends upon two truths: (1) The undeniable historical fact that David's tomb with his body in it was with them; and (2) the Word of God is inerrant.

Peter explicitly asserts the first truth above (2:29) to further assure the audience of the accuracy of his applying this prophecy to Jesus, while no one in his audience needed to be reminded of the second.[17] In the sermon in Acts 3, he calls Moses as a witness (3:22–23), and in both Acts 3 and 10, he simply states that "all the

[17] "'Men of Israel, listen to these words.' First Peter appeals to common ground, because both speaker and listeners accept the Scriptures as the Word of God." Ibid., 92.

prophets" bear witness to Jesus' suffering and to the salvation He would bring.[18] In Acts 13 Paul declares that Jesus is the promised seed of David. He proves this declaration by citing the well-known prophetic ministry of John the Baptist:[19] "And as John was finishing his course, he said, 'Who do you think I am? I am not *He*. But behold, there comes One after me, the sandals of whose feet I am not worthy to loose'" (Acts 13:25). Then Paul, after asserting that the "voices of the prophets" bear weekly witness to Jesus (13:27), quotes the same psalm that Peter did above and makes the same point about David's body decomposing to prove that its correct application is to Jesus: "Like Peter in his sermons delivered at Pentecost and at Solomon's Colonnade, Paul supports his sermon by quoting from the Old Testament Scriptures . . . to strengthen his message . . . he expects his listeners to ask why. . . . Therefore, Paul tells his audience the meaning."[20]

Witness of Jesus' Miracles

Next, we see the biblical preachers proving Jesus' exalted personage in general, and his resurrection in particular, from His miracles. Thus, Peter in Acts 2 interprets the miracle of speaking in tongues, which the people could "see and hear" (2:33) as supernaturally attested proof that Jesus was exalted to heaven and was now pouring out the Holy Spirit on all His people, even as Joel had prophesied. Peter makes miracle an even more direct witness to Christ earlier in the sermon in 2:22: "Men of Israel, hear these words: Jesus of Nazareth, a Man attested by God to you by miracles, wonders, and signs which God did through Him in your midst, as you yourselves also know." The word (ἀποδεδειγμένον) simply

[18] "Acts 3:19–20 . . . on the basis of the scriptural evidence that God has fulfilled the messianic prophecies, Peter commands his hearers to repent (compare 2:38)." Ibid., 134.

[19] "He proveth by the witness of John that Jesus is that Savior which should come." *1599 Geneva Bible*, Acts 13:23, 1112n1.

[20] Kistemaker, *Acts*, 482.

means to demonstrate or prove (BDAG 900). Calvin discusses the validity of miracle's witness to Christ:

> Notwithstanding, here may a question be asked, whether miracles do suffice to be a sufficient and just approbation (proof) or no? Because by this means inchanters might cause their legerdemain [impostures] to be believed. I answer, that the juggling casts of Satan do much differ from the power of God. Christ saith elsewhere, that the kingdom of Antichrist shall be in wonders, but he addeth by and by, *in lying wonders*, (2 Thess. ii. 9) . . . [the elect can be deceived] only from our own want of wit, because we are so dull; for God doth show His power manifestly enough. Therefore, there is sufficient approbation of the doctrine and of the ministry in the miracles which God doth work, so that we be not blind . . . Neither can Satan otherwise delude us, save only . . . through our own slothfulness."[21]

Peter does not hesitate to call miracle God's own attestation to Christ. Thus the preachers of biblical sermons echo their Lord who continually pointed to His signs as proof that He was from God:

> If I do not do the works of My Father, do not believe Me; but if I do, though you do not believe Me, believe the works, that you may know and believe that the Father is in Me, and I in Him. (John 10:37–38; see also Matt. 9:6; 11:2–6; 12:28; Mark 2:10; Luke 5:24; 11:20; John 3:2; 5:36; 9:30–33; 14:10–11; 15:24; etc.)

In Acts 3, Peter begins his sermon by denying that the miraculous power to heal the paralytic standing before the people came from him or John. He then introduces Jesus in messianic titles,

[21] Calvin, *Commentaries*, vol. XVIII, 94–95 (emphasis in original).

charges the crowd with His murder, and proclaims His resurrection and the apostles as witnesses. Then immediately he refers them back to the miracle: "And His name, through faith in His name, has made this man strong, whom you see and know. Yes, the faith which comes through Him has given him this perfect soundness in the presence of you all" (3:16). Thus, Peter refers to the restored man as tangible, sensory evidence that Jesus is alive, because it was by believing in Him that the man they all knew as a cripple was now standing before them supernaturally healed: "The cripple had been cured because Jesus had been glorified."[22] As in the gospels, miraculous healing proves the power of faith in Jesus' name. The apostolic miracles were a continuation of Jesus' power from on high, confirming the apostles' attachment to Him.

In Acts 10 Peter is sent for by Cornelius, who, through a miraculous vision, is given supernatural attestation that Peter is God's spokesman (vv. 4–6). When Peter preaches to these Gentiles he reminds his audience what they already knew, "how God anointed Jesus of Nazareth with the Holy Spirit and with power, who went about doing good and healing all who were oppressed by the devil, for God was with Him" (10:38). Like Nicodemus (see John 3:2), these Gentile God-fearers knew that a man could not do the powerful wonders and signs that Jesus everywhere did, unless God was with Him. Ministers today need to use this same motivation of the signs and miracles of Jesus to prove God was with Him. Although we cannot say of His miracles, as Peter could, "which God did through Him in your midst, as you yourselves also know" (Acts 2:22), yet we can magnify and proclaim the many mighty miracles of Christ recorded in Scripture, seen by thousands of witnesses, and attested to by His official apostles, which proved once and for all that God was indeed with Jesus!

Thus, biblical sermons emphasized the historical, bodily resurrection of Jesus and all of the signs and wonders He did as irrefutable

[22] Bruce, *Acts*, 80.

proof that He was from God. These early preachers were not at all ashamed to declare these things, even when, like Paul at Athens, they knew that the culture would laugh at and mock them for it. How different is the kind of preaching today, popularized in the nineteenth and early twentieth centuries, which is ashamed of or even outright denies Christ's miracles, His bodily resurrection, His virgin birth, and so on. Jesus was "demythologized" so that He could be more relevant and acceptable to modern man, who could no longer believe that a man could make the blind see, multiply loaves and fishes, walk on water, or rise bodily from the grave. They thought that by "modernizing" Jesus they could keep His ethic of morality, love, and mercy and that by making Jesus more—as they thought—*believable*, the world would be a utopia.

But a funny thing happened. When they demythologized the real Jesus, they created a mythical one, who cannot save, and who cannot sanctify. Totally depraved sinners need more than a made-up, godly example to do right, they need the power of God from on high—in them! But that power only comes to those who truly believe—yes, really and sincerely believe that Jesus Christ conquered sin, death, and Satan, and that He is right now alive in heaven. They must be convinced that this Jesus truly can and does send His Spirit to communicate His holy power and presence to all who believe in Him for their justification and sanctification. For if I am not convinced that Jesus is alive and in heaven, then I cannot possibly live by faith in Him. And seeing that Jesus is not physically present on earth, the only way I can know Him and be empowered by Him is by faith.

So then the morality, love, and mercy that the nineteenth-century liberals trusted in and hoped for more of, never came. And that which they did have grew cold in men's hearts, since they no longer looked to Him to give it, but to a mythical Jesus, a fantasy. And as with the idols of wood and stone that Israel turned to, the modern false Jesus was only words on a page. He could not save, He could not sanctify, and the natural sin of man's heart once again gained the ascendancy. All because we stopped believing in and preaching about the miracles of the Bible that proved once and for all that Jesus is the Son of God, alive in heaven, able to save and sanctify all who believe in Him, to the uttermost, in order that men, convinced of His reality, were moved to believe because they saw it was true. Preachers today must proclaim the miraculous testimony of Christ found in the Scriptures as an indispensable part of their proving that this Jesus, whom we crucified, is Lord! Sinners cannot be motivated to live for Christ except through their faith. And sinners cannot be motivated to believe in Christ except through the proof that His Word is true. The miracles, especially His bodily resurrection, are that proof in the sermons of Scripture.

Witness of the Apostles

Finally, we notice the official apostolic witness proves the exalted person of Jesus, particularly, that he rose from the dead. Here again is an element that all five of our sermons stressed, but that is given little to no attention today. Proclaiming the apostolic witness is crucial to proving that Jesus is the Christ, the Lord, and that He can and will save all who call upon Him and deliver them from their sins. Thus, unless the authoritative, apostolic witness to Jesus is proclaimed and proven, men cannot know for certain that the gospel is true or that God truly means it for them. For unless our audiences have assurance from God that the gospel message is true and from Him, and that they are officially called to this salvation by God Himself, they will not be moved to believe:

> For it is not sufficient to have the mercy of God preached unto us generally, unless we also know that the same is offered unto us by the certain ordinance of God. For this cause it is that Paul standeth so much upon the avouching of the calling of the Gentiles (Rom. 15:18; Eph. 3:3–4); because, if any man should think that the gospel came unto him by chance, when as it was scattered here and there, faith

> should quail [vacillate]; yea, there should be a doubtful opinion instead of faith.[23]

The believability of the message rests upon the authority of the one who sent it. How can we know that this offer of salvation is meant for us? Because Jesus assures us that He, Himself, offers it to us. How can we know that this offer of salvation is from God and not man? Because it comes to us through God's certified and appointed witnesses. How can we know that they were His appointed witnesses? Because the apostles were specifically appointed by Jesus to be witnesses for His resurrection (see Acts 1:21–22), and they performed confirming signs and wonders (see Heb. 2:3–4). All of these things are attested to in the sermons of our study, and in assuring us of these things, God gives us the greatest of all motivations to believe in Christ and live for Him, that it is all true and proven to be true. Thus, ministers, like the biblical preachers, must proclaim the assured truth and sincere offer of the gospel found in the official apostolic witness or sinful men will never believe it.

Accordingly, we see Peter in his first sermon declare that he and the apostles are the official witnesses of Christ's resurrection (see Acts 2:32), and we immediately find the apostles doing confirming signs and wonders (see Acts 2:43). Peter's second sermon is occasioned when he supernaturally heals the lame man at the beautiful gate (see Acts 3:1–10). With the crowd wondering over him and John, Peter specifically denies that they have any inherent power to do wonders (see 3:12–16), but that this power is from Jesus' name, and on this basis he proclaims that he and the apostles are Jesus' witnesses (see 3:15), because the miracle proves that He is with them.

In Acts 10, Peter explains more specifically what it means to be an official apostolic witness to the resurrected Christ:

[23] Calvin, *Commentaries*, vol. XVIII, 158.

> Him God raised up on the third day, and showed Him openly, not to all the people, but to witnesses chosen before by God, even to us who ate and drank with Him after He arose from the dead. And He commanded us to preach to the people, and to testify that it is He who was ordained by God to be Judge of the living and the dead. (Acts 10:40–42)

Peter makes this claim of being an official, chosen witness of the resurrection, and immediately, Christ confirms Peter's words by miraculously visiting the Gentiles of Cornelius' household with the supernatural gift of speaking in foreign, human languages that they did not naturally know. Thus, the Jews with Peter witnessed to this miracle with amazement (see 10:43–47) and rightly concluded that God had accepted them (see 11:17–18).

Furthermore, Peter reveals in this passage how the apostles were specifically appointed by Christ to be His official witnesses of His resurrection. To that end Jesus chose them, revealed Himself to them, and ate and drank with them. Thus, they did not just glimpse Him for a moment or from a distance. They sat down with Him for hours at a time, fellowshipping with Him, talking with Him, touching Him. It was no mistake. It was no mass delusion. It was not a ghost. They saw Him eat, and they saw Him drink. Having authenticated His resurrection to them, Jesus commanded them to preach to the people. Consequently, when an apostle preached, "Repent and believe and you shall be forgiven," that word came from God. The command and the promise are from Him, and thus, the ability to fulfill them comes from Him. Furthermore, Peter adds that Jesus also commanded them to "testify" (διαμαρτύρασθαι). As we saw before, this word means "to make solemn attestation or call to witness."[24] Jesus leaves nothing to chance. He accomplished our salvation. He appointed His official witnesses and sent them

[24] A. T. Robertson, *Word Pictures in the New Testament* vol. 3, *The Acts of the Apostles* (Nashville, TN: Broadman Press, 1960), 36.

forth by His authority and the signs of His power. Thus, the truth and credibility of their witness all goes back to Him.

> Therefore, let us assure ourselves of this, that the holy apostles were chosen by the holy decree of God, that by their testimony the truth of Christ's resurrection might stand . . . if we covet to have God the sure author of our faith, let us learn to be content with the witnesses whom in due time he hath brought forth, as it were, by his hand, being ordained by him before the world was made.[25]

Because Jesus appointed and sent out the apostles to preach, and because He authenticated them by His power, we know that their word is good. Again, the biblical preachers seek to motivate their audiences by firmly and irrefutably proving the truth of their message at every point. The messengers are official. They are from God. Therefore, we are *encouraged* to believe them in the true sense of that word. The apostles "were appointed witnesses by God . . . that they might by their preaching bring men unto the faith of Christ."[26] The apostle Paul likewise proclaimed "those who came up with Him from Galilee to Jerusalem . . . are His witnesses to the people," and after God raised Him from the dead, these witnesses saw Him "for many days," (Acts 13:30–31). Even in Athens, Paul preached as the official spokesman for the religion he was proclaiming (see Acts 17:23). Thus, Kistemaker has this understanding of Paul's words: "He speaks on behalf of God and thus his authority is divinely decreed."[27]

The apostles adamantly claimed to be Christ's official spokesmen and that they were to bring God's Word to the people and not their own. They "testified" of God's Word. They bore witness to Christ's Word while He was in heaven, and Christ, for His part,

[25] Calvin, *Commentaries*, vol. XVIII, 446.

[26] Ibid., 445.

[27] Kistemaker, *Acts*, 632.

proved that it was His Word by bearing witness to them through miracles. Thus, Bruce asserts of Acts 3:13:

> The cripple had been cured because Jesus had been glorified. From his place of exaltation Jesus had endowed his disciples with power to act in his name, and to perform mighty works such as he himself had performed in the days of his bodily presence among them.[28]

The miracles proved that the apostles' witness to Jesus was true as they gave all the glory for them to the power of Jesus' name. So when they preached to people, it was with His authority. Accordingly, when the apostles offered the gospel to their audiences, as we saw in the exegesis section, they grammatically emphasized that it was "to you." They proclaimed it as an official announcement of a king to his subjects, as if saying, "By the authority of king Jesus Himself, I, as His official spokesman and ambassador, declare to you this day:"

> "Repent, and let *every one of you* be baptized in the name of Jesus Christ for the remission of sins; and *you shall receive* the gift of the Holy Spirit. For *to you* is the promise and to your children, and to all who are afar off, as many as the Lord our God will call." And with many other words he *testified and exhorted* them, saying, "Be saved from this perverse generation." (Acts 2:38–40)

> *To you first, God*, having raised up His Servant Jesus, *sent Him* to bless *you*, in turning away *every one* of you from your iniquities. (Acts 3:26)[29]

[28] Bruce, *Acts*, 80.

[29] God was "sending" Jesus to them in the words of Peter's sermon, thus Peter was His official proclaimer. Peter hardly needed to declare his authority in Acts 3, seeing that he had to begin this sermon with a rebuke of the audience, who, witnessing the healing miracle were attributing supernatural powers

> And *He commanded us to preach to the people, and to testify* that it is He who was ordained by God to be Judge of the living and the dead. To Him all the prophets witness that, through His name, *whoever* believes in Him will receive remission of sins. (Acts 10:42–43)

> *To you* the word of this salvation has been sent . . . He was seen for many days by those who came up with Him from Galilee to Jerusalem, who are *His witnesses* to the people. And *we declare to you* glad tidings—that promise which was made to the fathers. God has fulfilled this for us their children, in that He has raised up Jesus . . . that *through this Man is preached to you* the forgiveness of sins; and by Him *everyone* who believes is justified from all things from which you could not be justified by the law of Moses. (Acts 13:26b, 31–33, 38–39)

> Therefore, the One whom you worship without knowing, Him *I proclaim to you*. (Acts 17:23)

The divinely appointed, sent, and miraculously attested apostles authoritatively speak for God to the people. They offer forgiveness to people who believe in Jesus. Therefore, what they tell us is infallibly true. We can trust it. We can believe it. The judgment and wrath they declare will surely come on all who do not repent. The blessed salvation of Christ will certainly be given to all who believe in Him.

What Does This Mean for Today's Ministers?

Ministers today are not apostles. They have not been directly chosen by Christ to be witnesses of His resurrection. They did not see His miracles. They did not eat and drink with Him after He rose from the dead. Christ does not do miracles through them. So how

---

to Peter and John (Acts 3:12).

can we imitate this motivation of the biblical preachers and give the same apostolic assurance of the truth of our message and the certainty of the offer, in order to motivate our congregations to believe in Christ?

First, because the minister preaches the same word of the apostles. In the Bible, we have the words of Jesus, given to us by the apostles, and therefore so long as what we preach is Scripture, it is just as much the Word of God as when Peter and Paul preached it.

Second, because when a minister is rightly called by a true church of Jesus Christ to preach the gospel and when that church vests the authority given to it in that man to be their preacher, that minister is just as truly called and authorized by Christ as any apostle was. The calling is indirect to be sure. The minister is not a vessel of inspiration or an empowered doer of confirming signs, nor does Jesus Himself call Him in a vision, but the same Jesus Christ who called and appointed the apostles calls and appoints him, through His Church. Under the authority of Jesus, the apostles could not ordain other apostles but they were commanded to appoint elders as ministers of the gospel who would continue to preach and to teach the word of Christ.

Jesus said, "I will build my church and the gates of hell will not prevail against it" (Matt. 16:18b). Jesus authorized his apostles to continue that building after them, through the ordaining of pastors and teachers (see Eph. 4:11). He gave the church the qualifications of those officers, so that the people of God could continue to have His authoritative word when the apostles died (see 1 Tim. 3; Titus 1). Thus, the minister who is duly called and ordained by a true Christian church is authorized by Jesus to preach His Word. And when the minister preaches that Word faithfully, it is just as much the Word of Jesus as it was when Paul preached it and when Peter preached it. Accordingly, ministers today need to give their congregations the divine assurance that they are authorized by Jesus Christ Himself to preach salvation and judgment to them. So that it is not the minister, but Jesus who promises them His Spirit and presence if they believe; and it is not the minister, but Jesus who threatens to cut them off from His people if they do not obey the preached Word. Thus, ministers motivate the people of God when they assure them that the gospel is truly for them and from God. The motivation comes once again through a confirming of what is true, on the part of God's official spokesmen: the duly called and ordained minister.

This is the chief motivation of the sermons of Scripture. It is the motivation of truth. Because the biblical sermons are carefully defended and logically argued treatises of proving the truth of God and of Jesus Christ, we see a definite progression in each sermon. The biblical preachers begin with a point of correction or explanation to their audiences about something that is before them, and then build their case from there until they have fully established the truth of their doctrine and can call upon their hearers to believe it. They do not shy away from expressing passion and emotion, but all of their effort is concentrated on the truth and certainty of their message as they develop it line upon line. Calvin notices this progression in Peter's sermon in Acts 2, where he brings his audience to the knowledge of Christ

> by little and little. For he doth not by and by in the beginning affirm that Jesus was Christ; but he saith only that he was a man sent of God; and that doth he prove by his miracles. Afterward he addeth, that he rose from death, when he was slain. Whereby it appeareth more certainly and more fully that he was not one of the prophets, but the very Son of God, who was promised to be the repairer of all things.[30]

Thus, the apostles build their case truth upon proven truth, for they seek to move their audiences by the truth.

[30] Calvin, *Commentaries*, vol. XVIII, 93.

18

Biblical Motivation, Part Two: The Approach

Next, we consider the approach that the biblical preachers use to address and speak to their audiences. Clearly both Peter and Paul speak in different ways from one another, and, in their own sermons, from one to the next. Various audiences and occasions seem to account for these differences. In four of the sermons the speaker began with a formal and respectful opening address that was suitable to the occasion. In the one sermon where this does not occur (Acts 10), the preacher actually goes even further to respect his audience. Peter begins his address to Cornelius' house apologetically, with an acknowledgment of his former Jewish pride and racism. He confesses to them that for the first time he realizes that God shows no partiality to men. It only took two visions from heaven, one repeated three times, and the Holy Spirit then speaking to him to learn this truth, but nonetheless he did learn it (when once he was convinced of the truth of it), and he humbled himself before his audience as a result.

In Acts 2, 3, and 13, the setting is one of God's people gathered to worship Him at a religious feast, at the temple, and at a synagogue. Accordingly, in all three sermons they refer to their audiences as "brethren." In Acts 3, Peter reminds them "You are sons of the prophets, and of the covenant which God made with our fathers," and he invokes the holy formula, "The God of Abraham, Isaac, and

Jacob, the God of our fathers." Similarly, Paul speaks to his synagogue audience, "sons of the family of Abraham, and those among you who fear God." These terms invoke the religious knowledge and moral convictions of their audiences. They call upon their audiences to hear them for the sake of all they profess to hold dear, for the sake of their God, the God of their fathers. Such phrases would be motivating to those who believed in God, for it would remind them of the true inheritance of God's people.

Furthermore, these titles are not made up, obsequious, or condescending. They are complimentary and blessed addresses right from the pages of Scripture. Thus, when Paul adds "and those among you who fear God," he is drawing from a rich concept of Scripture that is found throughout the Bible, as we noticed in the exegesis portion. That Paul included those who feared God in the same category as Israelites of God's covenant would have been a powerful motivation for them to hear Paul's message (if they were persuaded of the truth of it), for he was proclaiming their full acceptability to God, something that first-century Jews had largely denied or forgotten, as we already noticed in Peter's preaching to Cornelius' house.

What do we learn from this manner of speaking? Biblical preachers respect their audiences and believe in their message and they want their hearers to truly believe in it too. They seek to win them to Christ based solely upon the truth of their message. Thus, we read nothing about their attire or their mannerisms. We hear no powerful rhetoric or moving stories. Truth is their motivator and sincere faith is their goal. They would have their audiences believe in Jesus, and they would have that faith be real. Therefore they seek to win them to the truth, without any tricks, gimmicks, sentimentalism, or manipulation. If we reflect upon this fact, we will see that this approach has the greatest respect for people, treating them as equally-important-to-God human beings. Biblical preachers want their audiences to be won to God by the truth of His Word alone; so that each one will be able to know and serve God immediately and spiritually by faith in Him and be dependent upon no man or creature. They want their audiences to become their brothers and not their servants or admirers, and so they address them as equals in dignity, nature, and power: fellow "offspring of God" (Acts 17:29). They recognize that God has sent a message to their audiences, that they are merely the messengers, and God will hold them accountable. Thus, their entire effort is geared to winning their audiences to faith in that message by communicating and defending its truth.

Now admitting this fact is not to say that biblical preachers ignored things like using good speaking practices, etiquette, or hygiene! Of course they would have sought to be as personally inoffensive as possible and to speak as well as possible. Of course they would have been humble, kind, and patient in their speech, showing real love to their audiences. You can almost feel Peter's compassion for his hearers as he reminds them of their inheritance in Abraham and exhorts them continually to be saved (Acts 2)! Yet, even here, he does not do so with a shallow emotional appeal, with entertainment, sentimental stories, studied rhetorical devices, or flattering compliments. He does so by appealing to the truth and passionately warning them to resist the lie: "And with many other words he testified and exhorted them, saying, 'Be saved from this perverse generation,'" (Acts 2:40). He testified—he bore official witness as the God-appointed herald of this promise; and he exhorted—he admonished and urged them, "with many other words" to be saved from this "perverse" generation. A. T. Robertson comments on this word: "*Crooked* (*skolias*). Old word, opposite of *orthos*, straight . . . a perversity for turning off the truth. Cf. Luke 9:41; Phil. 2:15."[1] Thus, even when Peter pleads with men to be saved, his appeal is entirely based on their receiving and not rejecting the truth. Peter understands that God's true children will love and desire the truth above all else (see 2 Thess. 2:9–14).

Likewise, Paul passionately entreats the Jews at Antioch as he

[1] A. T. Robertson, *Word Pictures in the New Testament* vol. 3, *The Acts of the Apostles* (Nashville, TN: Broadman Press, 1960), 37.

multiplies addresses to assure them that God's promised salvation is their rightful Jewish heritage: "Men *and* brethren, sons of the family of Abraham." He protests that the gospel he brings is nothing more than "that promise which was made to the fathers," just "the sure mercies of David." This message was declared in Jerusalem by His witnesses and now "we declare [it] to you" for "to you the word of this salvation has been sent" (Acts 13:26, 31–32, 34). How could Paul get any more compassionate than that? Yet, in truly loving his audience, Paul does not keep his focus only on the "good" news of blessing, salvation, and peace. He does not hesitate to warn them in the most graphic terms, evoking the covenant curse seen in the Babylonian judgment: "Beware therefore, lest what has been spoken in the prophets come upon you: 'Behold, you despisers, marvel and perish! For I work a work in your days, a work which you will by no means believe, though one were to declare it to you'" (Acts 13:40–41). Understand that these bloodcurdling words of Paul are loving and "good," precisely because the danger of which he warns them is real and the judgment is certain; Paul believes it and he wants them to also, for their everlasting good.

Biblical Encouragement

Interestingly, both of these sermons are said to be words of "encouragement," (Acts 2:40; 13:15). The Greek verb is παρακαλέω, and the noun is παράκλησις. The word can mean to call to one's side, to encourage, to embolden, to exhort, to comfort. As we saw earlier, "encouragement" is a very popular word among the purveyors of the modern concept of internal motivation, and it is used to describe the boosting of one's self esteem and making him feel good about himself. J. I. Packer contrasts the biblical meaning of this word (sometimes translated "comfort") in Romans 8, with the modern use:

> Comfort is, of course, used here in the old, strong sense of that which encourages and nerves, not in the modern sense

> of that which tranquilizes and enervates. The quest for "comfort" in the modern sense is self-indulgent, sentimental and unreal, and the modern "I-go-to-church-for-comfort" religion is not Christianity.[2]

To "encourage" someone today is to always make them feel accepted, valued, and appreciated, and to never correct them or morally judge them. The phrase used repeatedly, as the slogan of the national contemporary Christian music station K-LOVE, captures this concept succinctly; they play music that is "positive and encouraging." Today, in modern motivational terms, those two words are nearly redundant. What is encouraging is by definition positive or else it would not be encouraging. That is not the case biblically speaking.

Thus in his sermon in Acts 2, Luke summarizes Peter's conclusion: "And with many other words he testified and *exhorted* them, saying, "Be saved from this perverse generation." The word "exhorted" here is παρακαλέω. Literally, Peter "encouraged" them by warning them to be saved from the perversion all around them. He encouraged them by proving the truth to them and warning them against the crookedness of the lie:

> Luke leaves the impression that Peter warned the inquirers to examine carefully the evidence he has presented. In fact, the tense of the verb *exhorting* (in Greek) indicates that Peter repeatedly appealed to his listeners with this request: "Save yourselves from this crooked generation."[3]

When Paul is asked to speak in Acts 13, the rulers of the synagogue said to him and Barnabas: "Men *and* brethren, if you have any word of *exhortation* for the people, say on" (Acts 13:15). The

[2] J. I. Packer, *Knowing God* (Downers Grove, IL: InterVarsity, 1993), 256.

[3] Simon J. Kistemaker, *Exposition of the Acts of the Apostles* (Grand Rapids, MI: Baker, 2004), 107–8.

word here is παράκλησις. They were asking Paul to give a word of encouragement to the people, and Paul did, though not according to the definers of encouragement today. We have already looked at both Paul's expressions of compassion and his bloodcurdling warning at the end. How can these two concepts go together in a word of encouragement? Because encouragement, as it is used here and in other places in the Bible, means to strengthen in what is right and to turn from what is wrong. Luke gives us a good example of this in Acts 9:31: "Then the churches throughout all Judea, Galilee, and Samaria had peace and were edified. And walking in the fear of the Lord and in the *comfort* of the Holy Spirit, they were multiplied." To walk in the fear of the Lord is to walk in the comfort, the encouragement, of the Holy Spirit. Scripturally speaking we are never more encouraged than when we truly fear the Lord, for this is when we are most strengthened in what is right and turned from what is evil. Thus, Paul and Peter include warnings and threatenings in their words of encouragement. Calvin gives his definition of biblical encouragement:

> An exhortation doth not exclude doctrine. But it seemeth that this word was commonly used among them; because it is properly the office of the teacher to utter no new thing of his own brain, but to apply the Scripture . . . unto the present use of the people. Thus, they do not only teach, but also apply the doctrine . . . unto the edifying of the Church, which I think is meant by the word exhortation.[4]

Passion and Truth

Biblical sermons display passion for the people of God that is real and unfeigned, yet they never employ anything other than the

[4] *Calvin's Commentaries*, vol. XVIII, trans. William Pringle, *John 12–21; Acts 1–13*, book 2, (Grand Rapids, MI: Baker, 2003), 514–15.

truth of their words to move them to believe. The preachers continually say, "Believe because you realize and are convinced that this is true. Do not believe because I smiled at, entertained, made you feel good, or even terrified you." Thus, I do not agree with those who see Paul using a certain level of deceitful or clever rhetoric in his opening address at Athens, in order to get the attention of the crowd through flattery. I strongly disagree with Kistemaker, where he asserts of Paul's opening address about them being "very religious": "Skillfully Paul addresses has audience with the same formula that had been used by the famous orator Demosthenes. With this address he touches the hearts of his hearers. Then he follows it with words of praise for their ostentatious religiosity."[5] I also disagree where he says "In the context of the speech, Paul uses the term affirmatively, because he is interested in gaining the attention of the Athenian crowd."[6] Similarly, A. T. Robertson says: "Paul was quick to use this confession on the part of the Athenians of a higher power than yet known to them. So he gets his theme from this evidence of a deeper religious sense in them and makes a most clever use of it with consummate skill."[7]

This is precisely the position that I am rejecting. Paul does not say these words for effect. He does not skillfully employ them to gain attention. He says them because they are true and he believed it, and meant it, and it was a loving thing to do to tell them about it. The Athenians *were* very religious. Who could deny that? They understood that the divine existed and they needed to worship that divine as I pointed out in the exegesis section. Now it is true that they messed up the number and types of gods that existed, and how they were to be worshipped, and a whole host of other things, and Paul would get to that, but at the very beginning Paul complimented them on the real truth that remained in their practice by the common grace of God. If I'm talking to a pagan and I see him treat his

[5] Kistemaker, *Acts*, 630.

[6] Ibid., 631.

[7] Robertson, *Word Pictures*, 286.

wife well, I praise him for that. I do not pretend that he is a Christian because of it, but neither do I notice it solely to point out to him how all his kindness to his wife is a stench in the nostrils of God. I use the remnants of civic virtue in him to prove to him the goodness of God and to eventually call him to repentance.

So also Paul does not speak to these Athenians like a teacher scolding children, for that would have been a prideful and hateful thing to do. Likewise, he did not attempt to flatter them into giving him a hearing, for that would have been a deceitful and cowardly thing to do. Paul understood that these Athenians were not *utterly* depraved and so he began his sermon to them noticing the truth of God that was still being acknowledged by them, and no doubt Paul was thankful to God for it. Thus, Paul said they were "very religious," because he believed it, and he had compassion for these lost souls at Athens, and he chose to point out to them first, a thing that they were doing right. These people were in such darkness for so long, that on spiritual things Paul has to address them little by little. Because he loved them and wanted them to turn from darkness to light, he praises the grain of truth that was being drowned in their puddle of falsehood, even as he prepared to take out his mop and clean up their mess.

Too many ministers will claim to do what Paul is doing here when they try to justify why they only preach "positive" messages about love and mercy and never preach against sin. "I don't want to offend baby Christians"; "I want to reach the unbeliever"; "I want them to hear the gospel"; "God's love, grace, and mercy will woo them to Christ," and so on. Unfortunately, if the only gospel they ever preach is the love, mercy, and non-judgment of Jesus, it is a false gospel which cannot save anyone. And God never authorized an apostle in Scripture to preach such a message. Therefore, it does not have God's-official-witness certification, and cannot be authentic, and consequently, those who preach it cannot truly do so out of an honest love for God's people. Conversely, Paul's compassion for his audience is genuine. It flows from love and not pride or cowardice, and so Paul immediately corrects one sin after another throughout the entire sermon at Athens. He corrects their idolatrous views of creation and worship (17:24–25); their false views of man's nature, and of God's sovereignty (17:26).

When he begins to given them the gospel, he continues to correct their sinful practices, but he does so in such a humble way that he even identifies with these pagan idol worshippers, showing them that while their practices were abominable, they were his equals who could be saved if they too would repent. Thus, notice where the passage goes from third to first person. Then observe how Paul continues to identify with them with the first person pronoun, even as he rebukes their idolatrous ways of which, being raised as a Jew, he had never been guilty:

> [S]o that *they* should seek the Lord, in the hope that *they* might grope for Him and find Him, though He is not far from each one of *us*; for in Him *we* live and move and have *our* being, as also some of your own poets have said, 'For *we* are also His offspring.' Therefore, since *we* are the offspring of God, *we* ought not to think that the Divine Nature is like gold or silver or stone, something shaped by art and man's devising. (Acts 17:27–29)

Again, Paul's compassion, his humility, his respect and love for these Athenians could not be greater. He wants them to come to the knowledge of the truth and be saved, to realize the noble and exalted purpose for which they were created, and that desire, and indeed love and respect, is what we see reflected in what Paul says and how he says it.

It is true that Paul does not directly quote Scripture in Acts 17, yet as was discussed in the exegesis section, everything he says to them can be found in the Bible. From general revelation, including the remnants of common grace seen in their own culture, we can easily see Paul in his sermon teaching monotheism, the nature of

God, the nature of man, divine sovereignty, human responsibility, the doctrines of creation, providence, worship, the resurrection, final judgment, and repentance. Paul recognized that the truth of God is what convinces men to believe in Christ, and so since these Greeks had no knowledge of the authority of Scripture, he spoke to them from that authority that they did know and could not deny: the reality all around and in them. However, as shown in the Doctrinal Similarities Chart, the sermon Paul preached at Athens is the same in substance as the other biblical sermons in our study. The same truth is communicated and proven though in a different way: "The man who calls himself 'a Hebrew of Hebrews' (Phil. 3:5) was at the same time, from another point of view, a Hellenist of Hellenists. The essential content of the speech is biblical, but the presentation is Hellenistic."[8] Had Paul been allowed to go on, it is certain that he would have begun to describe this judge of all the earth whom God raised from the dead. And in establishing the authority of Christ, Paul would have established the authority of Scripture.

Finally, since emotion is such a big part of today's definition and practice of motivation, we need to summarize the relationship between emotion and motivation in the biblical sermons of our study. We have already addressed what we believe to be the compassion of the preachers for their audiences as they spoke and we have shown how this compassion displayed itself in both their blunt rebukes and in their heartfelt entreaties. The texts of our passages give us no other conclusive evidence of any other feelings on the part of the speakers. Thus, we turn to consider the audiences of the biblical sermons, which is more important to examine anyway, since our purpose is to discover how sermons should motivate listeners. If we recall from our exegesis section, we saw very few words that conveyed emotion on the part of the audience. Plus, some of the words that appear to do so, under closer analysis, do not.

[8] F. F. Bruce, *The Book of the Acts*, rev. ed. (Grand Rapids, MI: Eerdmans, 1988), 341.

Thus, the "glad tidings" of Acts 13:32 (NKJV), is really just "we gospel" (εὐαγγελιζόμεθα), and is better rendered "bring good news" as in the ESV. So this word is not speaking to the emotional state of humans at all, but to the kind of news brought. It is not bad news but good news. In Acts 2:41, the NKJV, following the majority text, is the only modern evangelical translation that reads "gladly received." The others have "received," (ESV, NASB); or "accepted" (NIV). However, let's grant it as fact that the audience did "gladly receive" the Word of life. What could be more obvious than that they were very glad to become the heirs of salvation! Yet, right away we see that their gladness was in response to Peter continually exhorting them to "Be saved from this perverse generation" (Acts 2:40). As we noticed above, Peter is warning them not to be influenced by the lie, but to persevere in the truth. They were glad precisely because Peter had convinced them of the truth of his words and they believed that truth: both the promise and the threat, and they were glad.

Interestingly, this same audience was in sorrow to the point of utter despair just four verses prior, when "they were cut to the heart, and said to Peter and the rest of the apostles, "Men and brethren, what shall we do?"" (Acts 2:37). The Word of God pierced their hearts, in other words it killed them spiritually and emotionally. They had become convinced of the truth of Peter's proclamation: The Messiah had come and they had murdered Him, and now He sits enthroned in heaven ruling over all things and subduing His enemies. What in the world was left for them to do but to die? The words of Zechariah 12:10 had come to pass for these Jews: They looked upon the one whom they had pierced and they mourned for Him as one would mourn for and grieve the death of an only son. Their emotions were stirred as they came to believe the truth of the message. So they cry out to Peter in abject despair and he commands them to repent and be baptized with the promise that they will receive remission of sins and the gift of the Holy Spirit, the supernatural effects of whom they saw and heard all around them. So they become glad! Yes, I believe they were glad even if the critical text is the true reading.

What was it that Peter said or did that moved them from such sorrow to such gladness? Three specific things:

1. Repent and be baptized in the name of Jesus Christ for the remission of sins (see Acts 2:38).
2. You will receive the gift of the Holy Spirit for the promise is for you and for your children (see Acts 2:39).
3. Be saved from this perverse generation (see Acts 2:40).

Peter told them the truth. He told it to them officially and authoritatively, with compassion to be sure, but there is no textual evidence of any effort on his part to move them to Christ by any emotions, intimate images of how God loves you and accepts you just the way you are, moving sentimental stories, elaborate descriptions of how much Jesus suffered for you, macabre portrayals of the torments of hell, or anything other than the formal, yet personal, and passionate communication to them of the truth of the gospel. And of the three groups of instructions he gave them, which are all that stand between their despair and their joy, one included a command to repent, and another was a warning to be saved from the perversion all around you. It was not emotion or sentiment, but the truth communicated in the form of command, promise, and warning. And the audience believed Peter, to the point that they obeyed the command, embraced the promise, and heeded the warning. The proven truth of the gospel moved them, and they believed and obeyed, and were made to mourn and then to rejoice.

In the other sermons the reaction is similar. Although emotions are not explicitly stated, we can infer from the thrust and commands of the messages that those who were convinced of the truth were moved by mourning over their sin and being glad about salvation to repent and believe. Thus, we see them asking to hear more of these words (Acts 10:48; 13:42); and they then follow or join the preacher (Act 13:43; 17:34). While those who were not moved to believe left (13:42); or mocked (17:32). Interestingly, the negative reaction of mocking came as a result of rejecting the truth of the resurrection (Act 17:32). Thus, when men receive the truth by being persuaded and convinced of it, they believe and repent with joy; but when men are not convinced or persuaded of the truth, they do not receive it, but they reject it and mock.

This conclusion is true even in those sections of our sermons that focused on God's love and mercy. Thus, in Acts 17, where Paul most gently expounds on God's benevolent love, goodness, and patience to all mankind, and in Acts 13:17–25 where he recounts God's gracious, saving acts and loving care to Israel; and in Acts 2:16–21 where Peter extols God's faithfulness to His promises to the prophets, these truths are communicated not to break men's hearts in sympathy for God, so that they emotionally long to love Him the way they feel He loves them, but in order to see and be convinced of the truth of God's love toward them, as they are made to see His goodness and power in saving His people. However, when men are made to focus on God's goodness and power, the resulting emotion is not that sentimental sympathy, which is too often mistakenly called love, but it is fear.

The Fear of God

Throughout our sermons there was one emotion and its object that was specifically commended by the preachers to their audiences. It was commended by both Peter and Paul three times total in two of our five sermons (Acts 10:35; 13:16, 26). That emotion was fear and its object each time was God. We've mentioned the concept of the "fear of God" briefly throughout our study, but now we need to look at it specifically. Perhaps no title better summarizes what a sincere Christian is or ought to be than the phrase "God-fearing man." Thus, Calvin avers that in the church "true fear of Almighty God" distinguishes the sincere believer from the hypocrite.[9]

[9] Calvin, *Commentaries*, vol. XVIII, 516–17.

God Himself looks for and accepts the fear of Him in His people. Here are a few of the hundreds of passages of Scripture that commend to us the fear of the Lord:

1. The one thing God looked for in His people when He spoke to them on Mt. Sinai was fear. They were not to be terrified of God, yet at the same time, He wanted them to fear Him in the sense of reverence, so that they would not sin:

   "And Moses said to the people, 'Do not fear; for God has come to test you, and that His fear may be before you, so that you may not sin'" (Exodus 20:20).

2. The one thing God tested Abraham for was to see if he feared Him:

   "And He said, 'Do not lay your hand on the lad, or do anything to him; for now I know that you fear God, since you have not withheld your son, your only son, from Me'" (Genesis 22:12).

3. The one quality that God twice uses to describe Job's blamelessness and uprightness was that He feared God. Here we notice that to fear God is to turn away from evil:

   "Then the Lord said to Satan, 'Have you considered My servant Job, that there is none like him on the earth, a blameless and upright man, one who fears God and shuns evil?'" (Job 1:8; see also Job 2:3).

4. In one of the most famous messianic passages, the Messiah is twice known by the fear of the Lord. Jesus "delights" in the fear of the Lord, and the Holy Spirit is the Spirit of the fear of the Lord who rests upon Him:

"There shall come forth a Rod from the stem of Jesse, and a Branch shall grow out of his roots. The Spirit of the Lord shall rest upon Him, the Spirit of wisdom and understanding, the Spirit of counsel and might, the Spirit of knowledge and of the fear of the Lord. His delight is in the fear of the Lord" (Isaiah 11:1–3).

5. And in fact, when Jesus came, His prayer life was marked by fear:

   "Who, in the days of His flesh, when He had offered up prayers and supplications, with vehement cries and tears to Him who was able to save Him from death, and was heard because of His godly fear" (Hebrews 5:7).

6. The one quality that God declares makes the worship of His New Testament church acceptable to Him is fear. Here two different words for "fear" are in the text. Thus we could paraphrase that to worship (serve) God acceptably, we must do so with two different kinds of fear:

   "Therefore, since we are receiving a kingdom which cannot be shaken, let us have grace, by which we may serve God acceptably with reverence and godly fear" (Heb. 12:28).

7. Closer to our subject, when Luke wanted to show the faithfulness of the early church, he calls attention to their fear:

   > "And they continued steadfastly in the apostles' doctrine and fellowship, in the breaking of bread, and in prayers. Then fear came upon every soul, and many wonders and signs were done through the apostles" (Acts 2:42–43).

> "Then the churches throughout all Judea, Galilee, and Samaria had peace and were edified. And walking in the fear of the Lord and in the comfort of the Holy Spirit, they were multiplied" (Acts 9:31).

Thus, very clearly the Bible does commend to us the fear of the Lord, from all three persons of the Trinity, as a mark of a faithful church, and as the quality that makes our worship or service acceptable to God. Since the fear of the Lord is crucial to the Christian life, and it is the only emotion explicitly commended in the five sermons of Scripture, we have included an adult Sunday school course on "The Fear of the Lord," in Appendix C of this book. As ministers seek to see their congregations grow in the fear of God, they are seeking to biblically motivate God's people.

19

Conclusion

My findings are that biblical sermons seek to motivate by proving the truth of who God is and what he has done. As we noted earlier from Jonathan Edwards, man as a rational being must live by what he believes is true. He cannot live any other way. Even the wicked of Romans 1 can only continue in sin while they suppress the truth in unrighteousness. They cannot live evil lives and *know* that they are evil. They must convince themselves that what they want to do is right and good, and so they suppress God's truth. They deny it in general revelation by misinterpreting it and convincing themselves that they are right with theories like evolution. They deny it in Scripture by justifying misinterpretations, or by deceiving themselves with false arguments that the Bible is not God's Word, and in both instances they try to convince themselves that they are right. But the crucial thing for them is *they must believe that they are right!*

A man *must* live by the truth. He *will* live by what he believes is true. Thus, the motivational task of the minister is to do all that he can to prove the truth of the doctrines he is preaching. The ultimate truth to be proven, which we have seen repeatedly in the biblical sermons, is the resurrection of Jesus Christ. If Jesus rose from the dead, then everything He said about Himself, His Word, and His Church is true. And if I am persuaded of that truth then I will live by it. However, here is where we must remember our Reformed theology: We are totally depraved sinners, and even if I preach the Word perfectly and prove every point to the uttermost, unless the Spirit of God removes the self-inflicted blindness of the sinner, he cannot see. He will not see proven truth, and he will hate you for showing it to him. If you persist, he will shut his eyes and refuse to see it. And if you make him see it, he will deny it or make himself quickly forget it, or else he will do all that he can to silence you, so that he does not have to see it anymore. Thus, Jesus testified to man's wickedness: "But because I tell the truth, you do not believe Me" (John 8:45). What an astonishing assertion! They did not believe in Jesus. And it was not because He told them false things (which is blasphemy to consider), or because He did not tell them enough truth, or make it plain enough. They did not believe in Jesus *because* He told them the truth!

Until converted, sinful man is of his father the devil. He hates the light and will not come to the light lest his deeds be exposed (see John 3:20). However, as God pleases, by His will and not fallen man's, He will cause that truth to bring forth dead sinners to new life: "Of His own will He brought us forth *by the word of truth*, that we might be a kind of firstfruits of His creatures" (James 1:18). Thus, our job as ministers is still to tell them the truth, to tell them as well as we possibly can. We are called to do all that we can to remove every protest, answer every honest question, expose every lie and distortion, remove every doubt, and refute every critic. The truth is the seed. As we sow, God promises to cause it to sometimes find good ground. Likewise, hearers of sermons should be listening for the truth—considering it and wrestling with it, until all doubt is removed. The truth believed is what God uses to motivate His people to trust in Him, to repent, and to do good. My study has shown that this assertion is necessarily true for every doctrine of Scripture. Even God's love only biblically motivates as the sinner is convinced of the truth of it. Consider: It is not that I feel God's love so much that out of appreciation for that love I am moved to love God back. God does not sanctify us through our still sin-laden feelings of love, but through our God-given and growing faith. Christian faith can only exist where there is truth, and truth cannot be received by feelings but only by belief.

I believe this one distinction, chronicled by this study, throughout the sermons of Scripture, is the most important contribution it can make to the sound preaching of God's Word. The error of our day, as it was advocated in article after article, was in *the way* that preaching is said to motivate by love, mercy, and grace. As we have seen, it is true that God's love, mercy, and grace motivate God's people, even as it is true that His wrath and judgment do, but in the sermons of Scripture, the preachers do not proclaim these things with a view toward motivating through their audience's emotions or feelings but through their faith. Thus, I do not try to make listeners feel God's love, or get emotionally choked up about God's mercy or grace, for then, by not appealing to their faith (present or potential), I do no good to them whatsoever. My job is to set forth, prove, and establish the truth of these things; to show them that God's love, mercy, and grace for His people is true; it is real; it is proven by Scripture, by miracle, and by the facts of history; and it is for them *right now*. Then, as God is pleased to quicken that truth to them, so that they are motivated through their God-given faith, no doubt emotions and feelings will come. Depending on the character and situation of each listener, the emotions and feelings will vary in kind and in strength. But they will be produced by the truth of the Word of God as it is proclaimed, heard, and believed. Whether for the first time, in the case of unbelievers being converted, or for the ten-thousandth time in the case of believers being sanctified, the minister's job is to proclaim the truth, the listener's responsibility is to receive the truth, which by definition can only be by faith. Both should pray to God to give or to strengthen faith according to His good pleasure.

The sermons of Scripture seek to motivate in all the doctrines that they mention, but always by appealing to the truth of them, and never by appealing to *feelings about them*. Thus, it is true to say that God's love should be used to motivate in a sermon, but only if we mean the truth of God's love for sinners; only if we purport that men would be moved to believe it when they see that it is true, and not moved to feel it by trying to make it elicit an emotional response from them. Faith is the apple that by the grace of God grows on the branch of truth. Preachers must supply the branches and pray for God to give the fruit. Listeners must recognize and cling to those branches, while praying for God to give the fruit.

Consequently, all Christians, both preachers and listeners, must first study the Scriptures and the proof that they exhibit of themselves, so that *we* will become more convinced of their truth. Only as our doubts are answered and our persuasion of God's truth grows, can our faith grow too. Only as ministers believe in God's truth will we strive to proclaim, defend, establish, and prove the truth in our sermons. Only as listeners believe in God's truth will they seek to be rightly motivated by the truth as they hear sermons. Only then will we believe that God's Word can save and sanctify His people. Only then will we believe in God's power by faith in His Word: that He *will* save through His Word, and that He *will* sanctify through His Word. However, to the degree that I doubt God's Word, I will rely on other things to move God's people. I will seek to woo by sentimental stories, or wow by multimedia presentations, or will depend on our powers of persuasion, or rhetorical skill, or academic polish, or whatever. Likewise, listeners will look to other things to motivate them. They will seek to have their ears tickled or their pride flattered. They will demand entertainment to feel that rush of emotion, which comes without intellectual effort or soul-searching struggle. But unless or until each one is personally convinced of the power of God's truth, we will not strive to proclaim it or hear it because we will not believe that it is mighty to save.

Moreover, there are no shortcuts. Only through faithful and sincere use of the means of grace should we expect God to continually subdue our unbelief and strengthen our faith. I cannot make myself grow in my persuasion in the truth of God's Word. I cannot make my faith grow stronger. I cannot simply say, "I begin my thinking by presuming that all of God's Word is inerrant and infallible. Presto, now my faith is perfect!" Faith is the gift of God. I cannot make myself believe. I cannot make my faith grow. I cannot say something is true and really believe it any more than I can say I can fly and really believe it. It is impossible for me to fly and I know that. However, apart from the sovereign grace of God, it is impossible for me to believe in God's Word; *do you know that*? We know with our minds and confess with our mouths that God's Word is inerrant and infallible, but we cannot get that truth into our hearts. We sin and struggle precisely because our faith is weak. Still we come back to the undeniable fact that human beings only believe in what they are convinced is true. So holding onto Christ's promise to send to us the Spirit of truth (see John 14:17; Acts 2:38), and to sanctify us "by the truth" (John 17:17); with what little faith He is pleased to give us, we set forth His "word of truth" (Eph. 1:13) before our eyes and pray that it would continue to work effectually in us through our faith (see 1 Thess. 2:13). As we look to God to move us by faith in His truth, we must love God and His people enough to seek to incorporate that truth into our sermons. The biblical sermons were all united in their constant theme of proving the truth of their content for the glory of God and the good of His people. We must do the same.

You and I cannot live on fantasy, on sentiment, or on our own assertions. Sinful doubt is not overcome that way. My faith responds to truth. But I will not accept anything as truth unless or until I am persuaded and convinced of it. Therefore, as I grow in my persuasion of the truth of God's Word, I am able, by the grace of God, to grow in my faith. As I grow in my faith in the truth, I will be able to trust in the Word of truth alone to motivate God's people when I preach. And as I do all I can to prove and establish the truth of God's Word to His people, the promise of Jesus Christ Himself is, that by His sovereign power, that truth will be received by His elect as His Spirit quickens it to them so that they will be converted, believe, and grow in that faith. May God grant that these true words of Jesus will begin to strengthen your faith in the truth of His Word: "For this cause I was born, and for this cause I have come into the world, that I should bear witness to the truth. Everyone who is of the truth hears My voice" (John 18:37b). Jesus Christ swears to you that His elect *will hear His truth.* Will we believe Him enough to preach it and to hear it?

Appendix A: Doctrinal Similarities Chart

I. Sermonic Speech	**Sermon 1** Acts 2:14–40	**Sermon 2** Acts 3:11–26
1. Present with people 2. Public preaching 3. Facing one another	[14] But Peter, standing up with the eleven, raised his voice and said to them,	[12]So when Peter saw it, he responded to the people:
II. Concerning the Audience 1. Personal greetings 2. Commendations 3. Humble pleadings 4. Verses in brackets apply indirectly here; more directly to another point.	[14b]Men of Judea and all who dwell in Jerusalem, let this be known to you, and heed my words. [22]Men of Israel, hear these words: [29a]Men and brethren, [37b]Men and brethren, what shall we do?	[12a]So when Peter saw it, he responded to the people: "Men of Israel" [13]The God of Abraham, Isaac, and Jacob, the God of our fathers [17a]Yet now, brethren [25a]You are sons of the prophets, and of the covenant which God made with our fathers

Sermon 3 Acts 10:34–48	**Sermon 4** Acts 13:16–42	**Sermon 5** Acts 17:22–34
[34a]Then Peter opened his mouth and said:	[16]Then Paul stood up, and motioning with his hand said,	[22]Then Paul stood in the midst of the Areopagus and said,
[[34b]In truth I perceive that God shows no partiality. [35]But in every nation whoever fears Him and works righteousness is accepted by Him.]	[16b]Men of Israel, and you who fear God, listen [26a]Men and brethren, sons of the family of Abraham, and those among you who fear God [38a]Therefore let it be known to you, brethren	[22b]Men of Athens, I perceive that in all things you are very religious; [23a]for as I was passing through and considering the objects of your worship, I even found an altar with this inscription: TO THE UNKNOWN GOD. [28b]as also some of your own poets have said, "For we are also His offspring."

III. Sin Rebuked 1. Bluntly in columns 1, 2 2. By implication in columns 3, 4 3. Gently in column 5 4. Verses in brackets apply indirectly here; more directly to another point.	[15]For these are not drunk, as you suppose, since it is only the third hour of the day. [23b]you have taken by lawless hands, have crucified, and put to death; [36b]this Jesus, whom you crucified [[38b]Repent, and let every one of you be baptized in the name of Jesus Christ for the remission of sins] [[40b]saying, "Be saved from this perverse generation."]	[13b]whom you delivered up and denied in the presence of Pilate, when he was determined to let Him go. [14]But you denied the Holy One and the Just, and asked for a murderer to be granted to you, [15]and killed the Prince of life [17b]I know that you did it in ignorance, as did also your rulers [[19b]that your sins may be blotted out,] [[26b]in turning away every one of you from your iniquities.]
IV. Warning of Judgment Day 1. Wrath of God 2. God's/Jesus' wrath 3. End of this life	[19]"I will show wonders in heaven above and signs in the earth beneath: blood and fire and vapor of smoke. [20]The sun shall be turned into darkness, and the moon into blood, before the coming of the great and awesome day of the Lord."	[23]"And it shall be that every soul who will not hear that Prophet shall be utterly destroyed from among the people."

[34b In truth I perceive that God shows no partiality. 35 But in every nation whoever fears Him and works righteousness is accepted by Him.] 39 whom they killed by hanging on a tree. [43b through His name, whoever believes in Him will receive remission of sins.] [42c that it is He who was ordained by God to be Judge of the living and the dead.]	27 For those who dwell in Jerusalem, and their rulers, because they did not know Him, [nor even the voices of the Prophets which are read every Sabbath,] have fulfilled them in condemning Him. 28 And though they found no cause for death in Him, they asked Pilate that He should be put to death. [38b that through this Man is preached to you the forgiveness of sins] [41a Behold, you despisers, marvel and perish!]	23b Therefore, the One whom you worship without knowing 24b does not dwell in temples made with hands. 25 Nor is He worshiped with men's hands, 29b we ought not to think that the Divine Nature is like gold or silver or stone, something shaped by art and man's devising.
42c that it is He who was ordained by God to be Judge of the living and the dead.	40 Beware therefore, lest [what has been spoken in the prophets] come upon you: 41 "Behold, you despisers, Marvel and perish! For I work a work in your days, a work which you will by no means believe, though one were to declare it to you."	31 because He has appointed a day on which He will judge the world in righteousness by the Man whom He has ordained.

V. Prophetic Authority Claimed 1. Specifically in columns 1, 2, and 4 2. Generally in column 3 3. None in column 5 4. Authority of John the Baptist claimed in columns 3 and 4	[16]But this is what was spoken by the prophet Joel: [17a]"And it shall come to pass in the last days, says God" [25]For David says concerning Him [30a]Therefore [David], being a prophet	[18a]But those things which God foretold by the mouth of all His prophets, [21b]which God has spoken by the mouth of all His holy prophets since the world began. [22]For Moses truly said to the fathers [24]Yes, and all the prophets, from Samuel and those who follow, as many as have spoken, have also foretold these days. [25b]saying to Abraham, "And in your seed all the families of the earth shall be blessed."
VI. Official Apostolic Authority Claimed 1. Official witnesses to the resurrection in columns 1–4 2. Of Him generally or His gospel in columns 1–5	[32b]of which we are all witnesses. [40]And with many other words he testified and exhorted them.	[15c]of which we are witnesses

36The word which God sent to the children of Israel. . . . 37that word you know, which was proclaimed throughout all Judea, and began from Galilee after the baptism which John preached 43aTo Him all the prophets witness that . . .	27bthe voices of the Prophets which are read every Sabbath 35Therefore He also says in another Psalm 40bwhat has been spoken in the prophets 24after John had first preached, before His coming, the baptism of repentance to all the people of Israel. 25and as John was finishing his course, he said, "Who do you think I am? I am not He." 33bAs it is also written in the second Psalm:	
39aAnd we are witnesses of all things 42aAnd He commanded us to preach to the people, and to testify 41Not to all the people, but to witnesses chosen before by God	26bto you the word of this salvation has been sent. 30bwho are His witnesses to the people. 32"And we declare to you glad tidings—that promise which was made to the fathers.	23cHim I proclaim to you.

VII. Miraculous Attestation to Christ 1. Resurrection in columns 1–5 2. Other miracles in columns 1–3 3. Both are supernatural proof of His power and office, scripturally prophesied and sensorially fulfilled.	[22b]Jesus of Nazareth, a Man attested by God to you by miracles, wonders, and signs which God did through Him in your midst, as you yourselves also know— [24]whom God raised up, having loosed the pains of death. [32]This Jesus God has raised up [33b]He poured out this which you now see and hear. [17b]"That I will pour out of My Spirit on all flesh; your sons and your daughters shall prophesy, your young men shall see visions, your old men shall dream dreams. [18] And on My menservants and on My maidservants I will pour out My Spirit in those days; and they shall prophesy."	[12b]Why do you marvel at this? Or why look so intently at us, as though by our own power or godliness we had made this man walk? [16]And His name, through faith in His name, has made this man strong, whom you see and know. Yes, the faith which comes through Him has given him this perfect soundness in the presence of you all. [15b]whom God raised from the dead. [26]To you first, God, having raised up His Servant Jesus

[38a]how God anointed Jesus of Nazareth with the Holy Spirit and with power [38c]and healing all who were oppressed by the devil, for God was with Him. [39b]which He did both in the land of the Jews and in Jerusalem, . . . [40]Him God raised up on the third day, and showed Him openly. [41b]even to us who ate and drank with Him after He arose from the dead. [46]For they heard them speak with tongues and magnify God.	[29b]they took Him down from the tree and laid Him in a tomb. [30]But God raised Him from the dead. [31]He was seen for many days by those who came up with Him from Galilee to Jerusalem	[31b]He has given assurance of this to all by raising Him from the dead.

VIII. Prophetic Witness to the Resurrection	[26]"Therefore my heart rejoiced, and my tongue was glad; moreover my flesh also will rest in hope. [27]For You will not leave my soul in Hades, nor will You allow Your Holy One to see corruption. [28]You have made known to me the ways of life; you will make me full of joy in Your presence." [31]he, foreseeing this, spoke concerning the resurrection of the Christ, that His soul was not left in Hades, nor did His flesh see corruption.	
IX. Facts of History 1. Prove resurrection 2. Prove Jesus is the Christ 3. Verses in brackets apply indirectly here; more directly to another point.	[29b]Let me speak freely to you of the patriarch David, that he is both dead and buried, and his tomb is with us to this day. [[22c]which God did through Him in your midst, as you yourselves also know.]	[[12b]why do you marvel at this? Or why look so intently at us?] [[16b]has made this man strong, whom you see and know.] [[16d]in the presence of you all.]

	[33b]in that He has raised up Jesus. . . . "You are My Son, Today I have begotten You." [34]And that He raised Him from the dead, no more to return to corruption, He has spoken thus: "I will give you the sure mercies of David." [35b]"You will not allow Your Holy One to see corruption."	
[[39b]which He did both in the land of the Jews and in Jerusalem] [[40]Him God raised up on the third day, and showed Him openly]	[36]For David, after he had served his own generation by the will of God, fell asleep, was buried with his fathers, and saw corruption. [37]but He whom God raised up saw no corruption.	[[24]God, who made the world and everything in it, since He is Lord of heaven and earth] [[28]for in Him we live and move and have our being] [[29]Therefore, since we are the offspring of God.]

X. The Sovereignty and Goodness of God/Christ 1. Over all things 2. Fulfilling His word 3. Exalting Jesus 4. Doing good to all (love of benevolence) 5. Providence 6. Saving acts 7. Equity	[23]"Him, being delivered by the determined purpose and foreknowledge of God [24b]because it was not possible that He should be held by it. [25b]"I foresaw the LORD always before my face, for He is at my right hand, that I may not be shaken." [30b]and knowing that God had sworn with an oath to him that of the fruit of his body, according to the flesh, He would raise up the Christ to sit on his throne. [33]Therefore being exalted to the right hand of God, and having received from the Father the promise of the Holy Spirit [34]For David did not ascend into the heavens, but he says himself: "The LORD said to my Lord, 'Sit at My right hand, [35]till I make Your enemies Your footstool.'" [36]Therefore let all the house of Israel know assuredly that God has made this Jesus . . . both Lord and Christ.	[13b]glorified His Servant Jesus. [18b]that the Christ would suffer, He has thus fulfilled. [21]whom heaven must receive until the times of restoration of all things. [22b]"The LORD your God will raise up for you a Prophet like me from your brethren. Him you shall hear in all things, whatever He says to you."

34b In truth I perceive that God shows no partiality. 35 But in every nation whoever fears Him and works righteousness is accepted by Him. 36b Jesus Christ—He is Lord of all— 38b who went about doing good.	17 The God of this people Israel chose our fathers, and exalted the people when they dwelt as strangers in the land of Egypt, and with an uplifted arm He brought them out of it. 18 Now for a time of about forty years He put up with their ways in the wilderness. 19 And when He had destroyed seven nations in the land of Canaan, He distributed their land to them by allotment. 20 After that He gave them judges for about four hundred and fifty years, until Samuel the prophet. 21 And afterward they asked for a king; so God gave them Saul the son of Kish, a man of the tribe of Benjamin, for forty years. 22 And when He had removed him, He raised up for them David as king, to whom also He gave testimony and said, "I have found David the son of Jesse, a man after My own heart, who will do all My will." 23 From this man's seed, according to the promise, God raised up for Israel a Savior—Jesus 25b "But behold, there comes One after me, the sandals of whose feet I am not worthy to loose." 29 "Now when they had fulfilled all that was written concerning Him 33 God has fulfilled this for us their children.	24 God, who made the world and everything in it, since He is Lord of heaven and earth 25b as though He needed anything, since He gives to all life, breath, and all things. 26 And He has made from one blood every nation of men to dwell on all the face of the earth, and has determined their preappointed times and the boundaries of their dwellings, 27 so that they should seek the Lord, in the hope that they might grope for Him and find Him, though He is not far from each one of us; 28a for in Him we live and move and have our being. 29a Therefore, since we are the offspring of God

XI. Response 1. Conviction 2. Sorrow/Joy 3. Eagerness 4. Faith/Repentance 5. Obedience 6. Praise 7. Mocking	[37]Now when they heard this, they were cut to the heart, and said to Peter and the rest of the apostles . . . [41]Then those who gladly received his word were baptized; and that day about three thousand souls were added to them.	[4:4]However, many of those who heard the word believed; and the number of the men came to be about five thousand.
XII. Salvation Announced 1. "Repent" in columns 1–2, 5; implied in columns 3–4. 2. "Believe" in columns 1, 3–4; implied in columns 2, 5. 3. Forgiveness in columns 1–4; implied in column 5. 4. Other blessings: Holy Spirit (column 1) Refreshing (column 2) Presence of Christ (column 2) Sanctification (column 2) Peace (column 3) Justification (column 4)	[21]And it shall come to pass that whoever calls on the name of the Lord shall be saved. [38]Then Peter said to them, "Repent, and let every one of you be baptized in the name of Jesus Christ for the remission of sins; and you shall receive the gift of the Holy Spirit. [39]For the promise is to you and to your children, and to all who are afar off, as many as the Lord our God will call." [40b]saying, "Be saved from this perverse generation."	[19]Repent therefore and be converted, that your sins may be blotted out, so that times of refreshing may come from the presence of the Lord, [20]and that He may send Jesus Christ, who was preached to you before. [26b]sent Him to bless you, in turning away every one of you from your iniquities.

[44]While Peter was still speaking these words, the Holy Spirit fell upon all those who heard the word. [48]And he commanded them to be baptized in the name of the Lord. Then they asked him to stay a few days.	[42]So when the Jews went out of the synagogue, the Gentiles begged that these words might be preached to them the next Sabbath. [43]Now when the congregation had broken up, many of the Jews and devout proselytes followed Paul and Barnabas.	[32]And when they heard of the resurrection of the dead, [33]some mocked, while others said, "We will hear you again on this matter." [34]However, some men joined him and believed, among them Dionysius the Areopagite, a woman named Damaris, and others with them.
[36b]preaching peace through Jesus Christ [43b]through His name, whoever believes in Him will receive remission of sins.	[38b]that through this Man is preached to you the forgiveness of sins; [39]and by Him everyone who believes is justified from all things from which you could not be justified by the law of Moses. [43b]who, speaking to them, persuaded them to continue in the grace of God.	[30]Truly, these times of ignorance God overlooked, but now commands all men everywhere to repent.

Appendix B:
Structural Similarities Chart

I. Opening Preface	**Sermon 1** Acts 2:14–40 [14a]But Peter, standing up with the eleven, raised his voice and said to them	**Sermon 2** Acts 3:11–26 [12a]So when Peter saw it, he responded to the people
II. Introductory Address	[14b]Men of Judea and all who dwell in Jerusalem, let this be known to you, and heed my words.	[12b]Men of Israel. . . .
III. Correction of Sinful Misconception or Error/ Ignorance	[15]For these are not drunk, as you suppose, since it is only the third hour of the day.	[12c]Why do you marvel at this? Or why look so intently at us, as though by our own power or godliness we had made this man walk?

Sermon 3 Acts 10:34–48 34aThen Peter opened his mouth and said:	**Sermon 4** Acts 13:16–42 16aThen Paul stood up, and motioning with his hand said,	**Sermon 5** Acts 17:22–34 22aThen Paul stood in the midst of the Areopagus and said,
	16bMen of Israel, and you who fear God, listen	22bMen of Athens
34bIn truth I perceive that God shows no partiality. 35But in every nation whoever fears Him and works righteousness is accepted by Him.		22cI perceive that in all things you are very religious; 23for as I was passing through and considering the objects of your worship, I even found an altar with this inscription: TO THE UNKNOWN GOD. Therefore, the One whom you worship without knowing, Him I proclaim to you.

IV. Sermon Body God's Power, Goodness, Saving Acts, and Judgments (emphasis added)	[16]*But this is what was spoken by the prophet Joel:* [17]*"And it shall come to pass in the last days, says God, that I will pour out of My Spirit on all flesh; your sons and your daughters shall prophesy, your young men shall see visions, your old men shall dream dreams.* [18]*And on My menservants and on My maidservants I will pour out My Spirit in those days; And they shall prophesy.* [19]*I will show wonders in heaven above And signs in the earth beneath: blood and fire and vapor of smoke.* [20]*The sun shall be turned into darkness, and the moon into blood, Before the coming of the great and awesome day of the* LORD. [21]*And it shall come to pass that whoever calls on the name of the* LORD *shall be saved."* [22]Men of Israel, hear these words.	[13]The *God* of Abraham, Isaac, and Jacob, the God of our fathers

[36]"The word which *God* sent to the children of Israel, preaching peace	*[17]The God of this people Israel chose our fathers, and exalted the people when they dwelt as strangers in the land of Egypt, and with an uplifted arm He brought them out of it. [18]Now for a time of about forty years He put up with their ways in the wilderness. [19]And when He had destroyed seven nations in the land of Canaan, He distributed their land to them by allotment. [20]After that He gave them judges for about four hundred and fifty years, until Samuel the prophet. [21]And afterward they asked for a king; so God gave them Saul the son of Kish, a man of the tribe of Benjamin, for forty years. [22]And when He had removed him, He raised up for them David as king, to whom also He gave testimony and said, "I have found David the son of Jesse, a man after My own heart, who will do all My will."*	*[24]God, who made the world and everything in it,* since He is Lord of heaven and earth, does not dwell in temples made with hands. [25]Nor is He worshiped with men's hands, as though He needed anything, since *He gives to all life, breath, and all things. [26]And He has made from one blood every nation of men to dwell on all the face of the earth, and has determined their preappointed times and the boundaries of their dwellings*

V. Sermon Body: Jesus' Power, Goodness, Saving Acts, and Judgments (emphasis added)	22b"Jesus of Nazareth, a Man attested by God to you by miracles, wonders, and signs which God did through Him in your midst, as you yourselves also know—23Him, being delivered by the determined purpose and foreknowledge of God, you have taken by lawless hands, have crucified, and put to death; 24whom God raised up, having loosed the pains of death, because it was not possible that He should be held by it. *25For David says concerning Him: 'I foresaw the Lord always before my face, for He is at my right hand, that I may not be shaken. 26Therefore my heart rejoiced, and my tongue was glad; moreover my flesh also will rest in hope. 27For You will not leave my soul in Hades, nor will You allow Your Holy One to see corruption. 28You have made known to me the ways of life; You will make me full of joy in Your presence.'* 29Men and brethren, let me speak freely to you of *the patriarch David*, that he is both dead and buried, and his tomb is with us to this day. *30Therefore, being a prophet, and knowing that God had sworn with an oath to him that of the fruit of his body, according to the flesh, He would raise up the Christ to sit on his throne, 31he, foreseeing this, spoke concerning the resurrection of the Christ, that His soul was not left in Hades, nor did His flesh see corruption.* 32This Jesus God has raised up, of which we are all witnesses. 33Therefore being exalted to the right hand of God, and having received from the Father the promise of the *Holy Spirit*, He poured out this which you now see and hear. 34For *David* did not ascend into the heavens, *but he says himself: 'The Lord said to my Lord, "Sit at My right hand, 35till I make Your enemies Your footstool."'* 36Therefore let all the *house of Israel* know assuredly that God has made this Jesus, whom you crucified, both *Lord and Christ*." 37Now when they heard this, they were cut to the heart, and said to Peter and the rest of the apostles, "Men and brethren, what shall we do?"	13bglorified *His Servant* Jesus, whom you delivered up and denied in the presence of Pilate, when he was determined to let Him go. 14But you denied *the Holy One and the Just*, and asked for a murderer to be granted to you, 15and killed the Prince of life, whom God raised from the dead, of which we are witnesses. 16And His name, through faith in His name, has made this man strong, whom you see and know. Yes, the faith which comes through Him has given him this perfect soundness in the presence of you all. 17Yet now, brethren, I know that you did it in ignorance, as did also your rulers. *18But those things which God foretold by the mouth of all His prophets, that the Christ would suffer, He has thus fulfilled.* 19Repent therefore and be converted, that your *sins may be blotted out*, so that *times of refreshing* may come from the presence of the *Lord*, 20and that He may send Jesus *Christ*, who was preached to you before, 21whom heaven must receive until *the times of restoration of all things, which God has spoken by the mouth of all His holy prophets since the world began. 22For Moses truly said to the fathers, "The Lord your God will raise up for you a Prophet like me from your brethren. Him you shall hear in all things, whatever He says to you. 23And it shall be that every soul who will not hear that Prophet shall be utterly destroyed from among the people." 24Yes, and all the prophets, from Samuel and those who follow, as many as have spoken, have also foretold these days.*

[36b]through Jesus *Christ*—He is *Lord of all*—[37] that word you know, which was proclaimed throughout all Judea, and began from Galilee after the baptism which John preached: [38]how God anointed Jesus of Nazareth with the *Holy Spirit* and with power, who went about doing good and healing all who were oppressed by the devil, for God was with Him. [39]And we are witnesses of all things which He did both in the land of the Jews and in Jerusalem, whom they killed by hanging on a tree. [40]Him God raised up on the third day, and showed Him openly, [41]not to all the people, but to witnesses chosen before by God, even to us who ate and drank with Him after He arose from the dead.	[23]From this man's seed, according to the promise, God raised up for Israel *a* Savior—Jesus—[24] after John had first preached, before His coming, the baptism of repentance to all the people of Israel. [25]And as John was finishing his course, he said, "Who do you think I am? I am not He. But behold, there comes One after me, the sandals of whose feet I am not worthy to loose." [26]Men and brethren, sons of the family of *Abraham*, and those among you who fear God, to you the word of this salvation has been sent. [27]For those who dwell in Jerusalem, and their rulers, because they did not know Him, nor *even the voices of the Prophets which are read every Sabbath, have fulfilled them in condemning Him*. [28]And should be put to death. [9]*Now when they had fulfilled all that*[2] *was written concerning Him*, they took Him down from the tree and laid Him in a tomb. [30]But God raised Him from the dead. [31]He was seen for many days by those who came up with Him from Galilee to Jerusalem, who are His witnesses to the people. [32]And we declare to you glad tidings—that promise which was made to the fathers. [33]God has fulfilled this for us their children, in that He has raised up Jesus. *As it is also written in the second Psalm: "You are My Son; today I have begotten You."* [34]And that He raised Him from the dead, no more to return to corruption, *He has spoken thus: "I will give you the sure mercies of David."* [35]*Therefore He also says in another Psalm: "You will not allow Your Holy One to see corruption."* [36]For *David*, after he had served his own generation by the will of God, fell asleep, was buried with his fathers, and saw corruption; [37]but He whom God raised up saw no corruption.	[27]so that they should seek *the Lord*, in the hope that they might grope for Him and find Him, though He is not far from each one of us; [28] for in Him we live and move and have our being, as also some of your own poets have said, "For we are also His offspring." [29]Therefore, since we are the offspring of God, we ought not to think that the Divine Nature is like gold or silver or stone, something shaped by art and man's devising.

VI. Final Exhortation: Call to Repentance, Faith, Forgiveness of Sins, Salvation, and Warning of Judgment In Sermon 2, faith, repentance, and judgment is found more explicitly in the middle of the sermon (vv. 16, 19–20, 23). Yet these things can still be seen in the blessing of Abraham (v. 25); and in the blessing of Jesus in being turned from iniquities (v. 26).	38 Then Peter said to them, "Repent, and let every one of you be baptized in the name of Jesus *Christ* for the remission of sins; and you shall receive the *gift of the Holy Spirit.* 39 *For the promise is to you and to your children*, and to all who are afar off, as many as the *Lord* our God will call." 40 And with many other words he testified and exhorted them, saying, "Be saved from this perverse generation."	25 *You are sons of the prophets, and of the covenant which God made with our fathers, saying to Abraham, "And in your seed all the families of the earth shall be blessed."* 26 To you first, God, having raised up *His Servant* Jesus, sent Him to bless you, in turning away every one of you from your iniquities.

[42]And He commanded us to preach to the people, and to testify that it is He who was ordained by God to be *Judge of the living and the dead.* [43]*To Him all the prophets witness* that, through His name, whoever believes in Him will receive remission of sins. [44]While Peter was still speaking these words, the *Holy Spirit* fell upon all those who heard the word.	[38]Therefore let it be known to you, brethren, that through this Man is preached to you the forgiveness of sins; [39]and by Him everyone who believes is justified from all things from which you could not be justified *by the law of Moses.* [40]*Beware therefore, lest what has been spoken in the prophets come upon you:* [41]*"Behold, you despisers, marvel and perish! For I work a work in your days, a work which you will by no means believe, though one were to declare it to you."*	[30]"Truly, these times of ignorance God overlooked, but now commands all men everywhere to repent, [31]*because He has appointed a day on which He will judge the world in righteousness* by the Man whom He has ordained. He has given assurance of this to all by raising Him from the dead." [32]And when they heard of the resurrection of the dead, some mocked, while others said, "We will hear you again on this matter."

Appendix C: A Sunday-School Teaching Outline on the Fear of God

Class 1: What Is Fear?

I. Fear: dictionary definition and synonyms (Webster, Encarta)
   A. An unpleasant often strong emotion caused by anticipation or awareness of danger
   B. An unpleasant feeling of anxiety or apprehension caused by the presence or anticipation of danger
   C. Dread, alarm, fright, panic, terror, trepidation, worry, reverence, anxiety, apprehension, afraid

II. Words in the Bible used to convey fear: a rich, variegated theme throughout the whole Bible
   A. ארי—he feared; most common word: 385 times in the 39 books of OT
   B. רוג alt. of רגי—v. approximately a dozen times to convey fear (108 total: usually sojourner, stranger)
   C. דחפ—terror, dread: 75 times
   D. זגר—tremble, agitate, disturb: 49 times
   E. הָמֵיא—horror, fright: 17 times
   F. ץרע—terrified, be in dread: 15 times
   G. φοβέομαι—I feared: 93 times
   H. φόβος, φοβερός—fear; phobia: 44 times, 3 times

I. ἔκφοβος—afraid: 2 times
J. ἔντρομος—terrified, trembling: 3 times
K. εὐλάβεια—reverence, godly fear: 2 times
L. ἔμφοβος—afraid, terrified: 5 times

III. In general, fear is undesirable, yet fear of God is to be sought after, cultivated, and greatly prized.
   A. The object is what makes the emotional or mental state desirable or undesirable.
   B. This is true for most things: love God; do not love world. Hate evil, hate sin; do not hate your neighbor, do not hate your brother.
      1. "Do not love the world or the things in the world. If anyone loves the world, the love of the Father is not in him" (1 John 2:15).
      2. "Hate evil, love good; establish justice in the gate. It may be that the Lord God of hosts will be gracious to the remnant of Joseph" (Amos 5:15).
   C. The concept of fear is no different—the object of the fear determines the nature of it; likewise, the quality of the fear itself determines whether it is good or bad.
   D. There is a sense in which we are to fear God, and there is a sense in which we are not to fear God.
   E. This also is true for other concepts such as love and hate. We are commanded to love our spouses, parents, and children and we are not to hate them. However there is a sense in which we are to hate our closest family members. Likewise we are to love our lives and we are to hate them.
      1. "If anyone comes to Me and does not hate his father and mother, wife and children, brothers and sisters, yes, and his own life also, he cannot be My disciple" (Luke 14:26).
      2. So we love, hate, and fear, not in the same way or for the same reasons.

III. Even undesirable fear is often good for us.
  A. It is good to be afraid of the lion, the poisonous snake, or the spider.
  B. I have a "healthy" fear of the ocean, but not very much of saturated fats!
  C. Fear of failing can make us study harder, practice more.
  D. Fear of embarrassment or humiliation can help to keep us from shameful sins.
  E. Fear of my own weaknesses can keep me from sins of pride and from looking down on others: "Well said. Because of unbelief they were broken off, and you stand by faith. Do not be haughty, but fear. For if God did not spare the natural branches, He may not spare you either" (Rom. 11:20).

IV. Modern Christianity has all but abandoned a positive, desirable notion of the fear of God.
  A. If we followed the balance of the Bible we should hear more than twice as much teaching in our churches on the fear of God as we do on the love of God.
  B. The number of times the following phrases appear in NKJV; not the same as the concept but significant:
    1. fear of God: 8 love of God: 12
    2. fear God: 17 love God: 4
    3. fear the Lord: 35 love the Lord: 18
    4. fear of the Lord: 27 love of the Lord: 1
    Totals: fear God = 87 love God = 35
  C. According to Rev. Arnold Frank on the fear of God, apart from hymns that are Psalms, references to fear in the Trinity Hymnal are almost entirely the kind of fear that we should not have.[1]

[1] Arnold L. Frank, *The Fear of God, A Forgotten Doctrine* (Ventura, CA: Nordskog, 2008), 11.

D. The Psalms are filled with the admonition and blessing to fear the Lord.
E. What other category or books of the Bible are known for teaching on the fear of God?
F. The phrase "Not fear" occurs in the Bible seventy-six times; only ten in the NT!
G. "Not be afraid" occurs sixty-three times; only eighteen are in the NT!
H. If we added in the more "positive" English translations of "fear" (reverence, awe), which are overwhelmingly in reference to God, we would have another sixty times that the Bible commends to us fear as a desirable and good thing that we should seek in our relationship to God.

V. Ask if there any particular verses or concepts listeners would like to cover. Books to aid understanding:
   A. *The Fear of God: A Forgotten Doctrine* by Arnold Frank
   B. *The Fear of God, the Soul of Godliness* by John Murray
   C. *The Fear of God* by John Bunyan

VI. The Bible's teaching on fear.
   A. First appearance of the word fear: "So he said, 'I heard Your voice in the garden, and I was afraid because I was naked; and I hid myself'" (Gen. 3:10).
   B. First appearance of the concept?
   C. "Let all the earth fear the Lord; let all the inhabitants of the world stand in awe of Him. For He spoke, and it was done; He commanded, and it stood fast" (Ps. 33:8–9).
   D. Did Adam and Eve fear God before the Fall?
   E. Did sinless Jesus fear God?
   F. "And the Lord God commanded the man, saying, 'Of every tree of the garden you may freely eat; but of the

tree of the knowledge of good and evil you shall not eat, for in the day that you eat of it you shall surely die'" (Gen. 2:16–17).

G. "Who, in the days of His flesh, when He had offered up prayers and supplications, with vehement cries and tears to Him who was able to save Him from death, and was heard because of His godly fear" (Heb. 5:7).
H. "There shall come forth a Rod from the stem of Jesse, and a Branch shall grow out of his roots. The Spirit of the Lord shall rest upon Him, the Spirit of wisdom and understanding, the Spirit of counsel and might, the Spirit of knowledge and of the fear of the Lord. His delight is in the fear of the Lord, and He shall not judge by the sight of His eyes, nor decide by the hearing of His ears" (Isa. 11:1–3).
I. Will we fear God in heaven?

Class 2: A Natural Fear of God and the Restraining of Evil—Part 1

Intro: Hymns vs. Psalms: Ask people to read verses from hymns and Psalms about the fear of God.

A. Usually when fear is mentioned in the hymnal, it is the bad kind of fear we are delivered from.
B. Usually when fear is mentioned in the Psalms, it is the good kind of fear that we should seek.
C. For example: "For as the heavens are high above the earth, so great is His mercy toward those who fear Him; . . . As a father pities his children, So the Lord pities those who fear Him; . . . But the mercy of the Lord is from everlasting to everlasting on those who fear Him" (Ps. 103:11, 13, 17).
D. Discuss: What accounts for the difference? Be thinking about these two kinds of fear; we'll see this again.

I. Natural Law (the nature of things as God has created them) teaches the fear of God.
   A. "[T]here is a fear of God which flows from the light of nature. A people may be said to do things in the fear of God, when they act one towards another in things reasonable and honest betwixt man and man, not doing that to others they would not have done to themselves." John Bunyan[2]
   B. WCF 1.1: "Although the light of nature, and the works of creation and providence do so far manifest the goodness, wisdom, and power of God, as to leave men unexcusable . . ."—4 passages here cited.
   C. Discuss how each of these verses cite by the Westminster Assembly show men to be without excuse:
      1. "For when Gentiles, who do not have the law, by nature do the things in the law, these, although not having the law, are a law to themselves, who show the work of the law written in their hearts, their conscience also bearing witness, and between themselves their thoughts accusing or else excusing them" (Rom. 2:14–15).
      2. "Because what may be known of God is manifest in them, for God has shown it to them. For since the creation of the world His invisible attributes are clearly seen, being understood by the things that are made, even His eternal power and Godhead, so that they are without excuse" (Rom. 1:19–20).
      3. "The heavens declare the glory of God; and the firmament shows His handiwork. Day unto day utters speech, and night unto night reveals knowledge.

[2] John Bunyan, *The Fear of* God (Sterling, VA: G.A.M. Publications, 1990), 26; quoted in Frank, *The Fear of God*, 17.

There is no speech nor language where their voice is not heard" (Ps. 19:1–3).

4. "Who, knowing the righteous judgment of God, that those who practice such things are deserving of death, not only do the same but also approve of those who practice them; therefore you are inexcusable, O man, whoever you are who judge, for in whatever you judge another you condemn yourself; for you who judge practice the same things" (Rom. 1:32–2:1).

II. General revelation shows all mankind that there is a God and that He is to be feared.

A. Briefly describe the difference between general and special revelation.

B. The phrase "light of nature," which we saw above, is in the Westminster Standards fully ten times! "The light of nature showeth that there is a God, who hath lordship and sovereignty over all; is good, and doth good unto all; and is therefore to be feared, loved, praised, called upon, trusted in, and served, with all the heart, and with all the soul, and with all the might." (WCF 21.1)

C. Ask for some ways in which God's sovereignty over and goodness to all provoke the fear of Him.

D. Refer to the following verses in your discussion. Point out how Scripture views the thought of not fearing God as unthinkable.

1. "There is none like you, O Lord; you are great, and your name is great in might. Who would not fear You, O King of the nations? For this is Your rightful due. For among all the wise men of the nations, and in all their kingdoms, there is none like You" (Jer. 10:6–7).

2. "For who in the heavens can be compared to the

Lord? Who among the sons of the mighty can be likened to the Lord? God is greatly to be feared in the assembly of the saints, and to be held in reverence by all those around Him" (Ps. 89:6–7).

3. "The Almighty—we cannot find Him; He is exalted in power and He will not do violence to justice and abundant righteousness. Therefore men fear Him; He does not regard any who are wise of heart" (Job 37:23–24 NASB).
4. "'Do you not fear Me?' declares the Lord. 'Do you not tremble in My presence? For I have placed the sand as a boundary for the sea, an eternal decree, so it cannot cross over it. Though the waves toss, yet they cannot prevail; though they roar, yet they cannot cross over it'" (Jer. 5:22 NASB).
5. "For the kingdom is the Lord's, and He rules over the nations" (Ps. 22:28).
6. "They sing the song of Moses, the servant of God, and the song of the Lamb, saying: 'Great and marvelous are Your works, Lord God Almighty! Just and true are Your ways, O King of the saints! Who shall not fear You, O Lord, and glorify Your name? For You alone are holy. For all nations shall come and worship before You, for Your judgments have been manifested'" (Rev. 15:3–4).

III. The fallen nature of man, particularly marked by the absence of the fear of God, leads to all forms of evil.

A. There is no fear of God before their eyes (see Rom. 3:10–18).

1. The lack of the fear of God is here seen as both the culmination and the root of man's sin.
2. Discuss how the sins in this list are affected by a lack of fearing God.

B. "An oracle within my heart concerning the transgression of the wicked: There is no fear of God before his eyes. For he flatters himself in his own eyes, when he finds out his iniquity and when he hates. The words of his mouth are wickedness and deceit; he has ceased to be wise and to do good. He devises wickedness on his bed; he sets himself in a way that is not good; he does not abhor evil" (Ps. 36:1–4).
   1. Again "the wicked" are summarized as those who have "no fear of God before [their] eyes."
   2. Notice how the lack of fearing God leads to the lack of hating sin.

C. "But the midwives feared God, and did not do as the king of Egypt commanded them. . . ." (see Ex. 1:15–21).
   1. Talk about how Pharaoh's command to murder babies was a gross lack of fearing God.
   2. How does abortion today show a lack of fearing God?
   3. Connect how general revelation must be suppressed if men are going to not fear God.
   4. Discuss examples from Scripture where the fear of God can be found before the Law on Sinai. For example: "Select from all the people able men, such as fear God, men of truth, hating covetousness" (Ex. 18:21).

D. "In mercy and truth atonement is provided for iniquity; and by the fear of the Lord one departs from evil" (Prov. 16:6).
   1. Earlier we saw that where there is a lack of fearing God, men do not hate but embrace evil.
   2. Here we see affirmed the opposite; that where God is feared men depart from evil.
   3. Applying this truth to our nation, discuss how much our nation does or does not fear God.

E. "Rejoice, O young man, in your youth, and let your heart cheer you in the days of your youth; walk in the ways of your heart, and in the sight of your eyes; but know that for all these God will bring you into judgment. Therefore remove sorrow from your heart, and put away evil from your flesh, for childhood and youth are vanity" (Eccl. 11:9–10).
   1. How is the knowledge of judgment day conducive to the fear of God?
   2. In what ways do we see unbelievers showing the fear of God in their hearts?
   3. How does the fear of God in a believer's heart differ from the way an unbeliever may fear God?

Class 3: A Natural Fear of God and the Restraining of Evil—Part 2

I. General revelation as seen in natural law (the nature of created things) teaches the fear of God

II. The good effect of the natural fear of God as we see it in the Scriptures:
   A. Where there is no fear of God might makes right. Is this statement is true? Give examples.
   B. Scripture shows where there is fear of God, men restrain themselves from acting out of their passions:
      1. Genesis 12:11–14: Abram thought evil of the Egyptians and asked Sarah to lie to protect him.
      2. Genesis 12:16–20: Pharaoh was rightly offended (that Abram's hiding of the truth about his marriage almost caused Pharaoh to commit adultery), and he treated Abram with more integrity.
      3. Genesis 20:1–11: Abraham's reason for making his wife lie: He thought others didn't fear the Lord!

   4. Genesis 26:6–11: Abimelech, fearing God, rightly rebukes Isaac for what might've happened.

C. We cite these texts to show how the natural fear of God restrains the evil passions of all men. We should thank God for the common grace by which he causes unbelievers to have some fear of Him.

D. Ironically, Abraham's lying about his marriage showed a lack of the fear of God!

E. Scripture declares why it is good to fear God in speaking the truth: God will punish those who don't!

   1. "Conceiving and uttering from the heart words of deception" (Isa. 59:13b).
   2. "'And everyone deceives his neighbor, and does not speak the truth; they have taught their tongue to speak lies; they weary themselves committing iniquity. . . . Their tongue is an arrow shot out; it speaks deceit; one speaks peaceably to his neighbor with his mouth, but in his heart he lies in wait. Shall I not punish them for these things?' says the Lord. 'Shall I not avenge Myself on such a nation as this?'" (Jer. 9:5 NASB, 8–9).
   3. "He who walks uprightly, and works righteousness, and speaks the truth in his heart" (Ps. 15:2).
   4. "For rulers are not a terror to good works, but to evil. Do you want to be unafraid of the authority? Do what is good, and you will have praise from the same. For he is God's minister to you for good. But if you do evil, be afraid; for he does not bear the sword in vain; for he is God's minister, an avenger to execute wrath on him who practices evil. Therefore you must be subject, not only because of wrath but also for conscience' sake" (Rom. 13:3–5).

III. Where there is no fear of God, there is no justice, especially for the weak, poor, and powerless.
  A. "Ethical integrity is grounded in and is the fruit of the fear of God."—J. Murray[3]
  B. "You shall not curse the deaf, nor put a stumbling block before the blind, but shall fear your God: I am the Lord" (Lev. 19:14)
  C. "You shall rise before the gray headed and honor the presence of an old man, and fear your God: I am the Lord" (Lev. 19:32).
  D. "Therefore you shall not oppress one another, but you shall fear your God; for I am the Lord your God. . . . If one of your brethren becomes poor, and falls into poverty among you, then you shall help him, like a stranger or a sojourner, that he may live with you. Take no usury or interest from him; but fear your God, that your brother may live with you. . . . You shall not rule over him with rigor, but you shall fear your God" (Lev. 25:17, 35–36, 43).
  E. "Then Joseph said to them the third day, 'Do this and live, for I fear God'" (Gen. 42:18).
    1. If Joseph was trying to remain hidden from his brothers, why did he say he "feared God"?
    2. This shows that the fear of God was not exclusive to revealed religion (special revelation).
  F. "The former governors who were before me laid heavy burdens on the people, and took from them for their daily ration forty shekels of silver. Even their servants lorded it over the people. But I did not do so, because of the fear of God" (Neh. 5:15 esv).
  G. In the parable of the unjust judge, what is meant by

[3] John Murray, *The Fear of God, the Soul of Godliness* (Birmingham, AL: Solid Ground Christian Books, n.d.), 3.

"he neither feared God nor regarded man" (see Luke 18:1–5)?

1. What does it say about our society that few if any unbelievers talk about their fear of God?
2. What does it say about our churches that few if any Christians talk about their fear of God?

IV. Next week we will consider how the fear of God is reflected in the way mankind images God in maleness and femaleness.

A. Where this distinction is upheld with justice and integrity, God is feared and man prospers.

B. Where this distinction is blurred, abused, or denied, God is not feared and man suffers.

C. Consider the following questions for next week and look up the Scriptures referenced. Answer what our society would say about each one vs. what the Word of God says about them. Can you see how following God is always good and following man is always bad?

1. Why does God only number the men for war (see Num. 1)?
2. Why is the Bible always concerned about widows, but not widowers (see James 1:27)?
3. Why are only men allowed to be officers in the church (see 1 Tim. 3; Titus 1)?
4. Why is it said to be a great judgment of God when women rule over His people (see Isa. 3:12)?
5. Or when a nation's soldiers are said to become like women (see Isa. 19:16; Jer. 50:37; 51:30)?
6. Why doesn't Paul allow a woman to teach or to have authority over a man in the church (see 1 Tim. 2:12)?
7. Why must a woman have a symbol of authority on her head (see 1 Cor. 11:10)?

8. Why must a wife submit to her husband (see Eph. 5:22; Col. 3:18) and obey him (see 1 Peter 3:6)?
9. Why must husbands not be bitter with but love their wives, lay down their lives for them, and dwell with them in an understanding way, honoring them as the weaker vessel (see Eph. 5:25; Col. 3:19; 1 Peter 3:7)?
10. Why is long life and peace promised to children as they honor their parents (see Eph. 6:1–3)?

Class 4: Fearing God According to the Nature of the Created Order

I. Vestiges of the natural fear of God remain in sinful man by God's common grace. This fear of God flows out of man's natural knowledge of God, and is marked by the awareness of a day of judgment that is coming.
   A. "For the wrath of God is revealed from heaven against all ungodliness and unrighteousness of men, who suppress the truth in unrighteousness, because what may be known of God is manifest in them, for God has shown it to them. For since the creation of the world, His invisible attributes are clearly seen, being understood by the things that are made, even His eternal power and Godhead, so that they are without excuse, because, although they knew God, they did not glorify Him as God, nor were thankful, but became futile in their thoughts, and their foolish hearts were darkened" (Rom. 1:18–21). "In mercy and truth atonement is provided for iniquity; and by the fear of the Lord one departs from evil" (Prov. 16:6).
      1. As men consider God's judgment they are restrained from evil; as they forget it, they do evil.
      2. As men deny the knowledge of God from creation and their own natures, they turn to evil.

B. "Then one of the criminals who were hanged blasphemed Him, saying, 'If You are the Christ, save Yourself and us.' But the other, answering, rebuked him, saying, 'Do you not even fear God, seeing you are under the same condemnation? And we indeed justly, for we receive the due reward of our deeds; but this Man has done nothing wrong.' Then he said to Jesus, 'Lord, remember me when You come into Your kingdom'" (Luke 23:39–42).

1. Why did the second criminal appeal to the fear of God as he rebuked his partner from blasphemy?
2. His argument was based on the facts of their guilt and Christ's innocence.
3. What is it about mocking an innocent man when you are guilty that denies the fear of God?

II. Since God's wrath is revealed in this realm, all people know and cannot avoid knowing that God's judgment against sin has already begun. How we respond to this knowledge determines how much we fear God.

A. "And even as they did not like to retain God in their knowledge, God gave them over to a debased mind, to do those things which are not fitting; being filled with all unrighteousness, sexual immorality, wickedness, covetousness, maliciousness; full of envy, murder, strife, deceit, evil-mindedness; they are whisperers, backbiters, haters of God, violent, proud, boasters, inventors of evil things, disobedient to parents, undiscerning, untrustworthy, unloving, unforgiving, unmerciful; who, knowing the righteous judgment of God, that those who practice such things are deserving of death, not only do the same but also approve of those who practice them" (Rom. 1:28–32).

1. God judges by giving men over to the sins that they love.

2. It is only God's restraining hand (what Calvin called God's "preventing grace") that keeps us from falling into greater and greater sins.

B. "Woe to those who decree unrighteous decrees, who write misfortune, which they have prescribed to rob the needy of justice, and to take what is right from the poor of My people, that widows may be their prey, and that they may rob the fatherless. What will you do in the day of punishment, and in the desolation which will come from afar? To whom will you flee for help? And where will you leave your glory?" (Isa. 10:1–3).

1. Why is preying upon the weak considered to be a great evil in the eyes of God? What are some of the ways in which people show that they know this to be true?
2. Why was it right for Christians to hide Jews from Nazi murderers? For the Egyptian midwives to save the babies and not kill them?
3. Why does the Bible command children to obey their parents, and why is it is a sign of great judgment when children are not obedient to their parents (see Eph. 6:1; Col. 3:20; 2 Tim. 3:2)?

II. Where men suppress their nature, God justly gives them over to unnatural affections, sins against nature.

A. "For this reason God gave them up to vile passions. For even their women exchanged the natural use for what is against nature. Likewise also the men, leaving the natural use of the woman, burned in their lust for one another, men with men committing what is shameful, and receiving in themselves the penalty of their error which was due" (Rom. 1:26).

1. How is homosexuality a sin against the nature (biology) of man?

2. Though two people of the same sex can pleasure themselves why can't they become "one flesh"?
3. Since this passage plainly declares homosexual desires and practices to be a judgment from God on people who seek to forget Him, how do we comfort Christians who struggle with this sin?
4. A: Everyone struggles with sinful desires. The Christian, however, calls them evil and fights against them! Sinful desire does not define you. Sexual desire does not define you. Creation defines you!
5. God's Word shows the answer to sinful desires. God's will for every human being is to resist the sins we love (Rom. 6), seek to hate them, and put on the corrective obedience.

B. "Does not even nature itself teach you that if a man has long hair, it is a dishonor to him? But if a woman has long hair, it is a glory to her; for her hair is given to her for a covering" (1 Cor. 11:14–15).
   1. Consider the significance of Paul appealing to the "teaching" of nature! Consider how our language attests to the teaching of nature: common sense, common decency, common courtesy, chivalry, ladies and gentlemen, civil, morality, ethics, humane.
   2. That men and women are different and are to be treated differently is a mark of the fear of God
   3. Why is it folly for humans to deny either maleness or femaleness? Can we change our DNA?
   4. You are male or female objectively, genetically, unchangeably. To deny this is to deny reality and the will of God.

C. "For even their women exchanged the natural use for what is against nature" (Rom. 1:26b).

1. Because women more naturally resist vile sins, it is more repugnant for women to do gross things than for men to do them.
2. Consider how society views a man who has many women over against a woman who has many men. The foundation for this difference is in natural law.

D. A similar concept is found in Isaiah 49:15: "Can a woman forget her nursing child, and not have compassion on the son of her womb? Surely they may forget, yet I will not forget you."

1. Scripture considers it more shocking when a mother abandons her child than when a father does.
2. Consider which happens far more often in our society. What are the natural reasons for this fact?

E. "Deliver me, I pray, from the hand of my brother, from the hand of Esau; for I fear him, that he will come and attack me and the mothers with the children" . . . Now he [Jacob] arose that same night and took his two wives and his two maids and his eleven children, and crossed the ford of the Jabbok" (Gen. 32:11, 22 NASB).

1. Was Jacob a sexist or was he acting according to human nature based in objective reality?
2. Is it good, is it natural for a man to want to protect a woman and for a woman to look to a man for protection? How do we see this concept expressed in marriage (see Eph. 5:25)?

Class 5: Fearing God and the Family

I. The evangelical dilemma: Is the different treatment of men and women in the Scriptures due to deference to cultural norms and expectations (similarly to how we understand the Old Testament laws to regulate divorce, multiple wives, and monarchies), or is it due to the nature of the way God made man?

A. If God made man a certain way then it is a great sin against God to deny God's purpose and do differently.
B. Paul appeals to the order of creation and the order of the fall in setting forth some of the strongest commands with reference to the distinction between men and women.
C. "Let a woman learn in silence with all submission. And I do not permit a woman to teach or to have authority over a man, but to be in silence. For Adam was formed first, then Eve. And Adam was not deceived, but the woman being deceived, fell into transgression" (1 Tim. 2:11–14).
    1. There are two reasons why a woman is not permitted to teach a man or to have authority over a man in the church:
        a. Because Adam was formed first and then Eve
        b. Because it was not Adam but Eve who was deceived and fell into transgression
    2. These reasons are not drawn from or in deference to a cultural arrangement but from nature itself.
D. "Therefore, whether you eat or drink, or whatever you do, do all to the glory of God. Give no offense, either to the Jews or to the Greeks or to the church of God, just as I also please all men in all things, not seeking my own profit, but the profit of many, that they may be saved. Imitate me, just as I also imitate Christ. Now I praise you, brethren, that you remember me in all things and keep the traditions just as I delivered them to you. But I want you to know that the head of every man is Christ, the head of woman is man, and the head of Christ is God. Every man praying or prophesying, having his head covered, dishonors his head. But every woman who prays or prophesies with her head uncovered dishonors

her head, for that is one and the same as if her head were shaved. For if a woman is not covered, let her also be shorn. But if it is shameful for a woman to be shorn or shaved, let her be covered. For a man indeed ought not to cover his head, since he is the image and glory of God; but woman is the glory of man. For man is not from woman, but woman from man. Nor was man created for the woman, but woman for the man. For this reason the woman ought to have a symbol of authority on her head, because of the angels" (1 Cor. 10:31–11:10).

1. "Head" in verse 3 does not refer to "source" but to "authority" as the context plainly shows.
2. The issue of head coverings is one of authority. The type of covering is cultural, the acknowledgment of and deference to proper authority is not.
3. Again Paul appeals to creation itself as the reason for the woman culturally acknowledging she is under her spouse's authority, as well as the man culturally acknowledging that he is not.
4. The reference to angels is difficult, but again probably has reference to the great deference to authority among those heavenly beings, seeing that it was in some way a rebellion against proper authority that resulted in the fall of the demons (see Jude 1:6–9).

E. Conclusion: Though the Bible has been and will no doubt continue to be used by unscrupulous men to justify evil behavior, including the unjust oppression of women, yet the basis for the Bible's distinct roles for men and women are founded firmly in God's created order and not in deference to culture.

III. In about half of the passages that teach different roles for men and women, an appeal to the fear of God is explicitly part of the immediate context of the passage:

A. "Wives, likewise, be submissive to your own husbands, that even if some do not obey the word, they, without a word, may be won by the conduct of their wives, when they observe your chaste conduct accompanied by fear . . . as Sarah obeyed Abraham, calling him lord, whose daughters you are if you do good and are not afraid with any terror. Husbands, likewise, dwell with them with understanding, giving honor to the wife, as to the weaker vessel, and as being heirs together of the grace of life, that your prayers may not be hindered" (1 Peter 3:1–7).

B. ". . . submitting to one another in the fear of God. Wives, submit to your own husbands, as to the Lord" (Eph. 5:21–22).

C. "Wives, submit to your own husbands, as is fitting in the Lord. Husbands, love your wives and do not be bitter toward them. Children, obey your parents in all things, for this is well pleasing to the Lord. Fathers, do not provoke your children, lest they become discouraged. Bondservants, obey in all things your masters according to the flesh, not with eyeservice, as men-pleasers, but in sincerity of heart, fearing God. . . . Masters, give your bondservants what is just and fair, knowing that you also have a Master in heaven" (Col. 3:18–22; 4:1).
   1. As wives fear God they will submit to their own husbands.
   2. As husbands fear God they will honor their wives.
   3. As children fear God they will obey their parents.
   4. As parents fear God they will be patient and fair with their children.
   5. As servants fear God they will sincerely serve their masters.
   6. As masters fear God they will justly and kindly treat their servants.

IV. Even where the fear of God is not mentioned, it is implied as a motive for keeping to our distinct roles.

   A. "Husbands, likewise, dwell with them with understanding, giving honor to the wife, as to the weaker vessel, and as being heirs together of the grace of life, that your prayers may not be hindered" (1 Peter 3:7).

   B. "So husbands ought to love their own wives as their own bodies; he who loves his wife loves himself. For no one ever hated his own flesh, but nourishes and cherishes it, just as the Lord does the church" (Eph. 5:28–29).

   C. "Children, obey your parents in the Lord, for this is right. 'Honor your father and mother,' which is the first commandment with promise: 'that it may be well with you and you may live long on the earth'" (Eph. 6:1–3).

   D. "The wise woman builds her house, but the foolish pulls it down with her hands" (Prov. 14:1).

   E. "Charm is deceitful and beauty is passing, but a woman who fears the Lord, she shall be praised" (Prov. 31:30)

   F. "A Song of Ascents. Blessed is every one who fears the Lord, who walks in His ways. When you eat the labor of your hands, you shall be happy, and it shall be well with you. Your wife shall be like a fruitful vine In the very heart of your house, your children like olive plants all around your table. Behold, thus shall the man be blessed who fears the Lord. The Lord bless you out of Zion, and may you see the good of Jerusalem all the days of your life. Yes, may you see your children's children. Peace be upon Israel!" (Ps. 128)

   G. God's Word repeatedly holds out two external motivations to walking in the fear of God:

      1. Judgments are threatened to those who do not treat others according to the fear God.
      2. Blessings are promised to those who do treat others according to the fear of God.

Class 6: Fearing God and Not Fearing God!

I. Some claim that the Bible teaches that fearing God was for the OT, not the NT, which is now marked by love.

   A. "Love has been perfected among us in this: that we may have boldness in the day of judgment; because as He is, so are we in this world. There is no fear in love; but perfect love casts out fear, because fear involves torment. But he who fears has not been made perfect in love" (1 John 4:17–18).

      1. How does this verse square with all the other passages which extol the fear of God as a virtue?
      2. Because we truly fear God, we need not fear man—we need not even fear judgment day!

   B. "Inasmuch then as the children have partaken of flesh and blood, He Himself likewise shared in the same, that through death He might destroy him who had the power of death, that is, the devil, and release those who through fear of death were all their lifetime subject to bondage" (Heb. 2:14–15).

      1. What is the bad kind of fear mentioned here from which Christians are delivered?
      2. Why should you as a Christian not fear death (see 1 Cor. 15:54–55)?

   C. "For you did not receive the spirit of bondage again to fear, but you received the Spirit of adoption by whom we cry out, 'Abba, Father'" (Rom. 8:15).

      1. Is this verse saying that Christians should have no fear of God?
      2. What kind of fear brings people into bondage? How has God delivered Christians from this kind of fear?

   D. "Then the sky receded as a scroll when it is rolled up, and every mountain and island was moved out of its place.

And the kings of the earth, the great men, the rich men, the commanders, the mighty men, every slave and every free man, hid themselves in the caves and in the rocks of the mountains, and said to the mountains and rocks, 'Fall on us and hide us from the face of Him who sits on the throne and from the wrath of the Lamb! For the great day of His wrath has come, and who is able to stand?'" (Rev. 6:14–17).

1. What kind of fear is described in these verses?
2. Why would Christians not be afraid of what unbelievers are afraid of in these verses?

II. The Bible teaches that we are to *fear* God and yet that we are not to be *afraid* of God.

A. "Now all the people witnessed the thunderings, the lightning flashes, the sound of the trumpet, and the mountain smoking; and when the people saw it, they trembled and stood afar off. Then they said to Moses, 'You speak with us, and we will hear; but let not God speak with us, lest we die.' And Moses said to the people, 'Do not fear; for God has come to test you, and that His fear may be before you, so that you may not sin.' So the people stood afar off, but Moses drew near the thick darkness where God was" (Ex. 20:18–21).

1. Literally: Do not fear; for God has come to test you, so that you would fear!
2. What kind of fear of God should we not have? What kind of fear of God should we have?

B. "And you said: 'Surely the Lord our God has shown us His glory and His greatness, and we have heard His voice from the midst of the fire. We have seen this day that God speaks with man; yet he still lives. Now therefore, why should we die? For this great fire will consume us; if we hear the voice of the Lord our

God anymore, then we shall die. For who is there of all flesh who has heard the voice of the living God speaking from the midst of the fire, as we have, and lived? You go near and hear all that the Lord our God may say, and tell us all that the Lord our God says to you, and we will hear and do it.' Then the Lord heard the voice of your words when you spoke to me, and the Lord said to me: 'I have heard the voice of the words of this people which they have spoken to you. They are right in all that they have spoken. Oh, that they had such a heart in them that they would fear me and always keep all my commandments, that it might be well with them and with their children forever!'" (Deut. 5:24–29).

1. What were some of the reasons Israel expressed fear of God to Moses? What did they see, what did they hear, what did they realize?
2. Notice how Moses gives a fuller account of the situation thirty-nine years later as they are about to enter the land. What are some of the motivations of Israel that Moses brings out in Deuteronomy that were not explicitly mentioned in Exodus?
3. What does Israel ask Moses to do in both accounts, and how would that help them?
4. In Deuteronomy what did God say about Israel's fear, what did He think of it, and what did He say it would result in if they would keep it?
5. Considering all these things, what do you think Moses meant when he said in Exodus 20:20, "Do not fear"?
6. God did not come to destroy them, but to test them; God wanted the people to fear Him unto obedience to their good, not to fear Him unto despair for their destruction.

III. In Hebrews 12:11–29, the Jewish church at Mount Sinai is compared to the Christian church until end of the age.
   A. vv. 11–14: Discipline is hard but we must discipline ourselves for the good of others.
   B. vv. 15–17: We must especially be on guard against hypocrites, who:
      1. Cause trouble through bitterness, infecting others with sin.
      2. Trade the inheritance that comes to godliness for worldly gain and pleasure/status in this life.
      3. Do not repent of their sins, are not sorry for their evils, blame others, deceive with tears.
   C. Why did God come to the OT church in such fearfulness on Mt. Sinai? (See vv. 18–21.)
      1. What is it about God that we should fear?
      2. How does our faith in God relate to our fear and vice versa?
   D. Does God come to the NT church in a less fearful manner? (See vv. 22–24.)
      1. The reality, though not physically seen/heard/felt, is far more serious, far more awesome, and far more holy!
      2. Why should Christians fear God far more than the Israelites?
      3. How does the knowledge of God relate to the right kind of fear of God?
   E. vv. 25–29: The argument is clearly from the lesser to the greater, from the less fearful to the more.
   F. v. 28: "Acceptable" worship described with two words meaning "fear."
   G. v. 29: "For even/also our God is a consuming fire."
   H. Clear reference to Deuteronomy 4:23–24 "Take heed to yourselves, lest you forget the covenant of the Lord your God which He made with you, and make for yourselves

a carved image in the form of anything which the Lord your God has forbidden you. For the Lord your God is a consuming fire, a jealous God."

I. Since God has not changed we should still fear Him.

Class 7: Fearing God and Worship: Part 1

I. Worship is the most intimate time we have with God. It is when we are brought closest to Him.
   A. Read Isaiah 6:1–5.
      1. Even if we are without sin, we cannot meet the gaze of God without being burned up.
      2. If we trust in Jesus, we should have no fear of God casting us off on account of our sins.
   B. Jesus became man so that we could behold God. There is no beholding of God beyond Jesus.
      1. ". . . who alone has immortality, dwelling in unapproachable light, whom no man has seen or can see, to whom be honor and everlasting power. Amen" (1 Tim. 6:16).
      2. "No one has seen God at any time. The only begotten Son, who is in the bosom of the Father, He has declared Him" (John 1:18).
      3. "For it is the God who commanded light to shine out of darkness, who has shone in our hearts to give the light of the knowledge of the glory of God in the face of Jesus Christ" (2 Cor. 4:6).
      4. "'If you had known Me, you would have known My Father also; and from now on you know Him and have seen Him.' Philip said to Him, 'Lord, show us the Father, and it is sufficient for us.' Jesus said to him, 'Have I been with you so long, and yet you have not known Me, Philip? He who has seen Me has seen the Father; so

how can you say, "Show us the Father"?'" (John 14:7–9).

C. Jesus has all the glory of God: Revelation 1:10–18.

II. The acceptable way to worship God in the New Testament is "with reverence and godly fear."

A. We are not to serve God with sinful, faithless fear, which flows from a heart that has not received forgiveness and reconciliation. That is what these verses are referring to:

1. "The oath which He swore to our father Abraham: to grant us that we, being delivered from the hand of our enemies, might serve Him without fear, in holiness and righteousness before Him all the days of our life" (Luke 1:73–75).
2. "Therefore I remind you to stir up the gift of God which is in you through the laying on of my hands. For God has not given us a spirit of fear, but of power and of love and of a sound mind" (2 Tim. 1:6–7).
3. "Seeing then that we have a great High Priest who has passed through the heavens, Jesus the Son of God, let us hold fast our confession. For we do not have a High Priest who cannot sympathize with our weaknesses, but was in all points tempted as we are, yet without sin. Let us therefore come boldly to the throne of grace, that we may obtain mercy and find grace to help in time of need" (Heb. 4:14–16).

B. We are to worship God with a godly fear, precisely because we know that we have been forgiven of our sins and reconciled to God. This kind of fear is born of faith:

1. "Therefore, since we are receiving a kingdom which cannot be shaken, let us have grace, by which we may serve God acceptably with reverence and

godly fear. For our God is a consuming fire" (Heb. 12:28–29).

2. "But as for me, I will come into Your house in the multitude of Your mercy; in fear of You I will worship toward Your holy temple" (Ps. 5:7).

C. This is the kind of fear Jesus displayed as the perfect, sinless man in full assurance of God's love.

1. ". . . who, in the days of His flesh, when He had offered up prayers and supplications, with vehement cries and tears to Him who was able to save Him from death, and was heard because of His godly fear" (Heb. 5:7).

2. "There shall come forth a Rod from the stem of Jesse, and a Branch shall grow out of his roots. The Spirit of the Lord shall rest upon Him, the Spirit of wisdom and understanding, the Spirit of counsel and might, the Spirit of knowledge and of the fear of the Lord. His delight is in the fear of the Lord, and He shall not judge by the sight of His eyes, nor decide by the hearing of His ears" (Isa. 11:1–3).

III. The absence of the fear of God in worship led to the fall of the northern kingdom of Israel.

A. Fearing God is synonymous with worship: "To this day they continue practicing the former rituals; they do not fear the Lord, nor do they follow their statutes or their ordinances, or the law and commandment which the Lord had commanded the children of Jacob, whom He named Israel, with whom the Lord had made a covenant and charged them, saying: 'You shall not fear other gods, nor bow down to them nor serve them nor sacrifice to them; but the Lord, who brought you up from the land of Egypt with great power and an outstretched arm, Him you shall fear, Him you shall worship, and to

Him you shall offer sacrifice. And the statutes, the ordinances, the law, and the commandment which He wrote for you, you shall be careful to observe forever; you shall not fear other gods. And the covenant that I have made with you, you shall not forget, nor shall you fear other gods. But the Lord your God you shall fear; and He will deliver you from the hand of all your enemies'" (2 Kings 17:34–39).

B. Because Israel did not fear God, they did not obey Him, and instead provoked Him to anger (see 2 Kings 17:6–21).

C. Not fearing God led the northern tribes into the idolatry which eventually destroyed them.
   1. "And He will give Israel up because of the sins of Jeroboam, who sinned and who made Israel sin" (1 Kings 14:16).
   2. The OT repeatedly refers to this sin of Jeroboam: see 1 Kings 12:26–33; 2 Kings 13:11; 23:15.

D. If only Israel would have feared God they would not have run into the sins which eventually led to their exile and banishment: "Do not say, 'A conspiracy,' Concerning all that this people call a conspiracy, nor be afraid of their threats, nor be troubled. The Lord of hosts, Him you shall hallow; let Him be your fear, and let Him be your dread. He will be as a sanctuary, but a stone of stumbling and a rock of offense to both the houses of Israel, as a trap and a snare to the inhabitants of Jerusalem" (Isa. 8:12–14).
   1. Hallowing God, considering God to be holy is synonymous with fearing Him.
   2. God is a sanctuary, a fire of protection to those who fear Him.
   3. But He is a trap, a fire of destruction to those who do not.

Class 8: Fearing God and Worship: Part 2

I. Worship is the most intimate time we have with God. It is when we are brought closest to Him.

II. The acceptable way to worship God in the New Testament is "with reverence and godly fear."
  A. Some of God's most astonishing judgments came because of worship that lacked fear: consider Nadab and Abihu in Leviticus 10; Hophni and Phinehas in 1 Samuel 1:3 and 2:12–17, 22–25, 34; Uzzah in 2 Samuel 6:3–16; Uzziah in 2 Chronicles 26:16–21; and Ananias and Sapphira in Acts 4:32–5:13 and 1 Corinthians 11:23–34.
  B. We can have a fear of offending God, a fear of disrespecting Him, and a fear of His judgments should we engage in folly.
  C. Consider the fear a son has for the father he loves—a fear of offending or disappointing him because he loves him. Yet does he not also always have a healthy fear of his father's discipline, which he knows is for his good but which he also dreads and wishes to avoid?

III. Rightly fearing God is synonymous with worshipping Him.
  A. "If You, Lord, should mark iniquities, O Lord, who could stand? But there is forgiveness with You, that You may be feared" (Ps. 130:3–4).
    1. Because there is forgiveness with God, God ought to be feared.
    2. If I know God forgives me of my sins, I will fear Him.
  B. ". . . that all peoples of the earth may know Your name and fear You, as do Your people Israel" (see 1 Kings 8:43b).

1. Again, in this passage, forgiveness of sins results in people fearing God.
2. Solomon's prayer is that God's fear would be increased because of his temple.

C. "Serve the Lord with fear, and rejoice with trembling. Kiss the Son, lest He be angry, and you perish in the way, when His wrath is kindled but a little. Blessed are all those who put their trust in Him" (Ps. 2:11–12).

1. This verse refutes those who say if we fear God we cannot at the same time rejoice in Him.
2. The right fear of God complements true rejoicing in God.

D. "But as for me, I will come into Your house in the multitude of Your mercy; in fear of You I will worship toward Your holy temple" (Ps. 5:7).

E. ". . . saying with a loud voice, 'Fear God and give glory to Him, for the hour of His judgment has come; and worship Him who made heaven and earth, the sea and springs of water'" (Rev. 14:7).

F. "They sing the song of Moses, the servant of God, and the song of the Lamb, saying: 'Great and marvelous are Your works, Lord God Almighty! Just and true are Your ways, O King of the saints! Who shall not fear You, O Lord, and glorify Your name? For You alone are holy. For all nations shall come and worship before You, for Your judgments have been manifested'" (Rev. 15:3–4).

G. "Who is like You, O Lord, among the gods? Who is like You, glorious in holiness, fearful in praises, doing wonders?" (Ex. 15:11).

H. "Afterward the children of Israel shall return and seek the Lord their God and David their king. They shall fear the Lord and His goodness in the latter days" (Hos. 3:5).

I. "God is greatly to be feared in the assembly of the saints, And to be held in reverence by all those around Him" (Ps. 89:7).

J. "And they continued steadfastly in the apostles' doctrine and fellowship, in the breaking of bread, and in prayers. Then fear came upon every soul, and many wonders and signs were done through the apostles" (Acts 2:42–43).

   1. Everyone loves to point out the four marks of the early church's worship in v. 42, but they usually leave out the fifth mark in v. 43: the great fear of God that the early church had. There need to be church growth books on "How We Can Fear God Like the Early Church Did"!

IV. Principles to remember when we consider how we are to worship God.

   A. We worship God for who He is and for what He has done. This is also the reason we fear Him.
   B. Reverence and fear is the result of considering who God is; boldness is the result of considering what He has done for us
   C. God is not a creature like us. He is above us, beyond us, forever out of our reach.
   D. God has made us like Him, and to be like Him. We can and must seek to glorify Him. We live unto Him.
   E. We should fear to turn from trusting in Jesus, knowing that God will not accept a false profession.
   F. Thus, the closer we are brought to God, the more we should be bold in Him and yet fearful in ourselves.
   G. I must trust in God's strength and look to Him, I must not think I can do anything in myself.
   H. To hesitate to draw near to God, when I believe, is to slight what Christ has done and trust in myself

V. The fear of God is conducive to worship. Hypocrisy nullifies worship.
   A. The hypocrite's great sin is that he does not fear God. The man who fears God cannot be a hypocrite.
   B. "Therefore the Lord said: 'Inasmuch as these people draw near with their mouths and honor Me with their lips, but have removed their hearts far from Me, and their fear toward Me is taught by the commandment of men, therefore, behold, I will again do a marvelous work among this people, a marvelous work and a wonder; for the wisdom of their wise men shall perish, and the understanding of their prudent men shall be hidden.' Woe to those who seek deep to hide their counsel far from the Lord, and their works are in the dark; they say, 'Who sees us?' and, 'Who knows us?'" (Isa. 29:13–15).
      1. One kind of hypocritical worship replaces God's law with human inventions/traditions.
      2. A second kind of hypocritical worship keeps the letter of the law while hating it in spirit.
   C. "Hypocrites! Well did Isaiah prophesy about you, saying: 'These people draw near to Me with their mouth, and honor Me with their lips, but their heart is far from Me. And in vain they worship Me, teaching as doctrines the commandments of men'" (Matt. 15:7–9).
      1. What did Isaiah prophesy?
      2. Have different people in class read these verses: Isaiah 1; 8:12–14; 59:19.
      3. Discuss the different kinds of fear in these passages and their causes and effects.
   D. It is because of God's salvation that we fear Him.
      1. "I will cleanse them from all their iniquity by which they have sinned against Me, and I will pardon all their iniquities by which they have sinned and by which they have transgressed against Me.

Then it shall be to Me a name of joy, a praise, and an honor before all nations of the earth, who shall hear all the good that I do to them; they shall fear and tremble for all the goodness and all the prosperity that I provide for it" (Jer. 33:8–9).

2. "Surely His salvation is near to those who fear Him, that glory may dwell in our land" (Ps. 85:9).

E. If we are living hypocritical lives, where we have all kinds of secrets we hide from people, we cannot worship God correctly. Think of Adam and Eve after they sinned, of Achan, and even of Judas.

Class 9: Fearing God and Sincerity of Heart in True Obedience

Intro: "O Lord, why have You made us stray from Your ways, and hardened our heart from Your fear? Return for Your servants' sake, the tribes of Your inheritance" (Isa. 63:17).

A. We must fear God from the heart. When we do not, we stray from His ways. A hard heart does not fear God.

B. The one who does not fear God is far from Him, the one who is near Him is the one who fears Him.

I. Hypocrisy is a great sin. Fearing God is the antidote!

A. "The Lord is exalted, for He dwells on high; He has filled Zion with justice and righteousness. Wisdom and knowledge will be the stability of your times, and the strength of salvation; the fear of the Lord is His treasure. . . 'Now I will rise,' says the Lord; 'Now I will be exalted, now I will lift Myself up. You shall conceive chaff, you shall bring forth stubble; Your breath, as fire, shall devour you. And the people shall be like the burnings of lime; like thorns cut up they shall be burned in the fire. Hear, you who are afar off, what I have done; and you who are near, acknowledge My might.' The sinners in Zion are afraid; fearfulness has seized the hypocrites: 'Who among us shall dwell with the devouring fire? Who among us shall dwell with everlasting burnings?' He who walks righteously and speaks uprightly, he who despises the gain of oppressions, who gestures with his hands, refusing bribes, who stops his ears from hearing of bloodshed, and shuts his eyes from seeing evil: he will dwell on high; his place of defense will be the fortress of rocks; bread will be given him, his water will be sure. Your eyes will see the King in His beauty; they will see the land that is very far off" (Isa. 33:5–6, 10–17).

B. "Bondservants, obey in all things your masters according to the flesh, not with eyeservice, as men-pleasers, but in sincerity of heart, fearing God" (Col. 3:22).

C. "And Abraham stretched out his hand and took the knife to slay his son. But the Angel of the Lord called to him from heaven and said, 'Abraham, Abraham!' So he said, 'Here I am.' And He said, 'Do not lay your hand on the lad, or do anything to him; for now I know that you fear God, since you have not withheld your son, your only son, from Me'" (Gen. 22:10–12).
   1. Abraham's faith produced this great fear of God when provoked by God's test.
   2. Fear of God will do whatever God says no matter what the cost.

D. Cornelius is godly because he fears the Lord. When we fear the Lord we work righteousness.
   1. "[Cornelius,] a devout man and one who feared God with all his household, who gave alms generously to the people, and prayed to God always" (Acts 10:2).
   2. "And they said, 'Cornelius the centurion, a just man, one who fears God and has a good reputation

among all the nation of the Jews, was divinely instructed by a holy angel to summon you to his house, and to hear words from you'" (Acts 10:22).

II. God made a covenant with Levi because of his zeal for God before everything else.
   A. "'Then you shall know that I have sent this commandment to you, that My covenant with Levi may continue,' says the Lord of hosts. 'My covenant was with him, one of life and peace, And I gave them to him that he might fear Me; so he feared Me and was reverent before My name'" (Mal. 2:4–5).
      1. God gave this special covenant of life and peace to Levi so that Levi would fear Him.
      2. The Levites were the only people who could come near God in worship—because of their fear.
   B. "Now when Moses saw that the people were unrestrained (for Aaron had not restrained them, to their shame among their enemies), then Moses stood in the entrance of the camp, and said, 'Whoever is on the Lord's side—come to me.' And all the sons of Levi gathered themselves together to him. And he said to them, 'Thus says the Lord God of Israel: "Let every man put his sword on his side, and go in and out from entrance to entrance throughout the camp, and let every man kill his brother, every man his companion, and every man his neighbor."' So the sons of Levi did according to the word of Moses. And about three thousand men of the people fell that day" (Ex. 32:25–28).
      1. The sons of Levi, like Abraham had been prepared to do, carried out God's fearful command to slay.
      2. God blesses those to whom He gives difficult callings to perform, when they walk in them.
   C. "And of Levi he said: 'Let Your Thummim and Your

Urim be with Your holy one, Whom You tested at Massah, And with whom You contended at the waters of Meribah, who says of his father and mother, "I have not seen them"; nor did he acknowledge his brothers, or know his own children; for they have observed Your word and kept Your covenant. They shall teach Jacob Your judgments, and Israel Your law. They shall put incense before You, and a whole burnt sacrifice on Your altar" (Deut. 33:8–10).

D. "Phinehas the son of Eleazar, the son of Aaron the priest, has turned back My wrath from the children of Israel, because he was zealous with My zeal among them, so that I did not consume the children of Israel in My zeal. Therefore say, 'Behold, I give to him My covenant of peace'" (Num. 25:11–12).

E. "The law of truth was in his mouth, and injustice was not found on his lips. He walked with Me in peace and equity, and turned many away from iniquity. 'For the lips of a priest should keep knowledge, and people should seek the law from his mouth; for he is the messenger of the Lord of hosts. But you have departed from the way; you have caused many to stumble at the law. You have corrupted the covenant of Levi,' says the Lord of hosts" (Mal. 2:6–8).

III. God's name is called "fear" at least twice in Scripture. The fear of God protects His people from enemies without and within.

A. "Unless the God of my father, the God of Abraham and the Fear of Isaac, had been with me, surely now you would have sent me away empty-handed. God has seen my affliction and the labor of my hands, and rebuked you last night" (Gen. 31:42).

B. "'The God of Abraham, the God of Nahor, and the God

of their father judge between us.' And Jacob swore by the Fear of his father Isaac" (Gen. 31:53).

C. God gives His children the right kind of fear of Him: "Who is like You, O LORD, among the gods? Who is like You, glorious in holiness, Fearful in praises, doing wonders?" (Ex. 15:11)

D. "The LORD of hosts, Him you shall hallow; let Him be your fear, and let Him be your dread" (Isa. 8:13)

E. Those delivered from the terror of the Lord will fear Him with godly reverence.

Class 10: Zeal for God: Fearing God in our Behavior (Attitudes and Actions); Gospel Fear

I. Various verses show how the godly fear God and how that fear is evidenced in their attitudes and actions:

A. "Then the LORD said to Satan, 'Have you considered My servant Job, that there is none like him on the earth, a blameless and upright man, one who fears God and shuns evil?' So Satan answered the LORD and said, 'Does Job fear God for nothing? Have You not made a hedge around him, around his household, and around all that he has on every side? You have blessed the work of his hands, and his possessions have increased in the land. But now, stretch out Your hand and touch all that he has, and he will surely curse You to Your face!'" (Job 1:8–11).

1. The issue was hypocrisy. Satan was claiming that Job feared God for Job's benefit, that Job uses/manipulates God.
2. God's boast is that Job fears God truly, and not for any benefit Job is getting, but simply because of who God is. And Job passes the test when he loses everything and continues to fear God.
3. "Then the LORD said to Satan, 'Have you considered

My servant Job, that there is none like him on the earth, a blameless and upright man, one who fears God and shuns evil? And still he holds fast to his integrity, although you incited Me against him, to destroy him without cause'" (Job 2:3).

4. To continue to fear God in difficult situations is to be a person of integrity.

B. Consider and discuss the blessings of fearing God from the following verses:
   1. "Who is the man that fears the Lord? Him shall He teach in the way He chooses. He himself shall dwell in prosperity, and his descendants shall inherit the earth. The secret (counsel) of the Lord is with those who fear Him, and He will show them His covenant" (Ps. 25:12–14).
   2. Psalm 112: a psalm about the man who fears the Lord.
   3. Psalm 128: the blessings of the man who fears the Lord.
   4. The culmination of the godly woman of Proverbs 31 is her fear of God: "Charm is deceitful and beauty is passing, but a woman who fears the Lord, she shall be praised" (Prov. 31:30).

C. To fear God is to fear or keep His commandments. Like faith, obedience cannot be separated from the right fear of God.
   1. "He who despises the word will be destroyed, but he who fears the commandment will be rewarded" (Prov. 13:13).
   2. "He who walks in his uprightness fears the Lord, but he who is perverse in his ways despises Him" (Prov. 14:2).
   3. "A wise man fears and departs from evil, but a fool rages and is self-confident" (Prov. 14:16).

4. "Who among you fears the Lord, hearing/obeying the voice of His Servant that walks in darkness, and there is no light in it? Let him trust in the name of the Lord, and rely upon his God" (Isa. 50:10, translation mine).
5. "But in every nation whoever fears Him and works righteousness is accepted by Him" (Acts 10:35).

II. How the fear of God affects or influences our behavior, and how we can seek more fear of God!

A. "The fear of the Lord is to hate evil; pride and arrogance and the evil way and the perverse mouth I hate" (Prov. 8:13).

B. "In mercy and truth atonement is provided for iniquity; and by the fear of the Lord one departs from evil" (Prov. 16:6).

C. "Who is the man that fears the Lord? Him shall He teach in the way He chooses. He himself shall dwell in prosperity, and his descendants shall inherit the earth. The secret of the Lord is with those who fear Him, and He will show them His covenant" (Ps. 25:12–14).

D. "Also it shall be, when he sits on the throne of his kingdom, that he shall write for himself a copy of this law in a book, from the one before the priests, the Levites. And it shall be with him, and he shall read it all the days of his life, that he may learn to fear the Lord his God and be careful to observe all the words of this law and these statutes" (Deut. 17:18–19).

E. "Only take heed to yourself, and diligently keep yourself, lest you forget the things your eyes have seen, and lest they depart from your heart all the days of your life. And teach them to your children and your grandchildren, especially concerning the day you stood before the Lord your God in Horeb, when the Lord said to me,

'Gather the people to Me, and I will let them hear My words, that they may learn to fear Me all the days they live on the earth, and that they may teach their children.'" (Deut. 4:9–10).

F. "Gather the people together, men and women and little ones, and the stranger who is within your gates, that they may hear and that they may learn to fear the LORD your God and carefully observe all the words of this law, and that their children, who have not known it, may hear and learn to fear the LORD your God as long as you live in the land which you cross the Jordan to possess" (Deut. 31:12–13).

G. "Therefore, having these promises, beloved, let us cleanse ourselves from all filthiness of the flesh and spirit, perfecting holiness in the fear of God" (2 Cor. 7:1; see also Acts 9:31; Phil. 2:12; 1 Peter 1:17).

III. Fear and preaching: We preach the gospel, which is the good news of salvation from God's wrath.

A. Have members of the class read several of the following verses where the gospel delivers us from God's wrath: Matthew 3:1–12; John 3:36; Romans 2:5, 8; 5:9; Ephesians 2:3; 5:6; Colossians 3:6; 1 Thessalonians 1:10; 5:9; Revelation 6:16–17; 11:8; 19:15.

B. Similarly, the promise of salvation is deliverance from the terror of the Lord: "I will not execute the fierceness of My anger; I will not again destroy Ephraim. For I am God, and not man, the Holy One in your midst; and I will not come with terror" (Hos. 11:9).

C. God treats His enemies with terror:

1. "You have brought Your people Israel out of the land of Egypt with signs and wonders, with a strong hand and an outstretched arm, and with great terror" (Jer. 32:21).

2. "Enter into the rock, and hide in the dust, from the terror of the Lord and the glory of His majesty" (Isa. 2:10).
3. "Do not be a terror to me; you are my hope in the day of doom" (Jer. 17:17).

D. Therefore, it is good and right that we would call upon God to not treat us with terror, but to save us and deliver us for Christ's sake.

E. Rightly fearing God and being delivered from God's terror are both set forth as valid motivations for the preacher and for the believer.

1. "For we must all appear before the judgment seat of Christ, that each one may receive the things done in the body, according to what he has done, whether good or bad. Knowing, therefore, the terror of the Lord, we persuade men" (2 Cor. 5:10–11a).
2. "Then Paul stood up, and motioning with his hand said, 'Men of Israel, and you who fear God, listen'" (Acts 13:16).
3. "Men and brethren, sons of the family of Abraham, and those among you who fear God, to you the word of this salvation has been sent" (Acts 13:26).
4. "Let us hear the conclusion of the whole matter: Fear God and keep His commandments, for this is man's all. For God will bring every work into judgment, including every secret thing, whether good or evil" (Eccl. 12:13–14).

Bibliography

1599 Geneva Bible. White Hall, WV: Tolle Lege, 2010.

Ahmed, Wondimu and Marjon Bruinsma. "A Structural Model of Self-Concept, Autonomous Motivation, and Academic Performance in Cross-Cultural Perspective." *Electronic Journal of Research in Educational Psychology* 4, 3 (2006): 551–76. http://www.investigacion-psicopedagogica.org/revista/new/english/ContadorArticulo.php?144.

Arnold, M. B., ed. *Feelings and Emotions: The Loyola Symposium*. New York: Academic Press, 1970.

Baker, Derek, ed. *Religious Motivation: Biographical and Sociological Problems for the Church Historian*. Studies in Church History, Vol. 15. Oxford: Basil Blackwell, 1978.

Bauer, Walter. *A Greek-English Lexicon of the New Testament and Other Early Christian*

Literature. Frederick W. Danker, ed. 3rd ed. Chicago: University of Chicago Press, 2000. *BibleWorks* 9.

Blunt, Richard D. "A Causal-Comparative Exploration of the Relationship Between Game-Based Learning And Academic Achievement: Teaching Management With Video Games." PhD diss., Walden University, 2006.

Bock, Darrell L. *Acts*. Baker Exegetical Commentary on the New Testament. Grand Rapids, MI: Baker, 2009.

Bruce, F. F. *The Book of the Acts*, rev. ed. The New International Commentary on the New Testament. Grand Rapids, MI: Eerdmans, 1988.

Bullinger, E. W. *Figures of Speech Used in the Bible*. Grand Rapids, MI: Baker, 1997.

Bunyan, John. *A Treatise on the Fear of God*. The Works of John Bunyan. Vol. 1. Carlisle, PA: Banner of Truth, 2009, 437–91.

Burton, Ernest De Witt. *Syntax of the Moods and Tenses in New Testament Greek*. Grand Rapids, MI: Kregel, 1994.

Callahan, Kennon L. *Preaching Grace: Possibilities for Growing Your Preaching and Touching People's Lives*. San Francisco: Jossey-Bass Inc., 1999.

———. "The New Reality in Motivation: The Old Appeals Aren't Working Anymore. How to Deal with the Growing Gap Between Key Leaders and the Grassroots." *Leadership* 20, 4 (Fall 1999): 31–32.

Calvin, John. *Calvin's Commentaries*. Vol. XVIII, *John 12–21; Acts 1–13*, bk. 2, "The Acts of the Apostles." Translated by William Pringle. Grand Rapids, MI: Baker, 2003.

———. *Calvin's Commentaries*. Vol. XIX, *Acts 14–28; Romans 1–16*, bk. 1, "The Acts of the Apostles." Translated by William Pringle. Grand Rapids, MI: Baker, 2003.

———. *Calvin's Commentaries*. Vol. XX, bk. 2, "Commentary on the Epistles of Paul the Apostle to the Corinthians." Translated by William Pringle. Grand Rapids, MI: Baker, 2003.

———. *Calvin's Commentaries*. Vol. XXI, bk. 3, "Commentary on the Epistles of Timothy, Titus, and Philemon." Translated by William Pringle. Grand Rapids, MI: Baker, 2003.

———. *John Calvin's Sermons on the Epistles to Timothy and Titus*. Edinburgh: Banner of Truth Trust, 1983.

———. *Institutes of the Christian Religion*. Translated by Henry Beveridge. Grand Rapids, MI: Eerdmans, 1989.

Casey, Rod. "A Church for a Guy Like Me: Making the Case for Less Assumptive Preaching." *Preaching* 26, 1 (July/August 2010): 16–18.

Chapell, Bryan. *Christ-Centered Preaching*. Grand Rapids, MI: Baker, 1994.

Collins, Gary. *Man in Motion: The Psychology of Motivation*. Psychology for Church Leaders. Carol Stream, Illinois: Creation House, 1973.

Collins, Jim. "The Good to Great Pastor: An Interview with Jim Collins." *Leadership* 27, 2 (Spring 2006): 48–50.

Davis, Creath. *Beyond This God Cannot Go*. Grand Rapids, MI: Zondervan, 1971.

Dodd, C. H. *The Apostolic Preaching and Its Developments*. London, 1936; Quoted in F. F. Bruce. *The Book of the Acts*, rev. ed. The New International Commentary on the New Testament. Grand Rapids, MI: Eerdmans, 1988, 212, footnote 48.

Duncan, John D. "Preaching Out of a Slump," *Preaching* 6, 6 (May–June, 1991), 10–12. Reprinted, *Preaching* 13, 6 (May–June, 1998), 42–44.

Edwards, Jonathan. *Charity and Its Fruits*. Edinburgh: Banner of Truth, 2005.

———. *A Treatise Concerning Religious Affections*. In *The Works of Jonathan Edwards*, vol. 1. Edinburgh: Banner of Truth, 1995.

Finney, Charles. *Biblical Repertory and Theological Review* (1832). Quoted in Murray, Ian H. *Revival and Revivalism*. Carlisle, PA: Banner of Truth, 1994, 244.

———. "Selfishness Not True Religion." Lecture III, *Lectures to Professing Christians*. 1837. Quoted in Richard Hazelett and Dean Turner, *Benevolent Living, Tracing the Roots of Motivation to God*. Pasadena, CA: Hope Publishing House, 1990.

Frank, Arnold L. *The Fear of God: A Forgotten Doctrine*. Ventura, CA: Nordskog, 2008.

Garrison, Webb B. *Creative Imagination in Preaching*. Nashville, TN: Abingdon, 1960. Quoted in Bryan Chapell, *Christ-Centered Preaching*. Grand Rapids, MI: Baker, 1994.

Hanegraaff, Hank. *Christianity in Crisis*. Eugene, OR: Harvest House, 1993.

Hazelett, Richard and Dean Turner. *Benevolent Living, Tracing the*

Roots of Motivation to God. Pasadena, CA: Hope Publishing House, 1990.

Henry, Matthew. *Matthew Henry's Commentary on the Whole Bible Complete and Unabridged in One Volume*. Peabody, MA: Hendrickson, 2012.

Hybels, Bill and Mark Mittelberg. *Becoming a Contagious Christian*. Grand Rapids, MI: Zondervan, 1994.

Jones, W. Paul. "Joy and Religious Motivation." *Weavings* 8 (N-D, 1993): 38–44.

Keller, John M. "Using the ARCS Motivational Process in Computer-Based Instruction and Distance Education." Marilla D. Svnicki, series ed. *New Directions for Teaching and Learning* 78 (Summer 1999): 39–47.

Kistemaker, Simon J. *Exposition of the Acts of the Apostles*. New Testament Commentary. Grand Rapids, MI: Baker, 2004.

Kittel, Gerhard and Gerhard Friedrich, eds. *Theological Dictionary of the New Testament*. vol. II, V, VI, VII, X. Grand Rapids, MI: Eerdmans, 2006.

Knowling, R. J. "The Acts of the Apostles." In *Apostles, Romans, 1 Corinthians*. Vol. 2 of *The Expositor's Greek Testament*, edited by W. Robertson Nicoll. Peabody, MA: Hendrickson, 2002.

Lippitt, John. Review of *Divine Motivation Theory*, by Linda Trinkaus Zagzebski. *Faith and Philosophy* 25, 4 (October 2008): 451–54.

MacKinnon, Marjorie M. "CORE Elements of Student Motivation in Problem-Based Learning." Marilla D. Svnicki, series ed. *New Directions for Teaching and Learning* 78 (Summer 1999): 49–58.

Maxwell, John. "Communicating or Connecting? An Interview with John Maxwell." By Michael Duduit. *Preaching* 26, 1 (July/August 2010): 4–8.

———. "It's All About Them." *Preaching* 26, 1 (July/August 2010): 10–14.

May, Scottie. "A Look at the Effects of Extrinsic Motivation on the Internalization of Biblical Truth." *Christian Education Journal* 7, 1 (Spring 2003): 47–65.

McConnell, D. R. *A Different Gospel*. Peabody, MA: Hendrickson, 1995.

McConnell, Theodore A. *The Shattered Self: The Psychological and Religious Search for Selfhood*. Philadelphia: Pilgrim Press, 1971.

McMinn, Don J. *Strategic Living: How to Set and Accomplish Life-Changing Goals*. Grand Rapids, MI: Baker, 1988.

Merriam-Webster's Collegiate Dictionary, Tenth Edition. Springfield, MA: Merriam-Webster, 1994.

Moeller, Bob. "Saving a Sinking Ship." *Leadership* 17, 2 (Spring 1996): 47–51.

Moule, C. F. D. *An Idiom Book of New Testament Greek*, 2nd ed. New York: Cambridge University Press, 1998.

Moulton, Harold K., ed. *The Analytical Greek Lexicon Revised*, 1978 edition. Grand Rapids, MI: Zondervan, 1978.

Murray, Edward J. *Motivation and Emotion*. Englewood Cliffs, NJ: Prentice-Hall, 1964.

Murray, Ian H. *Revival and Revivalism*. Carlisle, PA: Banner of Truth, 1994.

Murray, John. *The Fear of God: the Soul of Godliness*. Birmingham, AL: Solid Ground Christian Books, n.d.

Olander, Mark A. "How to Be a Motivating Teacher." *Evangelical Missions Quarterly* 40, 2 (April 2004): 230–33.

Ortlund, Dane. *A New Inner Relish: Christian Motivation in the Thought of Jonathan Edwards*. Ross-shire, Scotland, UK: Christian Focus, 2008.

Packer, J. I. *Knowing God*. Downers Grove, IL: InterVarsity, 1993.

Panitz, Theodore. "The Motivational Benefits of Cooperative Learning." Marilla D. Svnicki, series ed. *New Directions for Teaching and Learning* 78 (Summer 1999): 59–67.

Robertson, A. T. *Word Pictures in the New Testament*. Vol. 3, *The Acts of the Apostles*. Nashville: Broadman Press, 1960.

Stevens, David. "Getting the Job Done Requires Motivating Your Volunteers." *Evangelical Missions Quarterly* 29, 1 (Jan. 1993): 12–15.

Sweet, Leonard. "The Quest for Community: But Today It's a Particular *Kind* of Community." *Leadership* 20, 4 (Fall 1999): 33–34.

Theall, Michael, ed., "Motivation from Within: Approaches for Encouraging Faculty and Students to Excel." Marilla D. Svnicki, series ed. *New Directions for Teaching and Learning* 78. Jossey-Bass, Summer 1999.

Thomas, Derek. *Acts*. Reformed Expository Commentary, eds. Richard Phillips and Phillip Ryken. Phillipsburg, NJ: P&R, 2011.

Thompson, Roger. "The Christian Art of Motivation." *Leadership* 15, 3 (Summer 1994): 52–59.

Vernon, M. D. *Human Motivation*. Cambridge: Cambridge University Press, 1969.

Warren, Rick. *The Purpose Driven Life*. Grand Rapids, MI: Zondervan, 2002.

Westminster Confession of Faith and Catechisms: As Adopted by the Presbyterian Church in America. Lawrenceville, GA: Christian Education & Publications, n.d.

Wlodkowski, Raymond J. "Motivation and Diversity: A Framework for Teaching." Marilla D. Svnicki, series ed. *New Directions for Teaching and Learning* 78 (Summer 1999): 7–16.

Wlodkowski, Raymond J. and Margery B. Ginsberg. "A Framework for Culturally Responsive Teaching." *Strengthening Student Engagement* 53, 1 (September 1995): 17–21.

Zagzebski, Linda Trinkaus. *Divine Motivation Theory*. Cambridge: Cambridge University Press, 2004.

Index of Scripture

Index of Subjects and Names

About the Author

Dr. Ray E. Heiple Jr. was born on December 6, 1968, in Latrobe, Pennsylvania, the second of three children born to Ray and Marcia Heiple. Baptized as an infant in the Sons of Zebedee Lutheran Church in Saltsburg, PA, Ray was not converted to Christ until 1989 through a tragic automobile accident. In 1991 he graduated from the Pennsylvania State University with a BA in Broadcast-Cable, and worked in television for ten years. During that time he embraced Reformed theology, got married, started taking classes part time at Reformed Presbyterian Theological Seminary (RPTS), became a father, and was ordained a ruling elder at New Life Presbyterian Church (PCA) in Harrison City, PA. In 2001, the congregation of New Life, believing that Ray was being called by God into pulpit ministry, pledged him two years of support so that Ray could quit his job and become a full-time student. At RPTS, Ray earned the Bruce C. Stewart Award for the highest cumulative grade point average as a middler in the spring of 2002.

The following year Ray received his M.Div. degree from RPTS and was called as an assistant pastor by Providence Presbyterian Church (PCA) in Robinson Township, near Pittsburgh, PA. In 2006, Providence called Ray to be their associate pastor. Then in 2010, upon the retirement of senior pastor Bailey Cadman, Ray was called by the congregation to be their senior pastor. While pastoring the church, Ray was able to complete his doctoral work at RPTS in 2013. His dissertation on motivation in preaching is the work upon which this book is based. In addition to serving Providence, Ray teaches senior high Bible and apologetics at Robinson Township

Christian School (RTCS), he is the host of the television series *Origins* on the Cornerstone Television Network (CTVN), and he regularly appears on the program *Hard Questions*. Ray has also been a featured speaker at several of the annual Prison Reformation Conferences in Cumberland, MD, and in 2014 he taught the Summer Institute at Greenville Presbyterian Theological Seminary (GPTS). Ray and his wife of twenty-one years, Robin, have four children: Calvin, Daniel, Jacob, and Sarah.

Available in the Reformed Academic Dissertation Series

◆

How Should We Treat Detainees? An Examination of "Enhanced Interrogation Techniques" under the Light of Scripture and the Just War Tradition,
by J. Porter Harlow

From Inscrutability to Concursus: Benjamin B. Warfield's Theological Construction of Revelation's Mode from 1880 to 1915,
by Jeffrey A. Stivason

Marks of Saving Grace: Theological Method and the Doctrine of Assurance in Jonathan Edwards's A Treatise Concerning Religious Affections,
by Eric J. Lehner

The Triune God of Unity in Diversity: An Analysis of Perspectivalism, the Trinitarian Theological Method of John Frame and Vern Poythress,
by Timothy E. Miller

It Has Not Yet Appeared What We Shall Be: A Reconsideration of the Imago Dei *in Light of Those with Severe Cognitive Disabilities*,
by George C. Hammond

The Doctrine of the Spirituality of the Church in the Ecclesiology of Charles Hodge,
by Alan D. Strange

Preaching with Biblical Motivation: How to Incorporate the Motivation Found in the Inspired Preaching of the Apostles into Your Sermons,
by Ray E. Heiple Jr.

Forthcoming

The Trinity, Language, and Human Behavior: A Reformed Exposition of the Language Theory of Kenneth L. Pike, by Pierce Taylor Hibbs

"King of Israel" and "Do Not Fear, Daughter of Zion": The Use of Zephaniah 3 in John 12, by Christopher S. Tachick

Do Good to All People as You Have Opportunity: A Biblical Theology of the Good Deeds Mission of the New Covenant Community, by John A. Wind

A Strategy for Incorporating Biblical Counseling in North American Church Plants, by Rush Witt

A Development, Not a Departure: The Lacunae in the Debate of the Doctrine of the Trinity and Gender Roles, by Hongyi Yang

Free to Be Sons of God
by Geoffrey M. Ziegler

Other Preaching Resources from P&R

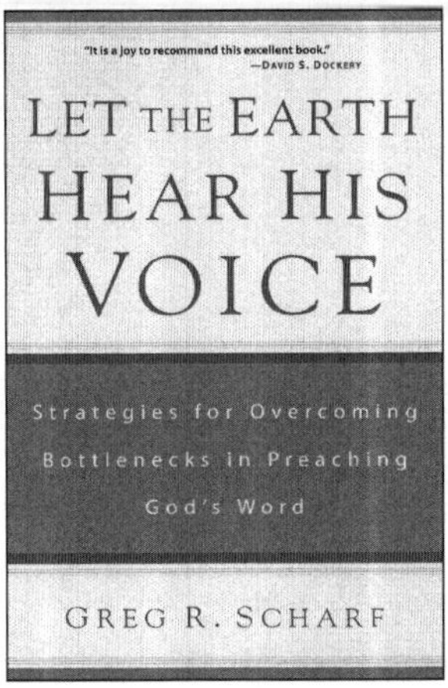

Uniting theological encouragement with practical advice, Greg Scharf identifies eight common bottlenecks that can clog a sermon's fruitfulness and faithfulness—humanly speaking—and gives diagnoses, strategies for addressing the problems, and exercises to overcome them. Seminary students, occasional preachers, and seasoned pastors will be given profound tools and insights for preaching faithfully, clearly, and applicably. A cross reference allows the book to be easily used alongside Bryan Chapell's *Christ-Centered Preaching*.

"I think highly of this book! . . . Its strengths are biblical//theological grounding, practical exercises, and a lack of posturing. Greg Scharf takes his craft very seriously, but not himself. He models humility, zeal, and wisdom."
—**Jeffrey Arthurs**, Professor of Preaching and Communication, Gordon-Conwell Theological Seminary

Other Preaching Resources from P&R

Murray Capill helps all preachers who want to change lives to make their preaching wholly applicable, avoiding the pitfalls of tacked-on application. He takes preachers through the living application preaching process—moving the Word of God, via the life of the preacher, to the lives of the hearers—and gives them the tools to systematically explore the application potential of any text. He himself applies this teaching to any preacher's situation by showing how it works out in some of the specific challenges and situations of preaching.

"Experienced preachers are well aware of the pitfalls that pervade the terrain of application in preaching. . . . *The Heart Is the Target* not only provides biblical and theological correctives to such errors and imbalances, but also offers practical guidance in preparing sermons that serve the transformative purposes of the Bible."
—**Dennis E. Johnson**, Professor of Practical Theology, Westminster Theological Seminary, California